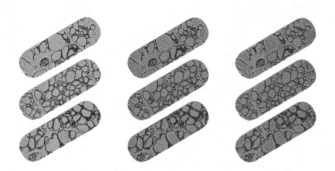

OXFORD BIOLOGY PRIMERS

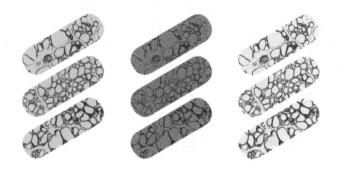

Discover more in the series at
www.oxfordtextbooks.co.uk/obp

Published in partnership with the Royal Society of Biology

ORGANS, SYSTEMS, AND SURGERY

OXFORD BIOLOGY PRIMERS

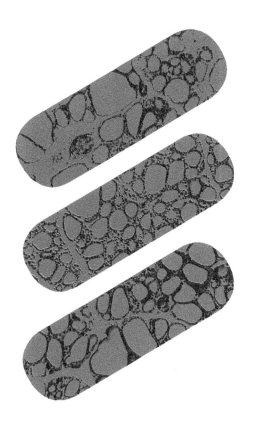

ORGANS, SYSTEMS, AND SURGERY

William Fullick and James Fullick

Edited by Ann Fullick

Editorial board: Ian Harvey, Gill Hickman, Sue Howarth, and Hilary Otter

OXFORD
UNIVERSITY PRESS

Royal Society of
Biology

OXFORD
UNIVERSITY PRESS

Great Clarendon Street, Oxford, OX2 6DP,
United Kingdom

Oxford University Press is a department of the University of Oxford.
It furthers the University's objective of excellence in research, scholarship,
and education by publishing worldwide. Oxford is a registered trade mark of
Oxford University Press in the UK and in certain other countries

Published in the United States of America by Oxford University Press
198 Madison Avenue, New York, NY 10016, United States of America

British Library Cataloguing in Publication Data

Data available

Library of Congress Control Number: 2023931419

ISBN 978-0-19-886187-4

Printed in the UK by
Ashford Colour Press Ltd, Gosport, Hampshire

PREFACE

There has never been a more exciting time to be a biologist. Not only do we understand more about the biological world than ever before, but we're using that understanding in ever-more creative and valuable ways.

Our understanding of the way our genes work is being used to explore new ways to treat disease; our understanding of ecosystems is being used to explore more effective ways to protect the diversity of life on Earth; our understanding of plant science is being used to explore more sustainable ways to feed a growing human population.

The repeated use of the word 'explore' here is no accident. The study of biology is, at heart, an exploration. We have written the Oxford Biology Primers to encourage you to explore biology for yourself—to find out more about what scientists at the cutting edge of the subject are researching, and the biological problems they're trying to solve.

Throughout the series, we use a range of features to help you see topics from different perspectives.

Scientific approach panels help you understand a little more about 'how we know what we know'—that is, the research that has been carried out to reveal our current understanding of the science described in the text, and the methods and approaches scientists have used when carrying out that research.

Case studies explore how a particular concept is relevant to our everyday life, or provide an intimate picture of one aspect of the science described.

The bigger picture panels help you think about some of the issues and challenges associated with the topic under discussion—for example, ethical considerations, or wider impacts on society.

More than anything, however, we hope this series will reveal to you, its readers, that biology is awe-inspiring, both in its variety and its intricacy, and will drive you forward to explore the subject further for yourself.

ABOUT THE AUTHORS

Dr William Fullick MBBS MRCGP

William trained at the University of East Anglia, gaining his MBBS in 2009. He moved to Cornwall to work as a junior doctor and embarked on his training as a general practitioner in 2012. He has worked as a GP since 2015, firstly in Cornwall and more recently in New Zealand. In addition to working as a GP, he continues to write medical and biological educational resources, including *Human Infectious Disease and Public Health* in the Oxford Biology Primers series. In his spare time, he enjoys exploring the beautiful countryside and coastline of New Zealand, kayaking, and skiing.

Dr James Fullick MBChB BSc (Hons) FRCA

James is an anaesthetist in South Wales. He studied medicine at the University of Bristol with an intercalated degree in neuroscience before going on to complete his Fellowship exams for the Royal College of Anaesthesia in 2021. James spends a lot of time teaching and wrote his dissertation on near-peer education. He is an instructor for advanced life support and also holds an honorary position at the University of Bristol for his work in the Resuscitation for Medical Disciplines scheme. Outside of work, James is a keen sportsman and spends his free time on hobbies and taking trips with his young family.

ACKNOWLEDGEMENTS

William Fullick

In completing this book I am once again indebted to Milly, my wife, for all her support, to my brother James, for all of his contributions to the really complicated bits, and to my mother, for her tireless work supporting her sons in their endeavours.

James Fullick

I would firstly like to thank my wife Sarah and daughter Jessica, who have been endlessly patient with me during this project and many others. Your support and love have been vital in allowing me to complete this book.

My brother William was my early inspiration to go into medicine and it has been an amazing experience to write this with him. I greatly value his expertise and guidance along the way.

My colleagues and seniors over the years have given me their time and shown me how to help and heal. It has been a privilege to weave some of this knowledge into the pages of this book and doing so has made me appreciate my teachers all the more. A sincere thanks to all those who have mentored and guided me through the complex world of medicine.

A final thanks must go to my editor (and mother) Ann Fullick, for teaching and inspiring me about the natural world as a child and instilling in me a passion for learning. Your love, guidance and wisdom have helped me throughout my life, and it seems only fitting that it has continued into the writing of this book.

CONTENTS

1 A BRIEF HISTORY OF SURGERY

Your body is an incredibly complex organism, made up of multiple organ systems and thousands of physiological processes, all acting to ensure that you continue to breathe, digest, move, and think. Most of these complex systems work with no conscious effort required on our part to keep them functioning. For the vast majority of people, the body systems function perfectly without any interference. But what happens if one of these organ systems malfunctions? Sometimes our body's own self-repair mechanisms fix the problem—but if the issue is severe enough, then external help may be required. For conditions as varied as blocked bowels, bleeds into the brain, or broken bones, surgery may offer help where the body's own systems cannot cope.

Surgery is not a new concept. It has existed for many thousands of years, in almost every society around the world. Early surgeries were crude, performed with no anaesthesia, and based on flawed understandings of human anatomy and physiology—but archaeological evidence suggests that people often survived these brutal procedures. Dental extractions, bone-setting, even drilling holes into the skull are all ancient operations. What's more, all of these ancient surgeries are still performed today—although the tools, processes, and reasoning behind each of them are very different.

To understand how to perform surgery safely, we must understand the anatomy and the physiology of the human body. Our initially rudimentary understanding of how humans are put together has evolved dramatically over the centuries, and modern surgical techniques take advantage of our advanced understanding of anatomy and physiology to make procedures safer and more effective than ever before. Coupled with other key developments such as antiseptic surgery and safe anaesthesia, surgery has become, to many people, almost routine. It's important to remember, though, that even the simplest surgical procedure involves cutting into the human body— and this comes with significant risks of harm.

In this primer you will look at the anatomy and physiology of the various organ systems in the body, along with the disease processes which affect them. You will discover the story of surgery and anaesthesia throughout the centuries, and look at some of the amazing advances made throughout the last two centuries and glimpse into the future—see Figure 1.1.

Figure 1.1 Nanobots—the future of surgery?

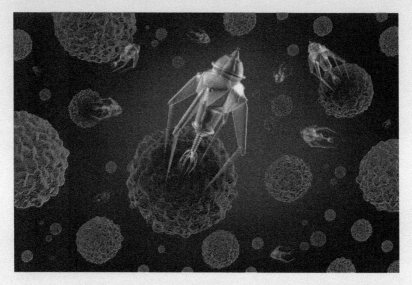

© Lightspring/Shutterstock.

Surgery through the millennia

The origins of surgery are lost in the mists of time, although findings by archaeologists and anthropologists help us understand just how ancient this branch of medicine may be. From the dawn of humankind, we have suffered from disease. Analysis of human remains from thousands of years ago shows evidence of sinus infections, tumours, dental caries, arthritis, and other medical problems which still plague humanity today. Of course, early humans probably had little understanding of the internal workings of the body, and very few ways to actually treat any of the diseases they suffered from. However, by the Neolithic period (between around 10,000 BCE and 4,500 BCE), there is some evidence of basic surgery.

Operations in the Ancient World

One of the earliest procedures for which we have conclusive evidence is **trephining**—cutting a hole in the skull. There is evidence of this operation in skulls from all around the world, from South America and China right through to Europe and Russia. Trephining would have been a primitive, brutal procedure, performed with stone tools and no anaesthetics. It is likely that many of the 'patients' who underwent this procedure died from infection, bleeding, or traumatic injuries to the brain. However, evidence of bony regrowth around certain skulls suggests that some individuals at least went on to live for several years after they had undergone trephining—see Figure 1.2.

What we cannot hope to understand in the twenty-first century is exactly why these procedures were performed. Neolithic societies had no written language, so no records exist to explain what appears to have been a relatively common procedure. Drawing on our understanding of cultures who have practised trephining more recently, it seems likely that the procedure was aiming to help people who had traumatic brain injuries, were suffering from epilepsy, or perhaps even were suffering mental health problems like schizophrenia. People affected by any of these conditions might have exhibited symptoms which Neolithic people interpreted as having a supernatural cause. One theory is that they believed making holes in the skull would allow evil spirits to pass out of the sufferer's body, so they would be cured.

It is even possible that this approach had a small degree of success, depending on the cause of the illness. When the brain suffers a traumatic injury, it often swells. This leads to symptoms such as confusion, personality changes, agitation, and coma. By making a hole in the skull, it is possible to relieve pressure on the brain caused by this **oedema**. This may occasionally have helped Neolithic victims of traumatic brain injuries or skull fractures. Certainly, some trephined skulls show evidence of trauma or fractures around the site of the trephining. Other skulls, however, do not—and without the benefits of soft tissue to examine (which might conclusively prove a traumatic brain injury) or any written records, it is difficult to draw definitive conclusions.

Figure 1.2 An example of a Bronze Age trephined skull. This example is from Jericho—globally, over 1,500 skulls have been found with similar holes.

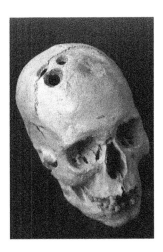

Trephining continued to be performed throughout most of medical history—and, indeed, it is sometimes still used to relieve cerebral oedema following traumatic injuries or **haemorrhages** in the brain or **meninges**. Nowadays, it is usually referred to as the creation of a burr hole—see Figure 7.8 in Chapter 7.

Gradually, our understanding of the human body and of surgery have improved. The causes of most diseases were still a mystery to people in the Ancient World, and they often used magico-religious ideas to explain why they became ill. But if there was a physically obvious problem, then surgeons in Ancient Greece, Rome, Baghdad, or China might have performed basic surgery to cure it. There is evidence that many cultures in the Ancient World were able to set broken bones, remove teeth, lance boils, and drain the lungs of fluid. Surgeons in the Islamic world even developed a sophisticated procedure for the treatment of **cataracts**—we still use the same basic principles today. However, all these procedures would have been performed with no **anaesthesia**, and the risk of infection would have been extremely high. The understanding of the microbial theory of disease, and the invention of antiseptic surgery, were still thousands of years in the future. This meant that surgery was only used as a last resort—although there are stories of great surgical successes (see The bigger picture 1.1).

Medicine in Medieval Europe

Despite the advances in understanding of anatomy and, to a certain extent, **physiology**, surgeons throughout most of human history had a very limited understanding of why their procedures worked. Without the ability to image the inner workings of the human body, or to examine the processes of disease under a microscope, doctors could only theorise based on what they could see with the naked eye. As a result, ideas such as the humoral theory of disease were commonly accepted for hundreds of years. First proposed by Hippocrates in around the fourth century BCE, this belief system suggested that every human being possessed four 'humours', which existed as liquids within the body—blood, yellow bile, black bile, and phlegm. As long as these humours remained balanced, then an individual would remain healthy. An imbalance in the humours would lead to disease—and could even affect a person's temperament, as you can see in Figure 1.3. Those with an excess of blood (sanguine) tended towards being talkative, enthusiastic, and active, whereas individuals with an excess of black bile (melancholius) were analytic deep-thinkers, obsessed with detail and often unsociable. People with too much phlegm (phlegmaticus) were thought of as being relaxed, easy-going, caring about others but often hiding their own emotions. Finally, those with an excess of yellow bile (cholericus) tended to be argumentative and quick to anger.

In this humoral model of disease, an excess of blood might lead to a surgeon performing bloodletting using tools or leeches in order to restore the humoral balance. Each season was felt to be associated with one of the four humours, as were different foods. A melancholic person might be advised to avoid eating meat and lettuce through the spring, as these were felt to be melancholic foods and, eaten in a melancholic month, could worsen

The bigger picture 1.1
Hua Tuo and the deer

One of the most famous figures in Ancient Chinese medicine is Hua Tuo (see BP1.1 Figure A), who lived around 140–208 CE, during the late Eastern Han Dynasty. Although he is famous for many different contributions to Chinese medicine, perhaps the most remarkable of his achievements is the theory that he may have developed an early form of anaesthesia or **sedation**.

Legend has it that, whilst gathering herbs in the wilderness, Hua Tuo noticed a wounded deer, staggering towards a pasture. After grazing on some of the herbs in the pasture, the deer seemed relieved of its pain. Intrigued, Hua Tuo sampled these herbs, and found some which made his mouth numb. This was, apparently, how he stumbled across the ability to create his ma-fei-sang—a potion or powder which possessed the ability to numb patients, and allow Hua Tuo to perform invasive surgery.

BP 1.1 Figure A A Chinese stamp showing Hua Tuo (c. 140–208) giving ma-fei-sang to a patient.

zhang jiahan/Alamy Stock Photo.

Contemporaneous reports suggest that, using this ma-fei-sang, Hua was able to perform operations such as the following.

- The removal of diseased bowels from a physician who suffered from abdominal pain. The man recovered, and lived for another ten years.

- The removal of half of the spleen of a man who had suffered from flank pain for ten days, and who had lost his hair and eyebrows during that time. The man allegedly recovered within a hundred days, and went on to lead a normal life.

- The removal of a snake-like worm from an ulcer on the leg of a twenty-year-old woman, the daughter of a military commander. This ulcer had been present on her left knee for seven or eight years, and would periodically heal, before breaking out again. Hua rendered the woman unconscious using the ma-fei-sang, and then tempted the worm out of the ulcer by using the blood from an exhausted dog. Once the worm had partially emerged from the ulcer, a hook was driven through its head, and the rest of the parasite was extracted. It measured three feet long, with an eyeless head and a scaly body. Hua then applied a healing salve to the ulcer, and the patient made a complete recovery.

The possible ingredients of this mystical ma-fei-sang are still relatively unclear. Some modern historians and scientists have suggested that a key ingredient may have been either *Papava somniferum* (opium poppy) or *Cannabis indica* (hashish). If this is the case, then Hua may indeed have been able to perform far more invasive procedures than were usual for the time.

❓ Pause for thought

Think about what you have learned about Hua and his ma-fei-sang. What diseases might Hua have treated in the three cases above? How reliable do you think written records from the Ancient World are likely to be? How could you attempt to verify the truth behind these stories?

the patient's condition. Doctors at the time felt that the humours would be concentrated in the patient's urine, and great importance was placed on the colour, consistency, smell, and taste of the urine as an indicator of the patient's health and general wellbeing!

Another popular theory of disease, particularly in Medieval Europe, was that of miasma. This was first recorded by the Ancient Greeks, who believed that 'foul air' was a cause of certain diseases. They thought that people living in environments affected by foul air or water, or by poor-quality food,

Figure 1.3 An eighteenth-century illustration of men displaying temperaments relating to their humours—sanguine (blood), phlegmatick (phlegm), cholerick (yellow bile), and melancholy (black bile).

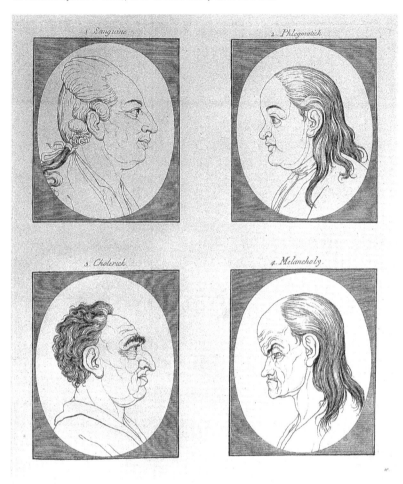

From J C Lavater, *Essays on Physiognomy* (1789). Wellcome Collection. Public Domain Mark.

would often be made ill by their conditions. With modern knowledge, we can theorise that perhaps some of these observations were based on scientific truths—but that infectious diseases and vitamin or mineral deficiencies were in fact the cause for the illnesses blamed on miasma.

Throughout the Middle Ages in Europe, most surgery was not conducted by doctors, but by barber-surgeons. Doctors were 'gentlemen', highly trained in the academic arts, and could not be expected to dirty their hands by operating on people! Surgery was felt to be a lesser profession, and not worthy of study in European universities. Most barber-surgeons trained as apprentices, learning their trade practically rather than academically. Many would travel from city to city, offering their services to anyone who could afford to pay them. Often they learned their craft during times of war, on the battlefield or at sea, where they would learn to perform swift amputations of limbs, extract teeth, dress wounds, and care for injured troops in whatever limited capacity they could. Some surgeons worked as apothecary surgeons, making their own medications from herbs. The use of herbs or alcohol to dull pain has been well-documented during this time period—but such practices were dangerous, and sometimes even led to the death of the patient whilst the surgeon was still sharpening his knife!

Printing presses and grave-robbing

Technological advances during the seventeenth and eighteenth centuries allowed significant improvements in how doctors and surgeons viewed the human body. The invention of the printing press facilitated the rapid spread of information, and mass production of anatomical texts allowed universities to teach anatomy to greater numbers of students (see Figure 1.4).

Figure 1.4 A page from Andreas Vesalius's Suorum de *humani corporis fabrica librorum epitome*, published in 1543.

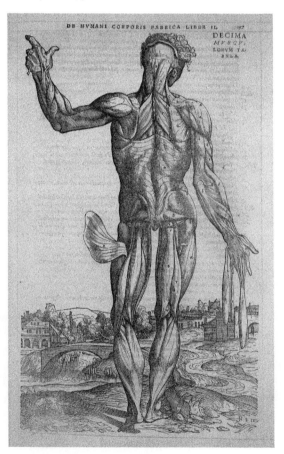

Wellcome Collection. Public Domain Mark.

This increased the numbers of **cadavers** required for **dissection**, as higher numbers of students progressed through their studies.

As a result of the increased need for bodies at medical schools, various charters were passed throughout Europe, permitting the use of executed criminals as cadavers. But this still wasn't sufficient to meet the growing demands. In the eighteenth century, the British Government increased the number of crimes punishable by death to increase the supply of executed criminals to medical schools! Across Europe, faced by high demand, many governments began to allow the use of the unclaimed bodies of paupers, prison inmates, and those who died in psychiatric or charitable hospitals for dissection.

This high demand for bodies to dissect may have led to some dubious laws being passed by governments—but it also led to unscrupulous practices by individuals. Grave-robbing became alarmingly commonplace in England, with poor people overwhelmingly targeted. Those who could not afford a deep grave and a sturdy coffin for their loved ones were at high risk of the bodies being exhumed and sold on to unscrupulous anatomists. And these so-called scientists often asked no questions about how these 'resurrectionists' had acquired their corpses. One of the most famous pair of grave-robbers, Burke and Hare (see Figure 1.5), even resorted to murder to supply anatomists and doctors with bodies. They killed as many as sixteen people, selling their bodies on at a profit, before they were caught and tried for murder.

Figure 1.5 Drawings based on court sketches of William Burke and William Hare—'resurrectionists' who profited from murdering their victims and selling the bodies to anatomists. Ironically, Burke himself was hanged for these offences, and his cadaver was donated for dissection.

(a)

(b)

WILLIAM BURKE.
(From a Sketch taken in Court.)

WILLIAM HARE,
(From a Sketch taken in Court)

From George MacGregor, *The History of Burke and Hare and of the Resurrectionist Times: A Fragment from the Criminal Annals of Scotland* (1884).

Eventually the Anatomy Act of 1832 was passed in an attempt to curtail grave-robbing and murder in the pursuit of new cadavers. This appears to have reduced the more obvious criminal aspects of acquiring cadavers—but it is likely that the bodies of many paupers were clandestinely diverted to the dissecting table before they ever reached the graveside, aided by unscrupulous funeral directors and workhouse owners.

The development of antiseptic surgery

Significant advancements in the field of lens-making were to have far-reaching effects on surgical procedures. In 1676 a Dutch draper by the name of Van Leeuwenhoek produced an early version of a light microscope, which was able to magnify objects to 266 times larger than their natural size. This allowed him to see micro-organisms (or 'animalcules' as they rapidly became known) for the first time, and opened up an entirely new speciality—the field of microbiology (see Figure 1.6). The significance of

Figure 1.6 Van Leeuwenhoek's initial drawings of the micro-organisms he had seen under his microscope, showing important features of bacteria that we recognize today. From Antonie van Leeuwenhoek *Arcana naturae detecta* (1695).

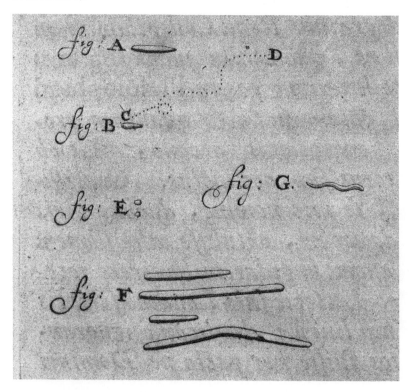

Wellcome Collection. Attribution 4.0 International (CC BY 4.0).

this discovery was not immediately apparent to the medical establishment, at least regarding the causes of common diseases. Many hundreds of different bacteria would be described over the following decades—but none of them were clearly associated with the many common infectious diseases at the time, with physicians still subscribing to the humoral or miasmic theories of disease.

Nearly two hundred years later, a Hungarian doctor named Ignaz Semmelweis made a connection between mortality rates on maternity wards and the hand hygiene habits of doctors and midwives. The midwife-led clinic at the Vienna General Hospital had a mortality rate of only 2–3 per cent—whereas the doctor-led clinic had a mortality rate of 10 per cent. The main cause of these deaths was a condition called childbed fever—now known as puerperal fever. This discrepancy troubled Semmelweis, and he set out to examine the differences between the two clinics.

After ruling out the climate, environment, and overcrowding—the climate and environments of the two clinics were identical, and the midwife-run clinic was always more crowded than the clinic run by the doctors—Semmelweis began to wonder whether the doctors were doing anything differently from the midwives. The breakthrough came about after the death of one of Semmelweis's close friends, who contracted symptoms similar to childbed fever after sustaining a puncture from a scalpel during an **autopsy**. Semmelweis immediately suggested a link between the dissection of cadavers and the high rates of childbed fever in the doctor-led clinic. The midwives who ran the second clinic did not perform autopsies and so avoided contamination. Doctors would often dash straight from a dissection to a delivery!

Semmelweis suggested that the doctors washed their hands with chlorinated lime (calcium hypochlorite) when moving from the autopsy room to the obstetric clinic. This swiftly reduced the mortality rates of the doctors' clinic to equal that of the midwives' clinic, confirming Semmelweis's theory that 'cadaveric particles' were being transferred from the bodies in the autopsy room to the patients in the clinic, causing childbed fever and ultimately killing 10 per cent of the women. He did not, however, make the link between these particles and micro-organisms. He then moved on to two other hospitals, taking his methods with him. Using what he had learned in Vienna, he was able to dramatically reduce the mortality rates from childbed fever in these hospitals as well. The medical establishment at the time was reluctant to believe Semmelweis, and he died at the age of 47 after developing an overwhelming infection whilst an inpatient at an asylum in Vienna.

Germ theory and antiseptic surgery

Semmelweis's theory would not become widely accepted by the general scientific population until later in the nineteenth century, after the experiments of a French scientist called Louis Pasteur. Pasteur conclusively proved that micro-organisms were not 'spontaneously generated' out of

Figure 1.7 Pasteur proved that microbes could not grow in a closed, sterilized environment—paving the way for the germ theory of disease.

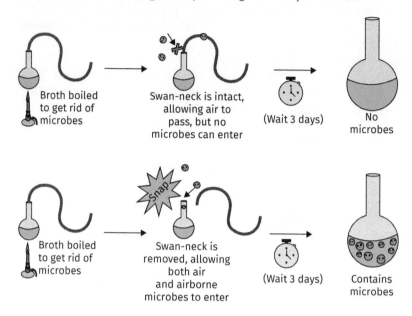

From William Fullick, *Human Infectious Disease and Public Health* (Oxford University Press, 2019).

thin air by conducting an experiment utilizing swan-necked flasks and sterilized nutrient broth (a liquid in which it was known that microorganisms would grow). You can see how Pasteur conducted his experiment in Figure 1.7.

An English surgeon named Joseph Lister took the ideas put forward by Pasteur, and used them to change the practice of surgery forever (Case study 1.1).

Surgery in times of war—the early twentieth century

Throughout much of human history, technological advancements have often been driven by—or as a result of—conflict. Surgery is no exception to this, and the first half of the twentieth century saw bloodier conflicts than any other era. Military innovations such as the machine gun, poison gas, and massed artillery barrages meant that horrific wounds could now be inflicted on hundreds—or even thousands—of individuals within minutes. The First World War (1914–1918) was a colossal conflict, introducing people to the concept of industrialized slaughter for the first, but sadly not the last, time.

Troops wounded on the front lines were stabilized in rudimentary field hospitals. Then they were evacuated, where possible, to have their injuries more comprehensively treated in a more sterile environment with a lower

Case study 1.1
Joseph Lister—pioneer of antiseptic surgery

Born in Essex in 1827, Joseph Lister (see CS1.1 Figure A) initially attended University College London to study botany. From this he went on to study medicine, entering the Royal College of Surgeons at the age of 26. From London, Lister moved to Edinburgh to study under the renowned surgeon James Syme.

In the mid-nineteenth century, surgery was still primitive. Post-operative infection rates were high, and there were no antibiotics to treat these infections. Surgical patients often died from overwhelming sepsis, even if their operation had been a success. Miasmic theory of disease was still widely held as the leading cause for these infections, and surgical wards were often 'aired-out' by opening windows during the day—the theory being that this would allow any miasma to escape, and allow healthy air to permeate the room.

Surgeons and their assistants did not wash their robes, and a patient's bedlinen was seldom laundered. Surgical tools were not routinely washed until they were due to be put away for storage, and the same surgical probe would be used on all patients on a ward to look for pockets of undrained **pus** in wounds. Most surgeons held that 'laudable pus'—pus expelled freely from a surgical wound—was a necessary part of the post-operative healing process, and the 'good old surgical stink' of the operating theatre was a natural part of life as a surgeon!

Lister read Pasteur's paper *Recherches sur la putrefaction* ('Research on decomposition'). He wondered whether the process described by Pasteur as fermentation could be responsible for causing infections in post-operative

CS 1.1 Figure A Joseph Lister (1827–1912) expanded on Pasteur's theories and developed a system of antiseptic surgery.

Photograph by Barraud's Ltd. Wellcome Collection.

wounds. Comparing the difference between closed fractures (breaks in bones which did not penetrate the skin) and compound fractures (broken bones which penetrated the skin, exposing the wound to the air), he noticed that rates of infection in the closed injuries were significantly lower than in fractures which broke the skin. This led Lister to suggest that infection was caused by exposure to the air without the protection of the skin.

Having heard of creosote being used to disinfect sewage, Lister looked around for a substance which might disinfect wounds and operating theatres. He settled on carbolic acid, and started by spraying the sweet-smelling substance on open wounds, both traumatic and post-operative. The results were immediately startling, and infection rates on wards utilizing Lister's 'anti-septic' approach plummeted. Lister also began using carbolic acid to sterilize surgical instruments, wash his own hands, and even to mist operating theatres with—all of which helped to lower infection rates still further (see CS 1.1 Figure B).

Lister published his findings in two papers in *The Lancet* in 1867, stating that it did not 'seem right to withhold it longer from the profession generally'. Initial scepticism from medical colleagues was quickly replaced by enthusiasm, as people quickly achieved similar results elsewhere. Germany led the way in adopting Lister's antiseptic surgical techniques, followed by the USA, France, and Great Britain.

Lister ushered in the age of antiseptic surgery, and his techniques have doubtless saved many millions of lives. Ultimately, however, Lister did not

CS 1.1 Figure B The carbolic acid misting apparatus used by Joseph Lister to pioneer antiseptic surgeries.

make the final connection between microbes and wound infections. That was down to a German scientist named Robert Koch. In the 1880s, Koch proved that he could infect mice with anthrax bacteria isolated from cows. Based on his findings, he wrote down what are now known as Koch's Postulates—a set of instructions to determine whether or not a particular micro-organism is responsible for causing a certain disease. This idea—that micro-organisms were responsible for infectious diseases, rather than humoral imbalance or miasma—is known as the germ theory of infectious disease.

Koch's postulates

1. The organism must be present in every case of the disease.
2. The organism must be isolated from a host of the disease and grown in pure **culture medium**.
3. Samples of the organism taken from the culture medium must then cause the same disease when inoculated into a healthy, susceptible animal in the laboratory.
4. The organism must be isolated from the inoculated animal and must be identified as being the same as the original organism isolated from the host and grown in pure culture medium.

⑦ Pause for thought

Think about the COVID-19 pandemic which swept the world in the 2020s. How have Koch's postulates been applied to our battle against SARS-CoV-2, the virus that causes the disease?

risk of enemy attack. By this time, the principles of antiseptic surgery were well established, and operations were conducted in conditions that were as **aseptic** as possible—although there were still no antibiotics to treat infections once they became established. Basic anaesthesia was possible by this point in time, meaning that surgeons no longer had to operate as quickly as possible—and patients could be spared the agony of enduring an operation whilst still awake! You can learn more about the history and development of anaesthesia in Chapter 2. **Analgesics** were also more readily available to treat pain both pre- and post-operatively.

Operations such as amputation of limbs or removals of bullets and shrapnel were not new to surgeons. The number of procedures needing to be performed were significantly higher than in previous conflicts, putting increased pressure on surgical staff—but the principles of the surgery itself were relatively well understood. However, with the advent of new ways to wage war came the potential for entirely new injuries, and new surgical techniques needed to be developed to treat these new problems. You can read more about one of the remarkable new branches of surgery in Case study 1.2.

Case study 1.2
The birth of reconstructive surgery

During the First World War, the nature of traumatic injuries changed. Trench warfare meant that the number of men presenting with facial injuries rose dramatically. Peering over the parapet of a trench often meant that the head was the only obviously exposed part of the body, and shells designed to scatter shrapnel over a wide area could instantly cause dozens of life-changing injuries for the men caught within their blast radius. These facial injuries were not easy to treat on the battlefield—and, in previous conflicts, those suffering from such injuries would probably not have survived. With more advanced medical care, however, these casualties were often evacuated to a field hospital, where they might end up having the ragged wounds sutured together to prevent catastrophic bleeding or infection.

Soldiers who survived this initial traumatic stage were often left significantly disfigured. As their wounds healed, the scar tissue would begin to contract, pulling their already damaged faces into even more unnatural shapes. Many men struggled to eat, drink, and even breathe properly as a result of the nature and severity of their injuries. Even if a soldier was able to overcome the physical nature of their injuries, they would often return to a society which was horrified by their mutilated appearance—friends and loved ones who could no longer bear to look them in the face, loss of employment, and even open hostility from members of the public.

Harold Gillies, a New Zealand surgeon, was posted to the front lines in 1915. There he witnessed first-hand the rise in horrific facial injuries and, on his return to England, he set up a surgical unit in Aldershot dedicated to treating them. He even sent his own casualty labels out to the front lines, to ensure that troops ended up being sent to him for treatment. Gillies' aim was to reconstruct the faces of these injured servicemen as fully as possible, to allow them to lead a normal life.

This was no small task, but Gillies knew that healthy tissue could be persuaded to grow over damaged tissue. Gillies devised a technique based on the existing surgical grafting techniques at the time. It was already known that by taking a flap of skin from somewhere else on the patient's body and keeping it attached to its original blood supply by a corridor of skin and blood vessels (a pedicle), a **skin graft** could be kept alive and healthy until it developed a blood supply to its new, transplanted site.

Whilst performing a particularly large skin graft procedure on a sailor named Willie Vicarage, Gillies noticed that the edges of the pedicle seemed inclined to curl in on themselves. He sutured the edges of the flap together, making a tube, and found that this gave the skin graft a better blood supply, and significantly reduced the risk of infection. This 'tubed pedicle' approach allowed larger areas of skin to be grafted successfully, and meant he could attempt more significant reconstructions. By surgically fixing areas of shattered bone into a more typical shape, and placing skin grafts on top of these newly contoured sites, Gillies and his team restored the facial features of

CS 1.2 Figure A Able Seaman Willie Vicarage was terribly injured during the Battle of Jutland in 1916. Gillies pioneered the tubed pedicle approach on him. You can clearly see the tubes of skin in the centre-right image. Vicarage's procedure was successful, restoring the young sailor's face to a remarkable degree and permitting him to eat, speak, and breathe normally once again.

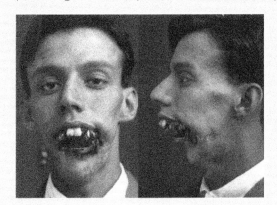  

From https://curiosociety.wordpress.com/2012/09/27/old-skool-plastic-surgery/.

many injured soldiers. You can see the remarkable results of Gillies' operation in CS 1.2 Figure A.

Gillies knew that, despite his team's best efforts, many of the young men he treated would still face significant difficulties when they returned to civilian life—both as a result of the psychological trauma from their injuries, and prejudice from the general public. He introduced vocational schemes for the men in his care, teaching them new skills which they could use once they were discharged from the hospital. Indeed, many of Gillies' patients would return to a relatively normal life once their injuries had healed—although some would spend the rest of their lives in hospital, too afraid or ashamed to show their faces to the general public. The hospital that Gillie helped to set up still exists today as Queen Mary's Hospital in Sidcup, south-east London.

Computers, robots, and microsurgery—the second half of the twentieth century and beyond

By the end of the Second World War, battlefield surgery had evolved almost beyond recognition. The tiled, disinfected operating theatres of hospitals in the mid-1940s were a far cry from the blood-stained, unhygienic tables of the barber surgeons which were a grisly reality only a century earlier. Antibiotics, better anaesthesia, and a variety of analgesia had all helped surgery to become safer and more effective than ever before. With greater understanding of how the human body worked both in health and disease, surgeons pioneered new operations, which would have been impossible without safe, aseptic surgery and anaesthesia. From the 1940s to the 1960s a rash of surgical firsts appeared: the first successful metallic hip replacement surgery in 1940; the first kidney transplant in 1950; the first cardiac pacemaker in 1955; the first heart transplant in 1967; and so on.

As the twentieth century progressed, advances in technology helped to make the diagnosis of disease (and subsequent surgery) significantly more precise. The **computed tomography** (or CT) scanner became commercially viable in 1972, allowing doctors to visualize their patients' internal organs in more detail than had ever been possible before without opening them up. The increasing power of computers meant that a CT scan could be used to accurately detect areas of disease that might not have been visible using traditional imaging techniques like X-rays, and also gave surgeons a detailed map of a patient's internal organs before they had made the first incision. You can see an example of an early CT scan in Figure 1.8.

In the late 1970s, the concept of nuclear magnetic resonance (**NMR**) was also found to have medical applications—something that had been suspected since the discovery of the phenomenon in the 1930s. NMR imaging uses powerful magnetic fields to change the spin of atoms within the body. Radio waves are able to pick up these changes, and computers can process this information into detailed maps of soft tissue. Unlike CT scanners, NMR scanning does not utilize radiation—and so is safer for the patient. In 1977 the first medically viable NMR scanner was produced (nicknamed 'Indomitable' by its creator, Raymond Damadian)—but, ultimately, it was

Figure 1.8 An image of the human brain (on the left) captured by an early CT scan in the 1970s. The resolution was low, but doctors and scientists were finally able to view the soft tissue inside the body. Compare this with a modern CT image of the human brain (on the right) to see just how much medical imaging has advanced over the last half century.

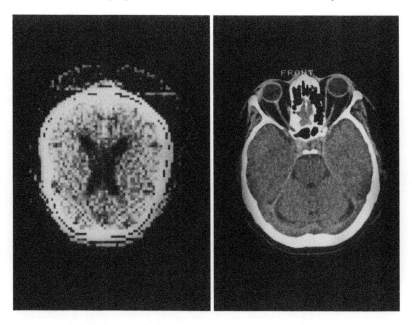

Courtesy of Siemens Medical Solutions USA, Inc.

the British physicist Peter Mansfield and American chemist Paul Lauterbur who were awarded a Nobel Prize for their contributions to what has become an incredibly important cornerstone of medical imaging. In order to make the scanning method more appealing to the general public, the word 'nuclear' was removed from its name. The imaging technique became known as **magnetic resonance imaging (MRI)** instead.

The 1980s saw a revolution in what would become known as robotic surgery. The first robot-assisted operations were performed in Vancouver in 1983, using a simple robot named Arthrobot—essentially a robotic limb which could reposition a patient's limb on voice commands from a surgeon. By the mid-1980s, the first robot-assisted neurosurgical biopsy had been taken, using a robot to position a biopsy needle based on information gathered from CT imaging. This was swiftly followed by robot-assisted **laparoscopic surgery** to remove gallbladders (**cholecystectomy**), and then prostate glands (**prostatectomy**)—but all of these robots were fairly simple, and required the operator to be in the same room during the procedure.

The idea of robots operated remotely to perform surgery on a patient hundreds of miles away from the surgeon was of immense interest to several different organizations—including NASA and the US military. The concept of 'bringing the surgeon to the soldier' via **telepresence** sounded like a dream come true in the field of combat medicine. It held out the potential for a highly trained surgeon to perform rapid surgery on wounded personnel, without risking the life of the surgeon and their team. This would, ultimately, prove to be the least useful application of robotic surgery—surgical robots, even today, are large, bulky devices, which are nevertheless extremely delicate. This makes them difficult to transport and challenging to use in extreme environments. However, various models of surgical robot were produced throughout the late 1980s and 1990s, gradually becoming capable of performing more and more sophisticated procedures.

The true value of current robot-assisted surgery is to reduce the size of incisions, increase the precision of the surgeon's work (by allowing smaller instruments and higher magnifications to be used), and to reduce some of the physical strain of surgery on surgical teams. Current surgical robots are capable of performing a wide variety of different procedures and have a huge array of different surgical tools they can use—although surgery is not usually performed remotely, and the surgeon will usually either be in the same room as the robot, or somewhere nearby. Although it certainly has its advantages, robot-assisted surgery is far from perfect—and some experts argue that its prohibitive costs reduce its significance. It is perhaps worth noting that, as of 2019, the Food and Drug Administration (FDA) in the USA have suggested that robot-assisted surgery is not suitable for cancer surgeries, as there is no significant evidence that it improves outcomes, and some studies suggest that it actually worsens prognoses for cancer patients. You can see an example of a robotic surgery system below, in Figure 1.9.

Along with robotic-assisted surgery, microsurgery has become more popular, allowing surgeons to perform increasingly delicate procedures. It has significantly altered how some operations are approached. From the 1950s onwards, some **otolaryngologists** (ear, nose, and throat surgeons) started to adopt microscopes for delicate procedures in the ear. Neurosurgeons, too,

Figure 1.9 The Da Vinci robotic surgical system—a three-part system which can perform a number of different surgical procedures.

WENN Rights Ltd/Alamy Stock Photo.

adopted the use of the surgical microscope, as it allowed for far more precise surgery. Through the late 1960s and early 1970s, reconstructive surgeons began to experiment with microsurgical techniques, utilizing tiny blood vessels (venules and arterioles) to attach grafted tissue, rather than relying on tubed pedicle grafts (as in Case study 1.2). This not only allowed 'single-stage' skin grafts (which could be completed all at once, rather than waiting for the skin graft to develop its own blood supply, necessary with the tubed pedicle approach), but also permitted surgeons to re-attach digits, parts of the face, and even entire limbs. Microsurgery also paved the way for more successful transplant surgery, with the transplanted organ receiving improved blood flow by the attachment of ever smaller blood vessels (see Figure 1.10).

Figure 1.10 Microsurgery involves the use of surgical microscopes to operate at a much smaller scale than is possible with the naked eye.

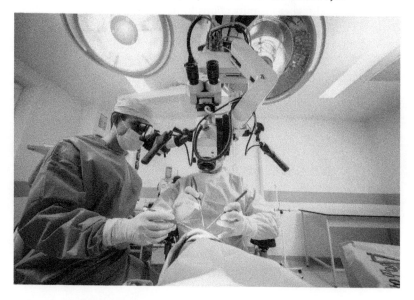

© Roman Zaiets/Shutterstock.

Surgery in the twenty-first century

The early years of the twenty-first century have brought with them still more remarkable surgical achievements. In addition to robot-assisted surgery and microsurgery, breakthroughs such as the world's first self-contained artificial heart have been developed and used, and 2008 saw the first full face transplant, performed on a woman who had lost her face to dog bites. In 2013, a replacement nose was successfully grown on the forehead of a patient in China, using cartilage from his ribs and skin from his face. Womb transplants, penile transplants, even bilateral arm transplantations have all been successfully demonstrated over the last two decades. Whilst most of these operations are unlikely to ever be performed in high numbers, they demonstrate the remarkable advances that the surgical profession has been able to make, using improved knowledge of anatomy, physiology, and technology to ensure safer, more effective operations.

 Chapter summary

- For much of early human history, surgery was crude and possibly performed for magico-religious reasons. Knowledge of anatomy and physiology was basic, and there were no antiseptics or anaesthetics available to improve the safety of any operations.
- Some very early healers may have discovered compounds which allowed them to treat pain or even administer very basic anaesthesia—but this was performed without any knowledge of how their concoctions actually worked.
- As anatomical knowledge advanced, surgeons were able to learn how they could safely operate on various parts of the body—but without fully understanding the causes of disease, such operations were not always based on sound scientific principles. Procedures such as bloodletting were common, and mortality rates were high.
- By the late nineteenth century, antiseptic surgery had become relatively well established as an effective way to reduce mortality from operations—and, once the germ theory of disease had been accepted by the medical establishment, the era of aseptic surgery would be truly ushered in.
- The horrifying casualties of the First and Second World Wars led to significant improvements in the fields of trauma surgery, and also reconstructive surgery—paving the way for these specialities to evolve throughout the twentieth century.
- Post-war, innovations such as organ transplantation, CT scanning, and microsurgery permitted ever more adventurous surgical procedures, with survival rates from more routine procedures also improving thanks to improved pre- and post-operative care, antibiotics, and standardized operations. These advancements have continued to the present day.

Further reading

Bishop, W J *The Early History of Surgery*. Barnes and Noble, 1995. https://
storage.googleapis.com/global-help-publications/books/help_early-
historyofsurgery.pdf
An excellent insight into surgery through the ages, from the dawn of humankind through to surgery after Joseph Lister.

Ghosh, Sanjib Kumar 'Human cadaveric dissection: a historical account
from ancient Greece to the modern era' *Anatomy and Cell Biology* 2015
(22 September) 48(3), pp 153–169. https://www.ncbi.nlm.nih.gov/pmc/
articles/PMC4582158/
An interesting look at how the study of anatomy using cadavers has
changed over the centuries, and why it is still relevant today.

National Army Museum 'The birth of plastic surgery'. https://www.nam.
ac.uk/explore/birth-plastic-surgery, accessed 8 August 2022
An article by the National Army Museum examining Gillies' role in plastic
surgery, and how his procedures affected the lives of those he treated.

Witzfeld, M D and Debra A 'A history of women in surgery' *Canadian
Journal of Surgery* 2009 (August) 52(4), pp 317–320. https://www.ncbi.
nlm.nih.gov/pmc/articles/PMC2724816/
An excellent examination of the role that female surgeons have played
over the centuries, which also looks at the difficulties women have (and
still have) in entering a profession largely dominated by men.

 Discussion questions

1.1   Think about an operation you or somebody you know has under-
      gone. How did you feel before the procedure? How did you feel
      afterwards? How long did it take you to recover? How might this
      have differed fifty years ago? How about a century ago?

1.2   Investigate other ways to learn about anatomy, other than by direct
      dissection of a cadaver. What advantages and disadvantages do you
      think studying anatomy 'traditionally' (i.e. by dissection) holds when
      compared to more modern techniques?

1.3   Apart from on the battlefield, suggest other situations where robot-
      assisted surgery might be beneficial.

1.4   Will developing technology lead to a time where repairs are done
      inside the body by nanobots, rather than by human surgeons in
      an operating theatre? What role would surgeons have if nanobots
      proved to be safer and more reliably successful at conducting sur-
      gical procedures than human surgeons? How might AI need to be
      involved?

2 THE STORY OF ANAESTHESIA

When the body is damaged or broken beyond its ability to heal itself, and when medical interventions don't work, surgery offers another way to promote survival and recovery. The problem with surgical techniques is that surgeons have to get inside the body to repair damaged tissue or remove diseased parts—and that is traumatic. Clean, sterile surgery is vital to make sure that the patient doesn't develop an infection as a result of any operation. Beyond that, the main challenges preventing the surgeon from operating come from the patient; an alert and conscious patient will experience fear, pain, and trauma, and will move about as a result. The human body is well adapted to avoid painful stimuli, and someone opening up your body is certainly a painful stimulus—so without anaesthesia, surgery is practically impossible. An unconscious patient who feels no pain and cannot move during an operation ensures optimal operating conditions for surgeon and patient alike!

Since we humans first started to write, we have described pain. For thousands of years early humans created legends of gifts or potions given by gods that could remove pain or induce sleep. Many of these legends have no basis in reality, and some are linked to the use of mind-altering drugs, but all expose the desire for a pain-free existence that has driven humanity since we recognized the sensation.

Anaesthesia is Greek for 'without sensation'. Today we use the term to describe the technique of reducing or obliterating the sensation of pain. As you saw in Chapter 1, until the nineteenth century operations were performed while the patient was fully awake and conscious, often held down by assistants, or with minimal sedation provided by herbs, alcohol or a blow to the head. In this chapter you will explore the history of anaesthesia both ancient and modern, and discover how we have arrived at the techniques and medications used for safe and comfortable surgery (see Figure 2.1).

Figure 2.1 Modern anaesthetics is a complex medical speciality requiring many years of training and a thorough knowledge of physiology and pharmacology.

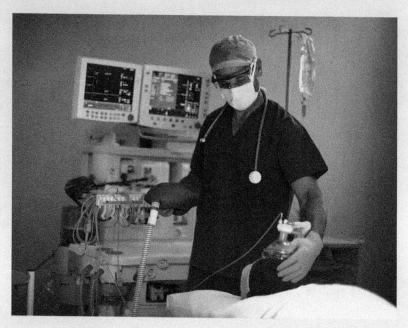

shapecharge/iStock.

The search for chemical sleep

Anaesthesia as we know it is a relatively modern medical speciality, only receiving recognition in 1948 and forming its own Royal College as late as 1992. There have been stories and reports of successful anaesthesia for thousands of years (such as the case of Hua Tuo discussed in The bigger picture 1.1 in Chapter 1). These stories are almost always impossible to verify, without any proof or cases reproduced by other practitioners. Often, they involve fantastical claims or a salve, herb, or mixture that induces 'sleep' in the patient, with complete recovery and no pain following the operation. The ingredients described within these potions range from crystals, herbal mixtures, and alcohol to divine gifts from the gods. Obviously, we cannot reproduce these tales, and none of these amazing mixtures survive today, but it is fascinating to glance backwards through time and appreciate how obsessed humanity has been with the relief or cessation of pain. It also makes us appreciate how lucky we are to live in the twenty-first century!

Pain is a stimulus like any other. It acts as a warning to your body that damage is occurring or imminent. Animals of every phylum react to painful stimuli, and humans are no exception—indeed we react with certain psychological elements that other animals lack. In the Age of Enlightenment in the mid-1700s there was huge interest in scientific discovery, and the science of pain was a hot topic.

A decade of discovery

The history of modern anaesthesia could be said to begin in the late eighteenth century, when a number of key discoveries were made, including a gas called **nitrous oxide** (N_2O—see Figure 2.4). This was the work of a scientist called Joseph Priestley who was also, along with Antoine and Marie-Anne Lavoisier, responsible for discovering oxygen. The effects of nitrous oxide on people were studied by Humphry Davy, a scientist working at the 'Pneumatic Institute of Medicine' in Bristol. New gases were being discovered regularly at the time, and it became fashionable to try to treat all sorts of diseases with the inhalation of different concentrations of the newly discovered gases, usually with very little success.

Davy documented the results of his experiments, in this case, the effects of nitrous oxide (see Figure 2.2), and showed that amongst the effects of this new gas were pain relief and euphoria—so much so that Davy coined the term 'laughing gas'. Nitrous oxide became very popular amongst Davy and his friends, who rather extended the definition of medical research—one of Davy's laboratory notebooks describes combining nitrous oxide with wine in a bid to cure a hangover!

Davy suggested the use of nitrous oxide as pain relief during surgery in his research notes, but this was not acted upon. We don't really know why it wasn't tried, but lost opportunities are a sadly recurrent theme in the history of anaesthesia. The idea of using nitrous oxide as an anaesthetic agent faded, whilst its use as a recreational drug became more commonplace,

Figure 2.2 Nitrous oxide may have taken a long time to be accepted as an anaesthetic, but it wasn't long before people used it to party, as this 1820 cartoon clearly shows! Doctor and Mrs Syntax, with other friends, taking laughing gas in the house of a tooth-drawer in Paris. Coloured aquatint, 1820.

and in America in 1844 a travelling showman demonstrated its powers to an audience. Within the crowd was Horace Wells, a dentist with an open mind and a willingness to experiment. He was keen to try to find a cure for the pain his patients had to undergo when he was pulling their teeth out, and with great enthusiasm he set about learning to manufacture and use nitrous oxide. Eventually he was confident enough to demonstrate his skill at a medical conference in Boston. To his dismay (and the delight of the audience of doubting surgeons) the patient on the day cried out as Wells removed the tooth. Even though the patient had no memory of the procedure or of any pain, Wells was labelled a charlatan and a fraud—and nitrous oxide was, once again, ignored.

Not everyone was put off by Wells's humiliation, though, and one of his students, William Morton, recognized the need for a better anaesthetic agent. In collaboration with Dr Charles Jackson he trialled the use of the volatile organic compound **ethoxyethane**, commonly called ether (see Figure 2.4). Ether was a well-known compound, and its effects were recognized long before it was considered as a possible anaesthetic agent. Many gentlemen and ladies of the day were fond of 'ether frolics', parties where they would attend and sample ether for its side effect of euphoria. After studying and trialling ether on animals, Morton successfully demonstrated the removal of a tumour from the neck from an anaesthetized patient named Gilbert Abbott at the Massachusetts General Hospital in 1846, to the astonishment of the audience (see Figure 2.3). Many people see this as the defining moment for modern anaesthesia—the true demonstration that surgery did not need to be a painful and dangerous affair, but could indeed be serene and painless for patient and surgeon alike.

Figure 2.3 The first demonstration of ether as an anaesthetic. In this illustration you can see Morton standing behind Gilbert Abbott, holding the vapouring equipment for the ether.

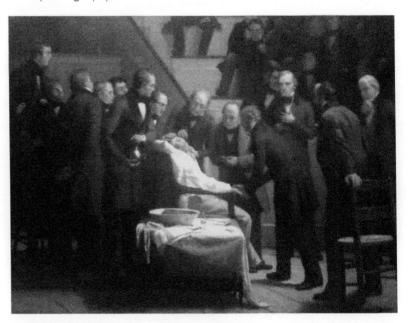

The History Collection/Alamy Stock Photo.

In fact, as so often happens in science and medicine, it subsequently emerged that another American doctor called Crawford Long had started using ether to perform surgery in 1842, and used it regularly in his practice both for surgery and childbirth. However, he did not publish his findings until years later, and so, even though the National Eclectic Medical Association declared in 1879 that Long was the official discoverer of anaesthesia (a year after his death), it is Moreton and Jackson, with their public demonstration of painless surgery using ether, who are still widely credited with the discovery of effective anaesthesia.

The final discovery of this extraordinary decade in the history of anaesthesia was when the Scot Sir James Simpson showed that **trichloromethane**, known as chloroform (see Figure 2.4), was a superior anaesthetic to both ethoxyethane and nitrous oxide. Trichloromethane received the royal stamp of approval when Queen Victoria herself used it during the deliveries of several of her children. Trichloromethane produces a deep sleep, but it is toxic and can cause liver damage. Interestingly, although trichloromethane is no longer used for pain relief during childbirth as it is too toxic, nitrous oxide is still very much present as part of the 'gas and air' mixture used by many women during labour (see Figure 2.5).

Figure 2.4 The first effective anaesthetics—a) nitrous oxide, b) ethoxyethane (ether), and c) trichloromethane (chloroform).

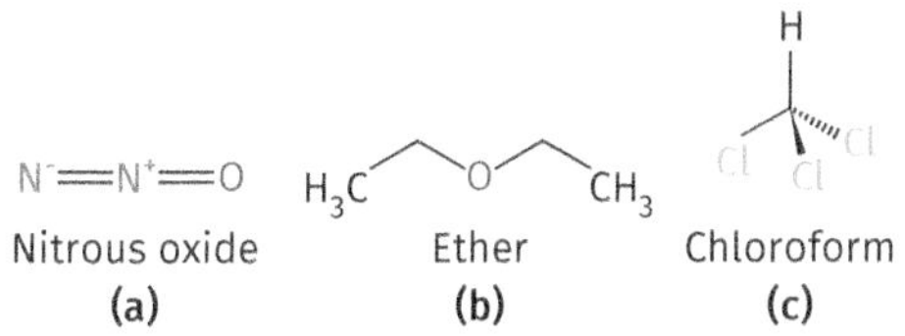

$$N^-\!\!=\!\!N^+\!\!=\!\!O$$

Nitrous oxide

(a)

Ether

(b)

Chloroform

(c)

Figure 2.5 Nitrous oxide is still used to help relieve pain during childbirth.

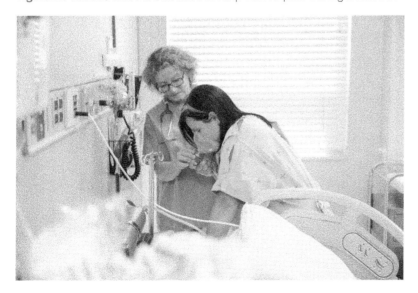

Into the twentieth century

It was not until the middle of the twentieth century that we made further strides in the development of anaesthetics. Demand grew for compounds which could readily be inhaled and produced deep sleep, yet were non-toxic and inflammable. By this time, organic chemists recognized two important features of organic compounds which helped them in their search.

- The substitution of a chlorine atom into a molecule of the organic family known as the alkanes results in a compound with anaesthetic properties—trichloromethane (chloroform) was a clear example. Increasing the number of chlorine atoms in the compound increased the depth of anaesthesia given—but unfortunately also made the compound more toxic.
- Carbon–fluorine bonds are very stable and so their presence in a compound leads to non-flammable, non-toxic and unreactive properties.

Given this information, thirty years ago organic chemists came up with **halothane** (2-bromo-2-chloro-1,1,1-trifluoroethane). With this effective compound giving deep yet safe anaesthesia, along with the similar compounds **enflurane** and **isoflurane** which followed, modern surgery really took off (see Figure 2.6). These anaesthetics are all halogenated alkanes.

Halothane and the anaesthetics which have followed it are deceptively simple molecules which have allowed surgery to progress so that operations are not only much safer for patients, but also an enormous variety of surgical procedures is possible. These range from operations carried out through minute openings made in the body wall to massive transplant operations involving both patients and doctors in many hours in the operating theatre. The lack of toxicity of modern anaesthetics even makes surgery lasting more than twenty-four hours a possibility.

Figure 2.6 Some of the twentieth-century anaesthetics that revolutionized surgery.

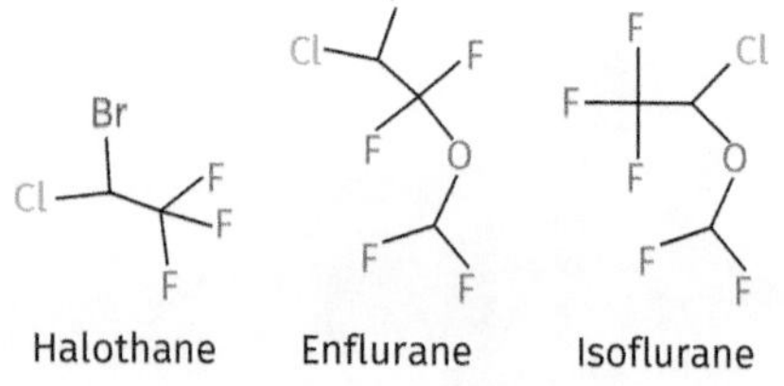

Halothane   Enflurane   Isoflurane

The anaesthetic challenges

Before we consider how anaesthetics work to send us into a chemically induced sleep, it makes sense to consider simply how the nervous system works when we are awake, conscious and perfectly capable of feeling pain and moving around.

The bigger picture 2.1
We *can* do it—but *should* we?

Over the last two chapters we have seen dozens of opportunities for anaesthesia to be refined and developed, from the Ancient World to the Age of Enlightenment. Many of these failed to thrive or were outright ignored. It is difficult to be certain why the practice of anaesthesia was ignored for so long, but it is almost certainly to do with the complexity of the body and brain.

Even after the introduction of anaesthetic agents such as ether, there was surprising reluctance to use them. Questions about their safety and even the morality of using such agents were rife from medical experts and members of the public alike, in spite of the obvious benefits. These complaints were not entirely baseless—even in the 1940s and 1950s, anaesthetics were still relatively dangerous and could result in significant complications or even death. As newer technologies and drugs have been developed in the last few decades, the risks of anaesthesia have significantly decreased.

What is fascinating about the many dozens of drugs available in modern anaesthetics is that the details of how many of them work remains a mystery. We have a reasonable understanding of which receptors the drugs may act on, and how they diffuse through different tissues, but how our brain is manipulated into a *reversible* unconscious state is something we cannot yet fully explain.

 Pause for thought

With what you have learned about the history of anaesthetics and surgery, why do you think people objected to anaesthetic agents? What complications and challenges were common in early anaesthetic practice? What are the challenges for the modern anaesthetist?

Nerve cell communications

If you sit down and think about moving your big toe, how long does it take for it to move? To move your toe, a dozen neurones have fired and sent a signal from your brain down to your legs in a tiny fraction of a second. This complex system is vital to allow our muscles, organs and brain to communicate almost instantaneously to allow rapid movements and adaptation to our environment.

The nervous system can be divided simply into a central and peripheral component. The central component contains the brain and spinal cord—located within the skull and spinal canal. The peripheral nervous system

Figure 2.7 The basic anatomical components of the nervous system.

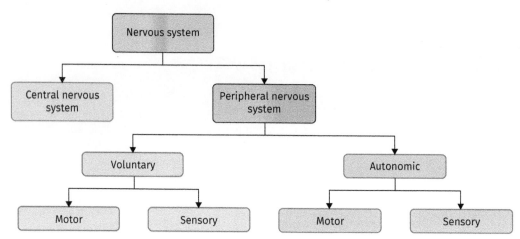

includes the voluntary and autonomic nervous system (Figure 2.7) controlling muscle movement and 'fight or flight' response respectively.

All of these systems have the same basic nerve cell, a neurone. A bundle of neurones makes a nerve. Nerves can be pure motor or sensory neurones but are often comprised of motor and sensory autonomic and voluntary neurones all mixed together. Neurones are specialized long, thin cells that carry signals in the form of electrical impulses. These impulses result from the movement of different ions in and out of the cell and are maintained by a special sodium/potassium 'pump' that requires ATP to, so neurones require lots of energy to send these signals. For example, the brain is less than 2 per cent of the body's total mass but consumes around 25 per cent of circulating glucose!

The flux of ions in and out the cell, causing a change in electrical potential and a wave of depolarization, allows a signal called an action potential to travel from one end of the cell to the other. In the case of the movement of your big toe, a motor signal would initialize from the pre-motor cortex, travel through the brain and descend in the spinal cord before exiting through the spinal nerve roots to descend further via the sciatic nerve to the leg. It will not be a single neurone that carries this signal, however. There will be several connecting steps where the impulse passes from one neurone to the next across a connecting **synapse**. This is a junction where signals can pass or be modulated between neurones by the release of specialist chemicals called **neurotransmitters**. There are dozens of different types of neurotransmitters, which stimulate or dampen down the neurone they act on. Specialized junctions also use neurotransmitters to carry impulses from motor neurones to effectors—for example, a **motor end plate** transfers impulses from a motor neurone to muscle fibres.

Post-synaptic receptors open or close depending on which neurotransmitter (or drug) binds to them, changing the post-synaptic potential. If it makes the post-synaptic potential more negative (hyperpolarized), the threshold for a new action potential in the post-synaptic neurone is less likely to be reached. This is an inhibitory post-synaptic potential (IPSP).

If the neurotransmitter makes the post-synaptic neurone more positive, it will depolarize and reach the threshold to trigger an action potential more easily—this is an excitatory post-synaptic potential (EPSP). After binding to the post-synaptic receptors many neurotransmitters are either broken down or reabsorbed into the pre-synaptic axon (see Figure 2.8). You will learn more about the nervous system in Chapter 7.

Figure 2.8 For a nerve impulse to pass from one neurone to another, neurotransmitters need to be released across the synaptic gap. The neurotransmitter molecules interact with receptors on the post-synaptic membrane and produce either excitatory or inhibitory post-synaptic potentials across the membrane.

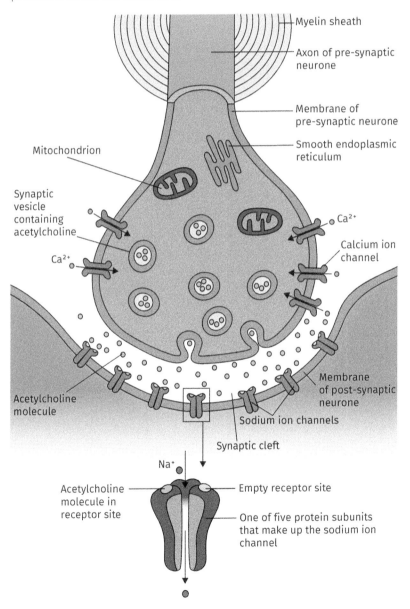

There are multiple ways that drugs can work on these junctions and receptors to modulate their normal function. The amount of neurotransmitter released by the pre-synaptic axon can be increased, the receptors can be stimulated or blocked, or the breakdown of the neurotransmitter can be inhibited to prolong its effects.

The anaesthetic triad

Modern anaesthesia involves precise doses of specially designed drugs that obliterate consciousness and provide pain relief. This, along with the scrupulous monitoring of a wide variety of physiological parameters, allows surgeons to carry out long and complex surgery, taking the time they need to do the job well with their patient safely unaware and unresponsive. Although standards have changed from the first anaesthetics—when keeping someone unconscious was an almost miraculous leap forward but awareness of dosages and adverse patient reactions was not a big part of practice—the principles behind anaesthesia remain the same. The ideal anaesthetic has three aims, often referred to as the anaesthetic triad: hypnosis (unconsciousness), analgesia (pain relief), and areflexia (muscle relaxation). Each part represents an important aspect of the anaesthetic process, and we need to use different medications to induce each aspect of full anaesthesia.

Hypnosis

The human brain is an amazing machine, and one we are still a long way from fully understanding. The concept of 'consciousness' is one that philosophers and scientists have argued about for millennia, an argument which continues to this day. One widely accepted description is that consciousness is the awareness of internal or external existence. Humans are not the only creatures thought to have awareness, but they are by far the most complex. Removing this awareness, and making sure that patients do not experience or remember the surgical procedure, is one of the key goals of anaesthesia—but how is this achieved?

Hypnosis refers to the loss of consciousness and ability to form memory that occurs in anaesthesia. While we have clearly mapped areas of the brain that respond to stimuli such as vision or scent, no one section of the brain is used for conscious thought. In spite of decades of research and years of use we still are far from understanding how the drugs used in anaesthetics work to cause a loss of consciousness. It is generally accepted that anaesthetic drugs decrease the transmission of nerve cell signals within the brain and that this results in a reduction and eventual loss of consciousness, and full anaesthesia.

If all nerve cells had the same type of receptors and the same neurotransmitters in the synapses and motor end plates, then a single drug would be able to create unconsciousness, paralysis, and pain relief with a single mechanism; unfortunately, it isn't that simple, and the nervous system has a huge array of receptor families and subtypes. A small sample is shown in Table 2.1.

Table 2.1 Cellular receptors

Receptor type	Receptor type	Location	Action
Muscarinic receptors	G-protein-coupled receptors	Autonomic nervous system—Parasympathetic	Sodium channel 'Rest and Digest'
Nicotinic receptors	Ion channels	Neuromuscular junction—Post-synaptic	Sodium channel Muscle contraction
Adrenoceptors	Ion channels	Autonomic nervous system—Sympathetic	Sodium channel 'Fight or Flight'
Glucose receptors	Tyrosine kinase receptors	Almost all cell tissues	Absorption of glucose in response to insulin
NMDA	Ion channel	Brain Spinal cord	Calcium channel Depolarizes nerve
GABA	Ion channel	Brain Spinal cord	Chloride channel Hyperpolarizes nerve
5–HT3 (Serotonin subtype 3)	Ion channel	Brain Pain receptors	Sodium, Potassium, Calcium channel Depolarizes cell Involved in anxiety, pain receptors and vomiting
Dopamine	G-protein-coupled receptors	Brain Blood vessels Heart	Multiple effects Modulation of motor effects

For sedation and hypnosis, the most important receptors are the GABA receptors. As you can see in Table 2.1, they are found in the neurones of the brain and spinal cord. GABA receptors are inhibitory receptors which, when stimulated, open to allow chloride ions (Cl^-) into the cell, hyperpolarizing the cell so it doesn't reach the required threshold to carry any signal. As the GABA receptors are found mainly in the central nervous system, it is thought that by stimulating GABA receptors the general level of activity in the brain is decreased. If this happens enough, then unconsciousness occurs and thus, anaesthesia. This also means that if a large enough dose of anaesthetic is given, it can fatally dampen the signals sent in the brain, so dosage must be calculated very carefully. To add even more complexity, each person's brain is unique; for example, a young, fit patient will have a far greater number of neurones than an elderly patient, and they will be firing more efficiently (see Figure 2.9). As a result, a younger patient may require much larger doses of anaesthetic drugs to induce unconsciousness. Along with natural patient variation, there are also lifestyle factors to consider. For example, alcohol also affects GABA receptors, and with chronic use a tolerance develops, so patients who are alcoholics often have huge tolerances to anaesthetic agents and need much higher doses than an equivalent person who does not drink heavily.

Figure 2.9 People vary in so many ways—age, gender, genetic makeup, body mass, alcohol use, pregnancy, etc. An anaesthetist needs to take all of these things into consideration to make sure effective, safe hypnosis is achieved during anaesthesia.

© Rawpixel.com/Shutterstock.

Analgesia

Pain is an unpleasant physiological and psychological phenomenon which alerts the body to current or impending damage. The perception of pain is a survival trait vital to normal human function, but it is a major limiting factor during and after surgery. Despite being anaesthetized during the surgery, the patient still undergoes controlled trauma and damage as the surgeon cuts into and through their tissues. This damage understandably causes pain. Modern pharmacology has a wide variety of techniques to improve or alter painful stimuli.

Pain is, at its root, a sensation, and is therefore carried by sensory nerves from the peripheries to the brain. Specific sensory neurones carrying painful stimuli are categorized as Aδ and C fibres. These begin with nerve endings in the periphery of the body which carry specific pressure, temperature, or chemical receptors. If triggered, these neurones transmit their signals to the spinal cord. Here they ascend up to the brain in the spinothalamic tract. Once at the brainstem, the nerve signals pass to many different brain structures including those involved in fear and emotional processing. This means that pain is not just a physical sensation but is also intrinsically linked to our psychological state.

When a small child hurts themselves, the grownups around them will often 'rub it better' or 'kiss it better'. Perhaps you remember the magic of this action! The 'gate' theory of pain is a model explaining the link between nociception (painful stimuli) and 'normal' sensation, which explains how 'rubbing it better' really works. The sensory neurones which carry messages to your brain about touch, light, etc. are **myelinated neurones** and so they conduct impulses very rapidly. Both Aδ and C fibres are thin and either poorly myelinated or **unmyelinated neurones**, and so they conduct impulses relatively slowly. As a result, the sensation of pain arrives in the brain slightly slower than normal sensory stimuli. There is a linked inhibitory neurone in the brain that is activated by both of these neurones. As normal sensation travels faster than pain, it arrives in the brain cell first and activates this inhibitory neurone, in turn causing decreased transmission of the painful stimuli to the brain (see Figure 2.10). So we all have our own built-in protection against pain—but this isn't enough when we are undergoing surgery. All the rubbing in the world won't stop a surgical incision hurting—so we need something stronger. Perhaps we can stimulate those inhibitory neurones using drugs?

Pain-relieving drugs use different mechanisms and work on many different receptors in the body. As a result, the drugs we have available to treat pain are most effective when a mixture of them is used, so multiple mechanisms of pain relief are brought into action. This is why even in large operations, patients are still given paracetamol and often a nonsteroidal drug similar to ibuprofen, both of which can be bought at the pharmacy. This multimodal analgesia offers much better pain relief than

Figure 2.10 The gate theory of pain. Note the inhibitory neuron that acts downstream to affect the final signal transmitted to the brain.

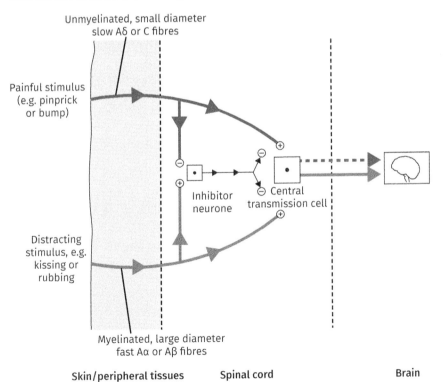

any single drug can do. It has the added benefit that each drug can be used in lower doses in a mixture than would be required if the drug were used by itself.

Areflexia

Even when the higher functions of the brain are decreased and a patient is unconscious, the body still has protective reflexes and mechanisms to defend itself from harm. Patients can move or twitch while still being in a plane of anaesthesia deep enough to reduce pain and render them unconscious. There are two main reasons why we want to minimize muscle movement during anaesthesia; one relates to anaesthetic technique and the second relates to surgical requirements.

- **For the anaesthetist:** When a patient goes under anaesthesia they lose some muscle tone—in other words, their muscles relax. Most importantly in this context, they lose tone within the oropharynx (throat) and upper airway. As a result, the airways collapse and the patient is unable to breathe. The anaesthetist must insert an airway device and breathe for the patient using a ventilator. Some airway devices simply require an adequate depth of anaesthesia as they do not pass through the vocal cords, these are known as supraglottic devices. Other devices, known as endotracheal tubes (ETTs), need to pass through the patient's vocal cords. If the anaesthetist uses an ETT, then the patient needs to be paralysed to relax the vocal cords enough to allow the tube to pass through them. The decision about which type of airway device to use depends on both the type of surgery and the preferences of individual anaesthetists.

- **For the surgeon:** If a patient moves when being cut in surgery, it could be very dangerous for the surgeon, and for the patient! Potentially disastrous errors could occur if the patient moves at the wrong time during a procedure, causing the surgeon to cut into tissues they wanted to preserve. This is especially relevant during surgery on very delicate or small areas of the body such as in neurosurgery or inner ear surgery, or when a surgeon is working near to major arteries. In these types of operation, it is often a surgical request rather than an anaesthetic decision to paralyse the patient in order to optimize the outcomes.

The neuromuscular junction is similar to a neuronal synapse (see Figure 2.8), but instead of a post-synaptic neurone there is a neuromuscular end-plate, a section of muscle fibre, which responds to the release of neurotransmitter, depolarizes and then contracts. Anaesthetic neuromuscular blockers can block the neuromuscular receptor to inhibit muscle contraction and stop patients moving. It is vital to note that these drugs *do not* affect consciousness. If they were used on an awake patient, they would be unable to move but still be aware and able to feel what was happening. In anaesthetics this is known as 'awareness' and is a critical complication, although thankfully a very rare one.

Case study 2.1
An ageing population

The number of compounds which can be used to deliver anaesthesia has expanded significantly since the days of Davy and Morton. Today we have many drugs available which act swiftly and precisely to deliver hypnosis, pain relief, and areflexia, and so offer optimal conditions during surgery with minimal side effects. The large range of drugs available presents both a blessing and a challenge for the modern anaesthetist, as their use and actions differ greatly depending on lots of factors. These include the type of patient to be operated on and the type of surgery to be performed.

A safe anaesthetic is a key part of modern surgery. When interviewing a patient to anaesthetize, an anaesthetist usually has three big considerations in mind: patient factors, anaesthetic factors, and surgical factors.

- **Patient factors**: These include age, past medical history, medications and allergies, normal activities, and what they are able to do. As anaesthetic drugs have significant effects on most organ systems, their baseline function may need to be reviewed and investigated with blood tests or physical examination. For example, the patient below, Mary (see CS 2.1 Figure A), is eighty years old and so likely to have reduced kidney function, which would make drugs that are filtered by the kidneys last longer than they would in a younger patient, as they are not excreted as effectively. Her artificial heart valve may mean she is on blood-thinning agents, depending on the type of valve, and this in turn would affect her ability to tolerate certain types of analgesia such as an epidural. Her heart arrhythmias may be controlled by drugs which

CS 2.1 Figure A Mary is eighty years old and although she still goes to aerobics classes and is very active in her family, she has an artificial heart valve, heart arrhythmias, and a recurrence of cancer. An anaesthetist has to take all of these factors into consideration before surgery.

© Ann Short.

reduce the heart rate, but many anaesthetic drugs also reduce heart rate and blood pressure and so this needs to be considered when calculating doses to give the patient.

- **Anaesthetic factors**: these include consideration of additional analgesic techniques, and working around options which are not open due to patient factors, to provide the best possible option for each patient. For example, if an epidural cannot be used, then other regional local anaesthetic infusions such as rectus sheath catheters could be placed instead. The use of muscle relaxants or the type of anaesthetic agent needs to be considered alongside the post-operative analgesic (pain-relief) plan as well.

- **Surgical factors:** these depend on what the patient requires to heal. Does Mary have a bowel obstruction caused by the cancer recurrence? Does she have a fractured hip from a fall? The length of the operation, the operation site, how painful the surgery is, and the associated complications or additional requirements all have to be woven into the anaesthetic plan. For example, in large vascular operations such as abdominal aortic aneurysm repairs there is often a point when the aorta is 'clamped off', causing a huge rise in blood pressure. At this point the anaesthetist needs to be ready with drugs to reduce the blood pressure rapidly or there could be serious complications. The anaesthetist and surgeon have to work in harmony and understand the key considerations of both of their specialities.

A fourth category is increasingly being included in these considerations; that of prehabilitation. The concept of rehabilitation is well known—a period of recovery and training after an operation to help patients return to baseline function. However, with an ageing and increasingly overweight population, current thinking is that the dangers of surgery can be minimized if a patient is given a period of prehabilitation, if there is time before the surgery is needed. For example, a patient may be encouraged to stop smoking, lose weight, or engage in specific exercises to strengthen key muscle groups that will mean they are at peak physical fitness before they undergo their surgery. This has had very promising results, improving outcomes for patients—it may well become commonplace for elective operations in the future!

❓ Pause for thought

Discuss the main issues with elderly patients and anaesthesia. There is some resistance to the idea of prehabilitation both from within the medical profession and from patients. Develop arguments both for and against the process. Some people might argue that if a patient refuses prehabilitation, they should not be offered elective surgery (surgery that is not vital for life, such as hip replacements). What are the arguments for and against this approach? Who is responsible for deciding if a patient is fit for surgery?

So how do anaesthetics work?

We don't know exactly how most anaesthetics actually have their almost miraculous effect, but we do have some understanding of how they affect the body—it isn't just a black box and magic!

Almost all drugs in anaesthesia act on two basic principles: activation or suppression of cellular receptors and/or dependence on a concentration gradient. Precise knowledge of the relationship between these two is vital for accurate prediction of the onset, duration, and offset of the drugs given for anaesthesia.

Receptors

A receptor is a membrane bound protein that binds to and is activated by an **endogenous ligand**—a ligand is a specific ion or molecule that binds to a metal atom to form a coordination complex. Receptors allow cells to communicate, and increase or decrease intracellular activity in response to chemical signals from other cells. Receptors are found in three major families: **G-protein-coupled receptors (GPCRs)**, **ligand-gated ion channels**, and **tyrosine kinase receptors**. Different types of receptors carry out different functions. They may be found in different types of cells, or in different areas of the body (see Table 2.1). Receptors are often the target of anaesthetic drugs, so it is useful to understand a bit about them. We will discuss two examples of receptors important in anaesthesia here.

G-protein-coupled receptors (GPCRs)

G-protein-coupled receptors (GPCRs) are involved in the way the body responds to many different substances, including adrenaline, the 'fight or flight' hormone. Adrenaline is vital for the anaesthetist. As mentioned previously, many anaesthetic drugs affect other organ systems; one of the most common side effects of anaesthesia is hypotension, or low blood pressure. Hypotension is sometimes needed to minimize bleeding and provide a good surgical field, but blood pressure that is too low causes reduced blood flow to vital tissues such as the heart, kidneys, or brain. Anaesthetists monitor the blood pressure of the patient all the time, using drugs which act on the adrenergic GPCRs to increase heart rate or blood pressure when needed to maintain blood flow to these vital organs. How do these adrenergic GPCRs work?

GPCRs are single polypeptide molecules folded and spanning the plasma membrane of the cell. When a ligand or drug binds to the extracellular receptor a conformational (shape) change takes place. This causes an energy-rich GTP molecule to bind to the G-protein, making it dissociate from the receptor. The G-protein travels to a membrane-bound enzyme called adenyl cyclase and changes its activity (see Figure 2.11). Adenyl cyclase is responsible for production of cyclic adenosine mono-phosphate (cAMP) which is a vital intracellular messenger. By increasing or decreasing activity of adenyl cyclase, G-protein-coupled receptors (GPCRs) cause an increase or decrease in cell activity. Some GPCRs are stimulatory (G-α_s) and some are inhibitory (G-α_i). As they work via enzymes, they are

Figure 2.11 G-protein-coupled receptors.

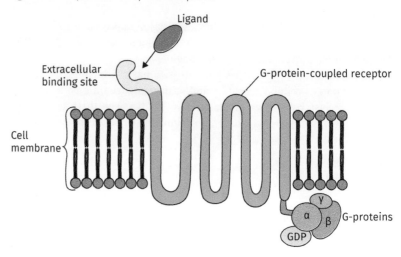

incredibly potent—a single α protein can cause adenyl cyclase to create thousands of cAMP molecules.

Ligand-gated ion channels

Ion channels are trans-membrane proteins that form 'pores' or holes within the membrane surface. In their resting state these receptors are closed, preventing any ions from crossing the cell membrane. When activated by a ligand or drug, the proteins undergo a conformational change and open to allow in a specific ion such as sodium (Na^+) or potassium (K^+) (see Figure 2.12). Ion channels are often found on cells which need rapid signal

Figure 2.12 Ligand-gated ion channels.

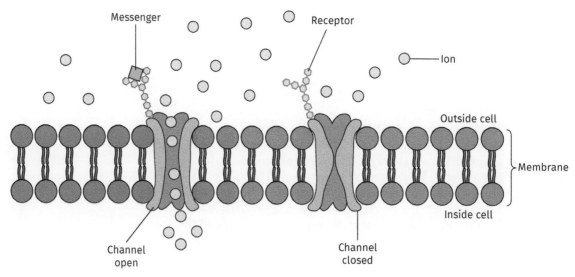

transduction to exert their effect, such as muscle and nerve cells. These cells rely on the electrochemical gradient between the outside and the inside of the cell. If these ion channels are disrupted, either through being activated or blocked, they can cause significant disruption to the functioning of these cells. In anaesthetics, ion channels are vital in areflexia, because at the neuromuscular junctions there are post-synaptic nicotinic receptors, which, when stimulated, cause muscle contraction and so movement. By blocking these receptors patients can be paralysed to ensure an ideal surgical environment.

Concentration gradients

A concentration gradient describes the concentration relationship between two areas. In a gas mixture or a solution, particles diffuse down a concentration gradient from an area with a high concentration of a substance to an area of lower concentration. If there is a permeable membrane in place, diffusion down a concentration gradient will take place freely through the membrane until there is an equal concentration on both sides. This is known as a state of equilibrium.

If a membrane is semi-permeable, rather than permeable, it allows some particles through but not others. The cell membrane, for example, allows in fat-soluble molecules but not water-soluble ones. The size of the molecule, whether it is ionized or not, and thickness of the layers all affect the ease with which the molecules can diffuse through the membrane and therefore the speed at which an equilibrium is reached.

The concept of concentration gradients is vital for the anaesthetist to understand, as it helps describe the actions and potential complications of a drug. In order to have an effect, a drug has to diffuse through tissues to the desired cell before binding to the receptor site. The characteristics of the drug affect how rapidly it will diffuse, and into which tissues, and thus how quickly it can cause its effect.

A useful example of the importance of diffusion is illustrated in the anaesthetic drug called Propofol. Propofol is the most commonly used agent to induce anaesthesia or provide sedation in the UK. Chemically it is 2,6-diisopropylphenol, a phenol-based molecule with 2 propyl side chains. It is very fat-soluble, and so it diffuses readily through cell membranes. When Propofol is injected into the blood stream it diffuses quickly into the body tissues, and can pass easily through the **blood–brain barrier**, reaching the conscious areas of the brain. As a result, it delivers sedation and anaesthesia rapidly, as it reaches the brain easily. On the other hand, it also stops acting very fast as it is rapidly redistributed to fatty tissue around the body. This rapid offset means that once a patient is anaesthetized with Propofol, they will require further anaesthetic drugs such as the halogenated vapours in Figure 2.6 or a constant infusion of a drug like Propofol. The rapid onset and offset also allows Propofol to be used for sedation, where a patient is made very sleepy but is not 'anaesthetized' as they may still be dimly aware of what is going on. This can be very useful for short, painful procedures such as relocating a dislocated shoulder, which requires extremely painful manipulation to put the shoulder back into place, but only takes a few seconds.

The anaesthetist at work: anaesthetic equipment and techniques

In the first part of this chapter we have looked at how modern anaesthetics work, but that theoretical knowledge is only a small part of what anaesthetists do in their day-to-day practice. There are a large variety of practical skills and techniques an anaesthetist uses to help monitor the patient and ensure safe, reliable anaesthesia. For many of us, our only experience of surgery is what we see on hospital dramas. Here we will consider each step as part of a patient's journey for a routine operation such as a repair of a hernia.

Patient arrives, clerking, and meeting with surgeon and anaesthetist

On arrival to the hospital, a patient is clerked in by the surgical doctors and gives their consent for the operation. A variety of checklists are completed to confirm the correct patient, the correct operation and the correct side of the body. The surgeon performing the operation will often discuss any final worries with the patient. The anaesthetist will also see the patient, ensuring any medication and allergy details are correct before discussing any additional procedures they may perform, and once again gaining consent from the patient (see Figure 2.13). The surgeon, anaesthetist, theatre nurses, anaesthetic assistants, and theatre 'runners' will have their morning meeting in the theatre and discuss what order they want to operate on patients and any concerns they have for each patient. These discussions will include issues with obese patients or patients with pre-existing medical conditions which will potentially complicate the surgery (see Case study 2.1).

Figure 2.13 Conversations between a patient and their anaesthetist allow for important exchanges of information.

© Monkey Business Images/Shutterstock.

Pre-operative checks and the anaesthetic room

When the patient is ready, they will be wheeled to the pre-operative area in a trolley or bed. They will have been changed into a gown and had identification bands placed on their wrists or ankles. In the pre-op area, they will again go through confirmation checks with a member of theatre staff. These may seem repetitive, but they are designed to avoid errors—no one wants to have the wrong bit of them operated on! Once these checks have been completed the patient will often stop in a designated anaesthetic room just outside of theatre. In the anaesthetic room there are several procedures that may be done and instruments that may be used, including the following.

- **Venous cannulas:** These are plastic tubes that are positioned within the veins of the patient. They allow the anaesthetist to put drugs straight into the venous system (see Chapter 3) so they are delivered rapidly to the rest of the body. Many, but not all, drugs can be given via the intravenous route, including anaesthetic induction agents like Propofol and neuromuscular blockers.

- **Arterial cannulas:** These are less common, and are used to measure blood pressure and cardiac output very accurately. They are used in frail patients who are likely to be very unstable, or in complex operations where large fluctuations in blood pressure are expected. Blood samples can also be taken from these cannulas.

- **Neuraxial analgesia:** Neuraxial analgesia and anaesthesia includes insertion of epidural catheters and spinal anaesthetic. Both of these are more complex procedures, which involve injecting local anaesthetic around the spinal cord. They don't make the patient unconscious, but they do remove any sensation below the anaesthetic intervention. These techniques can be used in childbirth, and can also act as postoperative analgesia for patients having lower limb or abdominal surgery.

- **Airway management:** This is the most important, and most dangerous, step of anaesthesia. As discussed above, the choice of airway device will depend on patient, anaesthetic, and surgical factors. The anaesthetist ensures that the patient is adequately anaesthetized and paralysed before inserting a device called a laryngoscope into the mouth of the patient, elevating the tongue and lower jaw to reveal a view of the vocal cords. They then insert an endotracheal tube to secure the airway and ensure that the patient has an effective supply of oxygen throughout the procedure. Once this step is complete, the patient is securely anaesthetized and ready for surgery.

- **Surgical theatre:** Once the airway is secure, the patient is moved into the theatre itself. Once in theatre, the patient is checked in once again using the namebands put on earlier, and a final checklist takes place. This was designed by the World Health Organization and so is often referred to as the 'WHO checklist'. These rigorous checks are in place to minimize the risk of performing the wrong operation on the wrong side on the wrong patient.

- **Ventilator and vaporizers:** As the patient is paralysed, they cannot breathe for themselves. A ventilator is used which pushes air into the patient. This is very different to how we normally breathe, by expanding our chest cavity, causing a drop in internal pressure and so 'sucking' air into our lungs (see Chapter 4). The ventilator can cause some significant changes to our lung physiology, particularly in those with pre-existing lung disease, and this can cause further problems for the anaesthetist. The ventilator often has vaporizers attached which deliver halogenated anaesthetic vapour to the patient, to sustain anaesthesia.

- **Recovery:** Once the operation is complete the patient is woken up in theatre, but often they are still very groggy due to low concentrations of anaesthetic agents still present in their system. They are transported to recovery where they are looked after by specially trained nurses. Once they have woken up and are out of the most common time frame for anaesthetic complications, they are returned to the ward to recover from their operation.

The bigger picture 2.2
Green anaesthesia

So far, we have considered how effective anaesthesia affects us. Now, in the twenty-first century, there is a new view of anaesthesia dubbed by some as 'green anaesthetics', looking at minimizing the environmental impact of anaesthesia.

Plastics are a large part of medical equipment, offering relatively cheap, sterile single-use equipment. This poses a problem of plastic waste—in the UK alone, National Health Service (NHS) providers generated 590,000 tonnes of waste in 2016/17, of which less than one-quarter was recycled. Many recycling firms refuse to handle medical waste for sanitary reasons, and currently there is no viable alternative to the single-use plastics found in syringes, cannulas, endotracheal tubes, and other vital pieces of medical equipment.

A further and arguably more important aspect of green anaesthesia is focusing on the greenhouse gas effect of the halogenated agents such as desflurane and sevoflurane. These halogenated agents are the most commonly used drugs to maintain anaesthesia. Vaporizers create a titratable flow of anaesthetic that is mixed with oxygen and air and delivered to the patient. As the patient breathes out, much of the anaesthetic is recirculated into the ventilator system, but some of it has to be 'scavenged' through an exhaust port to make room for more oxygen from the fresh gas flow. This scavenged gas is excreted from the hospital, usually directly into the atmosphere. Unfortunately, these halogenated carbon chains also produce a greenhouse gas effect. Modern anaesthetic gases make up 5 per cent of the carbon footprint of the NHS, and in total the NHS makes up 3 per cent of all carbon and greenhouse gases in the UK. As mentioned previously the greenhouse effect of different anaesthetic agents differs significantly, with desflurane being a major culprit; an hour-long anaesthetic with sevoflurane produces the same carbon footprint as a thirty-mile car journey while the same anaesthetic with desflurane would be the equivalent of a 230-mile trip!

In 2023, desflurane was banned in Scotland, NHS England plans to stop using it early in 2024 except in exceptional circumstances, and the EU plans the same action in 2026.

Pause for thought

- Investigate the similarity between anaesthetic drugs and the CFCs, widely used as refrigerants and aerosols in the twentieth century, but later discovered to cause huge damage to the ozone layer in the atmosphere.
- Banning anaesthetic gases such as desflurane may result in more difficult or less good anaesthesia. Discuss the ethics of banning these compounds, justifying all of your arguments.

Chapter summary

- Although surgery was performed in the ancient past, the pain and complications surrounding it made survival very low. Modern anaesthesia is imperative for comfortable, safe surgery.
- Anaesthetics truly began with the invention of inhalational agents such as nitrous oxide and ether. Since then, there have been many different anaesthetic drugs, which offer significant advantages over these early agents.
- Anaesthetists are responsible for maintaining normal physiology during an operation and providing the best operating environment for the surgeon. A theoretical triad for the perfect anaesthetic is described as hypnosis, analgesia, and areflexia.
- With the variety and complexity of modern operations the role of anaesthetist has expanded significantly to include considerations around the specific type of surgery being performed, the anaesthetic and analgesic requirement of this surgery, and the patient's comorbidities that may be affected by the anaesthetic or surgery.
- Modern anaesthetic vapours such as sevoflurane and desflurane are widely used but carry the unfortunate side effect of being greenhouse gases. One of the very new considerations for anaesthetists is how we

can reduce or remove the use of these agents without causing harm or detriment to patients.

- Despite a huge body of research into anaesthetic drugs there is still a large amount of debate on how they work. Most seem to cause an effect on GABA receptors to globally decrease neurone transmission within the brain, but this also has other effects on organ systems such as the heart and lung. Considerations around this are important to the anaesthetist during an operation.

 ## Further reading

Charlesworth, M and Swinton, F 'Anaesthetic gases, climate change and sustainable practice' *The Lancet* 2017 (14 June) 1(6). https://doi.org/10.1016/S2542-5196(17)30040-2
A well-written summary of the greenhouse effect of anaesthetic gases and a very important article highlighting the importance of sustainable healthcare.

Davies, H *Researches, Chemical and Philosophical, Chiefly Concerning Nitrous Oxide, or Dephlogisticated Nitrous Air, and Its Respiration.* J Johnson, St. Paul's Church-yard, London, 1800.https://archive.org/details/researcheschemi00davygoog
A delightful compendium of Humphry Davy's laboratory notes describing in detail how to make and store nitrous oxide. It includes details of experiments on the effect of nitrous oxide on amphibians, mammals, his lab assistants, and even himself (including while intoxicated). It includes the bizarrely titled chapter: 'Of the effects of nitrous oxide on vegetables'.

 ## Discussion questions

2.1   Imagine you were Davy or Morton (or one of their colleagues) when anaesthetic gases were first being investigated. How do you think you would have experimented with the gas? What problems do you think you might have faced from surgeons or scientists of the time?

2.2   What do you think makes the perfect anaesthetic drug? List some qualities you would want if you were to create the perfect drug for anaesthesia.

2.3   Investigate the potential for regional anaesthesia—a subspeciality of anaesthesia keeping people awake during operations by numbing specific groups of nerves. What advantages or disadvantages do you think this could have?

2.4   Have a go at making a list of all the ways (both direct and indirect) in which modern anaesthesia can contribute to rapid and effective post-operative healing.

3 THE HEART OF THE MATTER

Our heart and blood vessels form a complicated, largely automated system of organs. They function throughout our entire lives, usually without any conscious input, delivering oxygenated blood to the tissues of every organ system, and returning deoxygenated blood to the lungs. The heart is the very first organ to form during pregnancy—the most recent research from the University of Oxford in the UK suggests that the cells that will form your heart begin to beat just sixteen days after conception (see Figure 3.1). The cardiovascular system is made up of the heart, the blood vessels, and the blood which flows through them. A fully functioning cardiovascular system is essential for life.

But what happens when this system goes wrong? Globally, cardiovascular disease kills more people than any other health problem—it causes up to 31 per cent of all deaths, around 18 million people a year around the world; 85 per cent of these deaths are due to heart attacks and strokes. To prevent these deaths, we need to understand what causes them—and find out how surgery can help.

Figure 3.1 This striking image is a visualization of the heart of a human embryo at the beginning of the sixth week of pregnancy. The image is built up using data from a number of scans.

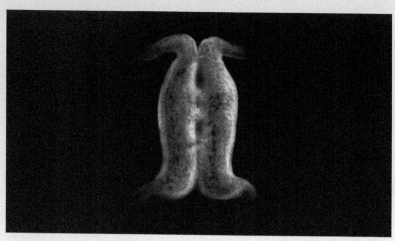

TheVisualMD/Science Source/Science Photo Library.

A summary of the cardiovascular system

To understand the problems that arise when the cardiovascular system goes wrong, we need a clear picture of what a healthy cardiovascular system looks like, and how it works. Here is a brief summary.

Veins, arteries, and capillaries—very different types of blood vessel

It has been estimated that if all of the blood vessels in an adult person were laid end to end, they would stretch between 60,000–100,000 miles. There are three distinctive types of blood vessels: **arteries**, **veins**, and **capillaries** (see Figure 3.2). Each has distinct adaptations for their very different functions in the body.

- **Arteries** (with the exception of the pulmonary artery, and the umbilical artery during pregnancy) carry oxygenated blood from the heart to the peripheries of the body—dividing into smaller arteries and then vessels called arterioles. Arteries function at high pressures, when the blood is pumped out of the heart. They have both smooth muscle and elastic tissues in their walls, as they must stretch and recoil back to shape with each pulse of blood (see Figure 3.2).

- **Veins** (with the exception of the pulmonary and umbilical veins) return deoxygenated blood from the body to the heart. This blood is not under such high pressure as blood in the arterial circulation, and so veins have relatively thin walls, with little smooth muscle or elastic tissue, and valves, which work to prevent the backflow of blood through the lower pressure system (see Figure 3.2).

Figure 3.2 This diagram shows the crucial differences between the three main types of blood vessel.

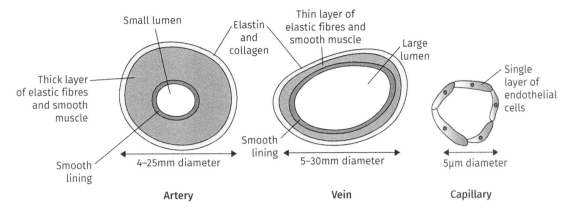

- **Capillaries** make up the tiny blood vessels between arterioles and venules. These fine, branching vessels form a matrix between the high-pressure arterial system and the lower-pressure venous system, allowing efficient exchange between the blood and the cells.

The heart

Angled very slightly to the left of the midline of the **thorax**, the human heart is a muscular, four-chambered pump.

The anatomy of the heart

Figure 3.3 shows the key structures of the heart.

Figure 3.3 The human heart is made of four chambers—but there are many other parts to this fascinating organ.

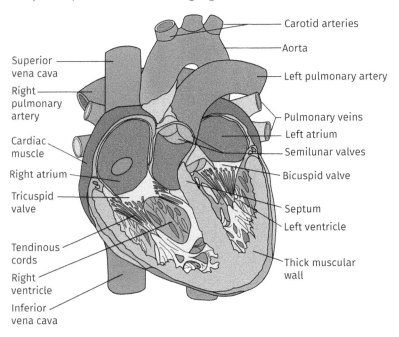

The physiology of the heart

To understand the normal functioning of the heart, we need to consider both the cycle of contraction and relaxation which moves blood through the heart (the **cardiac cycle**), and how the conducting tissue running through the myocardium regulates this cycle. Using modern technologies such as ultrasound and electrocardiograms (ECGs) it is relatively easy to visualize exactly how electrical impulses conducted through the heart affect its contraction and relaxation, and how blood moves through the various chambers. Physicians of the past did not have these technologies at their disposal—which led to some interesting and bizarre theories about how the heart works throughout the centuries. You can read about some of these in The bigger picture 3.1.

The cardiac cycle

The cardiac cycle can be broken down into two distinct phases—contraction (known as systole) and relaxation (known as diastole). During **systole** the chambers of the heart contract, pumping blood through the heart, to the lungs via the pulmonary circulation, and to the rest of the body via the aorta. During **diastole** the chambers of the heart relax, allowing blood to fill each chamber in preparation for the next period of systole. To allow the heart to pump blood efficiently, this must all take place in a certain order—see Figure 3.4.

Figure 3.4 The cardiac cycle can be broken down into three basic stages, based on what the atria and the ventricles are doing at the time.

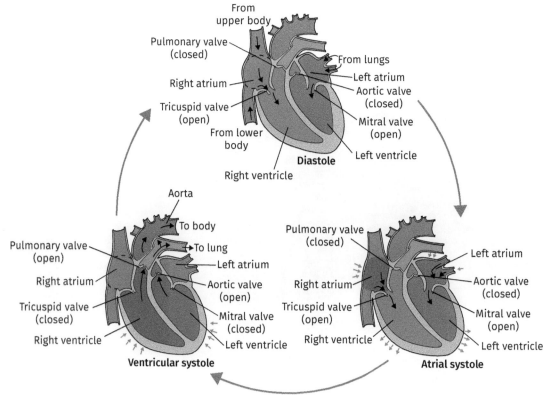

The bigger picture 3.1
Unravelling the mysteries of the circulatory system

Pliny the Elder, a Roman writer who lived 23–79 CE, and author of a thirty-seven-volume book entitled *Natural History*, wrote '*The arteries have no sensation, for they even are without blood . . . the veins spread underneath the whole skin, finally ending in very thin threads, and they narrow down into such an extremely minute size that the blood cannot pass through them nor can anything else*'—a bit confused by modern standards!

A century later Galen, a Greek doctor who lived in the second century CE, spent his lifetime in observation of the human body and its functioning. He performed extensive dissections and vivisections on animals. He studied the muscles, spinal cord, heart, urinary system, and proved that the arteries are full of blood.

Galen taught his students that there were two distinct types of blood, vital blood and nutritive blood. He thought vital blood was made by the heart and pumped through arteries to carry the 'vital spirits.' Galen believed that the heart acted not to pump blood, but to suck it in from the veins. His idea was that nutritive blood came from the liver and sloshed back and forth through the body, passing through the heart, where it was mixed with air by pores in the septum.

Galen, for all his mistakes, remained the unchallenged authority on the circulation for over a thousand years. After he died in 203 CE, serious anatomical and physiological research ground to a halt, because it was believed that everything there was to be said on the subject had been said by Galen! Galen was very enlightened for his time, but he made many mistakes—and these mistaken ideas were repeated for centuries.

Then, in 1208 CE, Ala'El-Deen Ibn-Al-Nafis was born in Kersh, a small town near Damascus. He studied medicine and philosophy in Damascus, and spent most of his life in Cairo. He was a physician, a linguist, a philosopher, and a historian. He was the first chief of Al-Mansuri Hospital in Cairo and the dean of the School of Medicine in 1284 CE.

He worked out the correct anatomy of the heart and the way the blood flowed through it. In his writing he stated clearly:

> the blood from the right chamber of the heart must arrive at the left chamber, but there is no direct pathway between them. The thick septum of the heart is not perforated and does not have visible pores as some people thought or invisible pores as Galen thought. The blood from the right chamber must flow through the vena arteriosa (pulmonary artery) to the lungs, spread through its substance, be mingled with air, pass through the arteria venosa (Pulmonary vein) to reach the left chamber of the heart.

Ibn-Al-Nafis also worked out the correct anatomy of the lungs and was the first person known to record the coronary circulation—the vessels supplying blood to the heart itself (see BP 3.1 Figure A).

BP 3.1 Figure A An illustration of Ibn-Al-Nafis—an enlightened man way ahead of his time.

Art Directors & TRIP/Alamy Stock Photo.

Ibn-Al-Nafis's work was based on extensive reading and the study of anatomy. But the significance of his ideas was not really understood even in his own country. Around 300 years later, in 1547, some of Ibn-Al-Nafis's work was translated into Latin. His important observations became available in Europe—shortly before some European scientists and doctors began to make the same discoveries! A coincidence or not?

It was only in the twentieth century that his work was brought to light again and people became aware of how early he had reached his conclusions on the workings of the heart and that some 'borrowing' of ideas may have occurred!

One of those who may have 'borrowed' ideas from Ibn-Al-Nafis was William Harvey (1578–1657). Harvey was an English doctor who studied in Italy before joining the Royal College of Physicians in London, where he continued his physiological studies. Observing the hearts of living animals, Harvey noticed that the muscular contraction of the ventricles (known as systole) resulted in blood being pumped out of the heart and through the arteries. By performing **vivisection** on dogs, Harvey proved conclusively to other members of the Royal College of Physicians that the volume of blood pumped around the body by the heart was far too great for the tissues of the body to simply absorb it. Harvey calculated that around 6g of blood was pumped with each contraction of the ventricles of a dog's heart, and that they contracted around one thousand times every half hour. This equates to around 6kg of blood being pumped every half hour—or 245kg of blood every day! Harvey hypothesized that this was an impossible amount of blood for the body to create every day, and that therefore the heart must pump around an existing volume of blood, rather than creating it anew.

Turning his attention to veins and arteries, Harvey noticed that the valves described by his mentor Fabricius appeared to only permit the flow of blood in one direction. Tying a ligature around the arm of a human subject, Harvey was able to demonstrate the dilation of the veins, as well as the valves themselves. Trying to force blood down towards the fingers proved impossible,

BP 3.1 Figure B An illustration from Harvey's work *De Motu Cordis*, showing distention of the veins of the forearm when a tourniquet is applied above the elbow. What do you think is being demonstrated in the second diagram? From Guilielmi Harvei [William Harvey]. *Exercitatio anatomica de motu cordis et sanguinis in animalibus.*

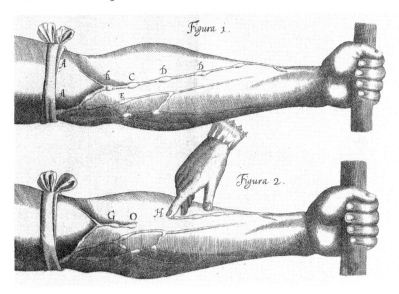

whereas moving blood back towards the body was relatively easy, as you can see in Harvey's diagram in BP 3.1 Figure B. Harvey demonstrated that venous blood flowed towards the heart. He also suggested that the circulatory system was divided into two circuits, with blood flowing from the heart to the lungs (pulmonary circulation) and then to the rest of the body (systemic circulation). He did not, however, predict the existence of capillaries, stating instead that the blood 'passes through pores in the flesh, from which it returns from the periphery everywhere to the centre'. His observations of dissected hearts helped to prove his theory that the circulatory system was unidirectional, as the valves in the heart functioned in the same way as the valves in the veins, preventing backflow of blood through the heart itself. Whether or not Harvey's ideas began with reading the ideas of others, his subsequent work helped to lay the foundations of our modern understanding of cardiology, and ultimately paved the way for some of the interventions and treatments you will read about later in this chapter.

The entire cardiac cycle is repeated many times every minute. When measured, this is known as the heart rate—or pulse. In healthy people, this varies from around 50 to 90 beats per minute.

The electrophysiology of the heart

Having studied the cardiac cycle, it is clear that the order of systole and diastole must be tightly linked. If the ventricles contract before the atria, then insufficient blood will be pumped to the pulmonary and systemic circulations, resulting in poor oxygen supply to vital organs. Similarly, if the atria contract whilst the ventricles are still contracted, then the ventricles won't fill adequately. Fortunately the cardiac cycle is regulated by a system of specialized cells, which transmit electric impulses through the cardiac muscle, stimulating it to contract in sequence to allow efficient pumping of blood. This conduction system is made up of a series of specialized nodes and conduction cells, seen in Figure 3.5.

The passage of electrical impulses through the conduction system mirrors the cardiac cycle, starting in the sinoatrial node (SA node, or SAN) in the right atrium, and finishing in the Purkinje fibres (sometimes called the Purkyne fibres) at the base of the ventricles.

1. An electrical impulse is generated at the SAN, and travels through the atria via the internodal pathways to the atrioventricular (AV) node (or AVN). As the impulse travels through the internodal pathways, it causes the atria to contract (atrial systole).

2. The impulse is delayed for a short period of time (around 120 milliseconds) at the AV node, allowing complete contraction of the atria. The atria start to repolarize and relax.

3. The impulse then passes into the ventricles, travelling into the bundle of His in the ventricular septum. This bundle of electrically conducting fibres then divides into the left and right bundles, conducting the impulse into the Purkinje fibres of the left and right ventricles respectively.

4. The Purkinje fibres are highly specialized cells, able to rapidly transmit electrical impulses to the muscular walls of both ventricles. This triggers contraction of the ventricles (ventricular systole).

5. The final stage of the conduction cycle is repolarization of the ventricles, allowing them to relax in preparation for a return to step 1.

The electrocardiogram—measuring electrical activity

To make clinical use of our understanding of the electrical conduction system of the heart, we need to measure the electrical activity in a quantifiable

Figure 3.5 The anatomy of the cardiac conduction system.

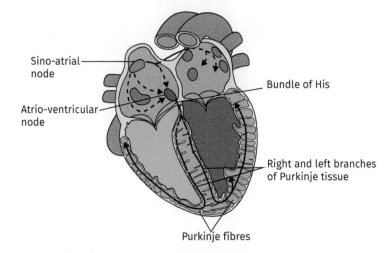

Sino-atrial node

Atrio-ventricular node

Bundle of His

Right and left branches of Purkinje tissue

Purkinje fibres

fashion. First developed in 1887 to record a tracing of the patient's heartbeat, the electrocardiogram (otherwise known as an ECG) has become a crucial tool in the investigation and diagnosis of cardiac conditions. The original ECG machines used in the late nineteenth and early twentieth centuries were large and cumbersome—but these days, portable ECG machines can be worn by patients for days at a time to record long periods of cardiac activity. This can help to identify problems with the conducting system of the heart, and allow medical or surgical correction of these problems. You can see the evolution in equipment in Figure 3.6.

Figure 3.6 Early ECG machines were big, and often required patients to immerse one or more limbs in a bath of an electrically conducting salt solution. Modern ECG machines like the example below are much smaller—often even handheld—and significantly easier to both use and interpret.

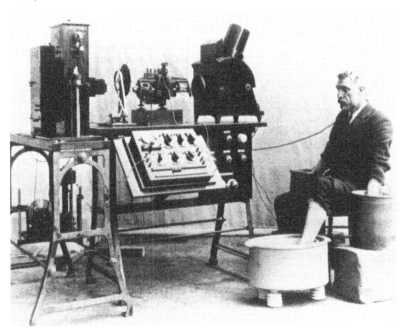

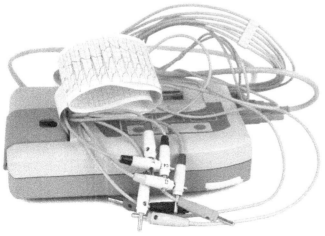

Early ECG machine: Science Photo Library. Modern ECG machine: © oksana2010/Shutterstock.

Figure 3.7 This diagram shows how the different phases of the ECG are related to the physical stages of the cardiac cycle.

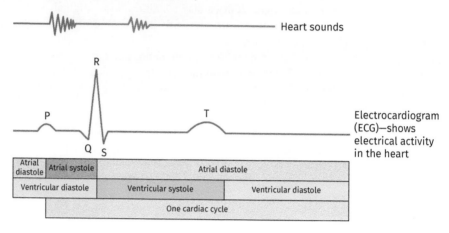

Modern ECGs are known as 12-lead ECGs. This is because they obtain twelve different electrical 'views' of the heart—although, confusingly, they only use ten separate leads to do so! The different views obtained by a 12-lead ECG can be helpful to doctors looking for problems in specific areas of the heart. Figure 3.7 shows you an ECG tracing, demonstrating the electrical activity of one complete healthy heartbeat alongside the systolic and diastolic stages of the cardiac cycle. Doctors learn to interpret changes in these patterns and link them to specific heart problems.

The blood supply of the heart

The heart is active all the time. It needs a good blood supply to enable the cardiac muscle to pump huge volumes of blood, day and night. So a rich blood supply has evolved, consisting of a series of coronary arteries which carry oxygenated blood to the main areas of the heart, and the associated veins. You can see these vessels clearly in Figure 3.8.

Figure 3.8 The coronary arteries branch off from the ascending aorta. They are essential to provide an adequate blood supply to the musculature of the heart itself.

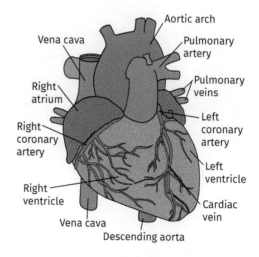

When the cardiovascular system goes wrong

Knowing how important the cardiovascular system is in the body, it's not hard to see why it is such a potential problem when things go wrong. Let's consider some of the more common problems. We cannot cover them all, so we'll focus mainly on issues solved by surgery.

Ischaemic heart disease

By far the most common medical condition affecting the heart is ischaemic heart disease (or IHD). Ischaemia means 'lack of oxygen' in Latin, so ischaemic heart disease refers to a disruption to the blood supply of the heart itself through the coronary arteries. There are a number of reasons for this, but the commonest is atherosclerosis, the gradual infiltration of fatty deposits into the lining of the coronary arteries, causing **atheromatous plaques**. The process starts with the accumulation of foam cells—**macrophages** which absorb fatty deposits onto the wall of a blood vessel. The fatty deposits continue to accumulate and harden, forming a plaque on the wall of the blood vessel.

These plaques gradually increase in size, narrowing the lumen of the coronary artery. Initially atherosclerosis may have no noticeable effect, but as the coronary arteries narrow, sufferers begin to experience symptoms when their heart requires more oxygenated blood. This usually manifests itself as a temporary dull, aching, heavy sensation in the chest, experienced on exercise—a sign that the coronary arteries are struggling to provide adequate oxygenated blood to the heart muscle. Once oxygen demands fall again, symptoms subside, usually within minutes of stopping exercising. This condition is known as **angina**. We classify it as stable (defined as angina that predictably occurs on exertion) or unstable (occurring both at rest and on exertion).

Unstable angina is usually a symptom of severe IHD, and requires urgent medical intervention. It may be a precursor to the most severe form of IHD—a heart attack, or **myocardial infarction**. This occurs when the blood supply to the myocardium is disrupted for a prolonged period—usually by a complete blockage of one or more of the coronary arteries. One of the most common causes of these blockages comes from the growing plaque, which attracts inflammatory cells and compounds. These destabilize the plaque and may cause it to rupture, potentially leading to the formation of a **thrombus** (blood clot) which in turn suddenly and completely blocks the blood vessel. You can see the stages of atherosclerotic plaque formation and rupture in Figure 3.9. If the affected area of myocardium remains without oxygenated blood for a prolonged period of time, then the cells die, leading to areas of heart muscle which cannot contract and relax properly. Myocardial infarctions usually present as severe chest pain which is not eased with rest. People experiencing one may feel sick, sweaty, clammy, and faint. If it is not treated promptly, a myocardial infarction can quickly prove fatal.

Peripheral vascular disease

The processes which result in IHD may also occur in any of the other blood vessels in the body. Depending on where an atheroma forms, it can lead to

Figure 3.9 Formation of atherosclerotic plaques takes place over decades, and may begin surprisingly early in life.

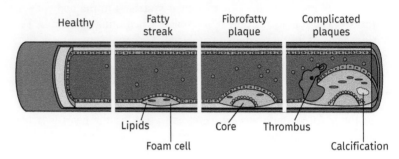

© Designua/Shutterstock.

a number of different symptoms, grouped together as peripheral vascular disease (or PVD). The lower limbs are commonly affected, initially causing colour changes in the legs and feet. Eventually it leads to symptoms such as claudication—similar to angina but experienced in the muscles of the legs and buttocks—and even acute ischaemia if the blood vessel involved becomes completely blocked. If the delicate blood vessels in the kidneys or eyes are affected, this can lead to chronic kidney disease or blindness. If PVD affects the blood vessels of the penis, men suffer erectile dysfunction.

Cerebrovascular disease

The blood vessels supplying the brain may also be affected by atherosclerosis. Gradual narrowing and blocking of small blood vessels in the brain can lead to chronic cerebrovascular disease, gradually causing memory loss and affecting higher brain function—a condition called vascular dementia. If a blood vessel becomes completely blocked, or if an area of atherosclerotic plaque ruptures, then symptoms occur much more rapidly—within seconds. If this leads to permanent death of brain tissue and therefore permanent effects on the body, this is known as an ischaemic stroke or cerebrovascular event (CVE). If the disruption to the blood supply is temporary, occurring without long-term damage to the brain, then it is known as a transient ischaemic attack (TIA). We will look at CVEs and TIAs in more detail later on in Chapter 7.

Mending a broken heart

Having something wrong with your heart or circulation system is without a doubt frightening—but surgery offers many different options for successful treatments in those parts of the world where health care is accessible and affordable.

Ischaemic heart disease and peripheral vascular disease are usually initially treated with medication—antiplatelet agents to reduce the likelihood of thrombus formation, statins to reduce cholesterol levels and stabilize atherosclerotic plaques, antihypertensive agents to reduce blood pressure, and nitrates to dilate blood vessels and ease temporary discomfort from angina or claudication.

However, if atherosclerosis reaches a critical stage, or if plaque rupture and thrombus formation go on to cause acute ischaemia, medical management may not be sufficient. At this point, two surgical options are commonly considered—stenting and grafting.

Angioplasty is a significantly less invasive process than grafting, requiring no open surgery. Using X-ray guidance, a thin guidewire attached to a **catheter** is passed through a peripheral artery (usually in the wrist or groin). The guidewire, pulling the catheter, is then slowly advanced to the area of narrowing (confirmed by releasing **radio-opaque** dye from the top of the catheter to visualize areas of reduced flow). At this point, a small balloon at the end of the catheter is inflated, dilating the affected artery, compressing the atheromatous plaque, and restoring blood flow. After blood flow has been restored, a mesh stent may be left behind to keep the artery open and functioning normally. You can see how angioplasty and stenting works in Figure 3.10.

Sometimes angioplasty is not possible. If a blood vessel is badly diseased, or if many areas of narrowing are present, then graft surgery may be required instead. This is far more invasive, requiring open surgery and a general anaesthetic—and is therefore higher risk than angioplasty. For graft

Figure 3.10 During angioplasty, a thin guidewire is inserted past the area of blockage, allowing a small balloon to be passed directly over the blockage itself. This balloon is then inflated, and a stent may or may not be left behind to keep the artery open.

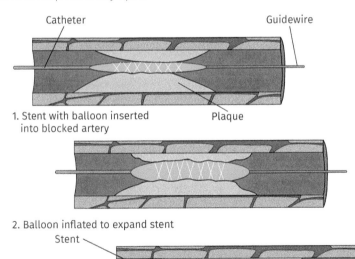

1. Stent with balloon inserted into blocked artery

2. Balloon inflated to expand stent

3. Balloon removed from expanded stent

Scientific approach 3.1
Grafting vs stenting: a tale of two specialities

Angioplasty and stenting are not new procedures—in fact, they have existed since the late 1970s. Over the decades, the procedure has evolved from using a simple balloon catheter, to bare metal stents, to modern drug-releasing stents and biodegradable stents. These procedures allow us to correct blocked arteries without the risk of open-heart or vascular surgery—and without the need for a general anaesthetic. This not only meant that angioplasty and stenting was, in theory, less risky than open surgery—it also meant that patients needed to stay in hospital for shorter periods, making it an economically attractive option, too. During the mid-2000s, the medical press predicted the decline of traditional cardiothoracic surgery in favour of the speciality of 'interventional radiology'—which includes angioplasty and stenting, but also other surgical type interventions, such as the insertion of feeding tubes. There were rumblings and suggestions that coronary artery bypass graft (CABG) surgery might be consigned to a few, rare cases—and that the expertise to perform these procedures would be lost to all except a few specialist centres.

More recently, though, studies have started to show that CABG procedures can show significant advantages over stenting in certain patient groups—particularly those with multiple coronary arteries affected by disease. However, even in people with single-vessel disease (only one coronary artery affected by atherosclerotic plaque), the longer-term survival rates appear to be improved in people undergoing CABG procedures compared to individuals who had undergone angioplasty and drug-eluting stent insertion. These differences in outcomes can be quite marked—in a study reported on by the American College of Cardiology, people with multi-vessel disease undergoing CABG rather than stenting had a 47 per cent lower risk of an adverse outcome (listed as 'death, heart attack or further surgical/interventional radiology procedure').

Does this newly emerging data spell the end of angioplasty and stenting? As with almost any question in medicine, the answer is not simple. Read the following articles from various medical journals to help you gain a better understanding of the data on stenting vs grafting:

- American College of Cardiology, 'Heart bypass surgery outperforms new generation stents' (https://www.acc.org/about-acc/press-releases/2015/03/16/15/56/heart-bypass-surgery-outperforms-new-generation-stents)

- ScienceDaily, 'Open heart surgery outperforms stents in patients with multivessel disease' (https://www.sciencedaily.com/releases/2019/05/190502113601.htm)

- Park, Duk-Woo et al. '10-year outcomes of stents versus coronary artery bypass grafting for left main coronary artery disease'. *Journal of the American College of Cardiology* 2018, 72(23). Part A, pp. 2813–2822. (https://www.ncbi.nlm.nih.gov/pubmed/30261236)

The data presented may seem relatively clear—longer-term outcomes of those undergoing CABG seem to be statistically better than those of people who had stents inserted. However, when examining any data, you need to ask certain questions about the data itself. In this case, we need to think about the individuals chosen for each procedure. For example, the patients chosen for CABG surgery would all need to be fit enough to undergo a prolonged general anaesthetic. This might mean that some of those chosen for stenting had significant **comorbidities**, preventing them from being considered for CABG, but making them much more likely to have further problems.

Even with seemingly compelling evidence as presented in the studies above, this is still a hotly debated topic. In fact, you can easily find studies which show that there is very little difference in outcomes between the two procedures—along with studies which show that using medication, rather than surgery, is actually associated with lower complication rates in certain groups of patients!

❓ Pause for thought

Can you think of any other potential confounders you would need to know about before making an informed decision on the findings of these studies? How might the cost of each procedure, staff availability, operating theatre time, and staff training impact on the ability of a hospital to offer CABG versus stenting? Can you think of any other factors which might influence whether a person is offered CABG surgery vs stenting?

surgery (also known as bypass surgery), a new route is created for blood to flow around the diseased vessel. This new route may be created by harvesting a healthy vein from elsewhere in the patient's body, or a synthetic graft may be used. The choice of whether to use a tissue graft or synthetic graft will depend on the location of the narrowing, the shape of the blood vessel itself, and the surgeon's own expertise.

Thickening and flopping: valvular disease

Some forms of heart disease have nothing to do with blocked blood vessels— they are caused by problems with the valves in the heart. There are two main ways in which the normal functioning of the valves is disrupted— **stenosis** and **prolapse** (see Figure 3.11).

Figure 3.11 Stenotic valves do not open properly compared to a normal valve. Prolapsed valves do not close properly, resulting in regurgitation.

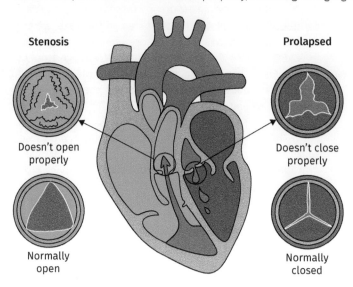

Image used with permission of the National Heart Foundation of New Zealand. heartfoundation.org.nz.

In stenosis, the valves become thickened or stiffened. Sometimes two or more of the valve leaflets become fused together. The heart must work significantly harder to pump blood through this stiffened valve, which can lead to a reduced oxygen supply to the rest of the body. This may present with symptoms of angina, especially if the coronary arteries also have significant atherosclerotic plaques. Sufferers of stenotic heart disease may also complain of breathlessness.

Prolapsed valves have the opposite problem to stenosis. Rather than being excessively stiff, prolapsed valves are too floppy and they fold the wrong way, allowing the backflow of blood and reducing the heart's efficiency. This results in a reduced oxygen supply to the body, which in turn can give symptoms of breathlessness or angina. Prolapsed valves also increase the pressure in the chambers of the heart, resulting in an excessively muscular 'hypertrophic' heart, or in a heart with dilated chambers.

In both types of valve disease, the ability of the heart to pump blood efficiently becomes significantly impaired, but the treatments differ—so doctors need to identify exactly what is wrong. When valves do not open or close properly, your heart sounds change—often picked up by your GP when listening to your heart. Ultrasound scans, known as echocardiograms, use sound waves to build up a picture of your heart. This is the most widely used technique for diagnosing valve disease, once a problem has been identified. It sounds simple but you need to be an expert to interpret the images!

More mending: valve surgery

Any of the heart valves can become diseased over the course of an individual's life—however, the mitral and aortic valves suffer from disease more commonly than the right heart valves. Additionally, some people may be born without properly developed heart valves—so-called **congenital** valve defects. The treatment for valve disease will depend upon the degree of severity—often, in mild to moderate disease, patients are simply placed under surveillance with a periodic echocardiogram to assess the state of their valvular disease, and its impact on the rest of the heart.

Once valvular heart disease has progressed past a certain point, the diseased valve will need to be replaced. Historically, this involved using metallic replacement valves—and these are sometimes still used today. However, modern valve replacements are often made partially from organic tissue—usually sourced from bovine (cow) or porcine (pig) heart valves, which are very similar to our own. Very rarely, a human donor valve may be used. Metallic valves are very durable, but can damage the red blood cells as they travel through the valve. This means that a person with a metallic valve replacement needs to take anticoagulants (which thin their blood) for the rest of their lives, to reduce the risk of blood clots associated with the new valve. People who have bioprosthetic (or tissue) valves do not need to take anticoagulants, and the red blood cells are protected, but this type of artificial valve only lasts for ten to twenty years. This means that, particularly in younger people, further replacement valve surgery may be necessary as the bioprosthetic valve ages.

Often, valve surgery requires a large incision to be made on the front of the patient's chest—a sternotomy. This so-called **open-heart surgery** is a major operation—and people with complex health needs may not be fit enough to undergo the anaesthetic, or the procedure itself. Sometimes in aortic valve disease it is possible to replace the valve using a catheter, a little like the one used for angioplasty. This procedure is known as a trans-aortic valve insertion (TAVI)—and does not remove the diseased valve. The new valve is inserted along a guidewire, and then deployed over the damaged valve. This approach is only possible in certain cases—but can be performed under local anaesthetic, causing significantly less trauma to the patient.

More malfunctions . . .

High blood pressure

High blood pressure is when the pressure in your arterial system is regularly above the normal systolic and diastolic pressures of 120/80. Your blood pressure varies all the time as a result of many different factors including activity levels, stress levels, time of day, your body mass index (BMI), how fit you are, and your genetics. If your blood pressure is regularly above 140/90, you are at risk of developing many other cardiovascular diseases. Unfortunately, raised blood pressure can be both a symptom of cardiovascular disease and a cause, so once diagnosed, the first priority is to lower it and the second is to discover why it was raised in the first place. High blood pressure is usually controlled using drugs, which work in many different ways—for example, by increasing urine output to reduce the total circulating volume, or by dilating the blood vessels, reducing the pressure in the arterial system.

Cardiomyopathy—thickened or baggy hearts

Cardiomyopathy refers to a group of disorders affecting the heart muscle, causing it to become stiffened, thickened, or enlarged. All of these conditions affect the heart's ability to contract and relax effectively, which in turn affects the flow of blood to the lungs and the rest of the body. Most forms of cardiomyopathy are the result of inherited problems rather than lifestyle factors. Cardiomyopathy causes symptoms of heart failure, angina, arrhythmias, and even sudden death, and can affect people at any age. There are no surgical treatments available for cardiomyopathy apart from heart transplantation in severe cases. Management usually focuses on medication to improve the efficiency of the heart's contractions, manage excess fluid in the legs or lungs, and relieve symptoms such as breathlessness or chest pain.

Electrical issues: arrhythmias

Disruption to the electrical conducting system of the heart causes abnormal conduction of electricity through the heart, leading in turn to arrhythmias—abnormal heart rates and rhythms. Arrhythmias can be broadly broken down into tachyarrhythmias—in which the heart beats too quickly—and bradyarrhythmias—in which the heart beats too slowly. An arrhythmia may be regular or irregular, depending on the part of the conducting system which is involved. It may involve the whole heart, or different parts of the heart. Atrial fibrillation is relatively common and treatable, ventricular fibrillation is much more serious, for example. ECGs are the main diagnostic tool for arrhythmias as you can see in Figure 3.12.

Ablation and pacemakers

Heart arrhythmias may occur at many different points in the electrical conducting system of the heart. They may be caused as the conducting system ages, or by damage to the heart through myocardial infarction or cardiomyopathy. Arrhythmias can also occur as a result of strain placed on the heart by valvular disease. The treatment for arrhythmias will depend on the type of arrhythmia, and its location within the conducting system. Many people with tachyarrhythmias respond well to medication, and may not need surgical intervention. However, if the tachyarrhythmia is caused by aberrant electrical pathways in the heart, it may be possible to destroy those individual pathways. This procedure is known as cardiac ablation. In theory, it preserves the correct electrical pathways, restoring normal heart rhythm. Ablation procedures use a catheter to apply heat, cold, or simply physical scarring to the area of the heart with the conduction problem—usually within the atria, or the AV node. The damage caused to the cardiac tissue disrupts the abnormal conduction.

Ablation isn't always the answer, because bradyarrhythmias—along with certain tachyarrhythmias—are not suitable for the treatment. Additionally, ablation is not always successful. In some of these cases, a pacemaker or

Figure 3.12 ECGs show simple tachycardias and bradycardias, but they also show up other problems in the heart.

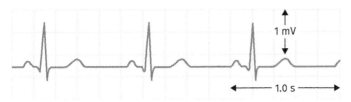

1 mV

1.0 s

(a) Normal ECG—beats evenly spaced, rate 60–100/min

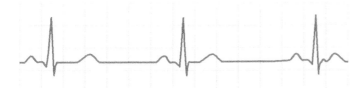

(b) Bradycardia—slow heart rate—beats evenly spaced,
    rate <60/min

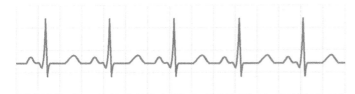

(c) Tachycardia—fast heart rate—beats evenly spaced,
    rate >100/min

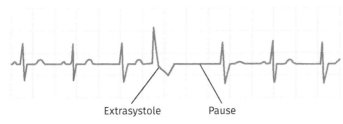

Extrasystole   Pause

(d) Ectopic heartbeat—altered rhythm, extra beat followed
    by longer than normal gap before the next beat

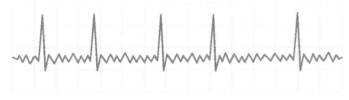

(e) Atrial fibrillation—abnormal irregular rhythm from atria,
    ventricles lose regular rhythm

implantable cardiac defibrillator (ICD) may be required. These devices consist of a box containing a battery and computerized generator, implanted under the skin. Leads (also called electrodes) extend from this box into one or more chambers of the heart, allowing the computerized generator to detect when the heart's rhythm falls outside its programmed parameters. When this occurs, the generator sends electrical impulses through the electrodes, adjusting the heart's rhythm. You can see what a pacemaker looks like in Figure 3.13.

An ICD is implanted instead of a PPM if the patient's arrhythmia leads to periods of significantly decreased or disorganized electrical activity in the heart's conducting system. An ICD is programmed to deliver a higher energy electrical impulse to the heart, re-synchronizing cardiac muscle cells and preventing fatal cardiac arrhythmias—a mini, personalized version of the defibrillators you see regularly on medical dramas and everywhere from the local sports centre to the pub.

Figure 3.13 This chest X-ray shows the battery and generator of a permanent pacemaker (PPM) located in the left side of the patient's chest. You can clearly see the electrodes extending from the battery/generator box into the chambers of the heart.

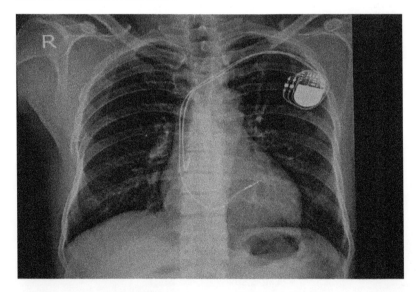

© April stock/Shutterstock.

Ballooning arteries: aneurysms

Blood vessels may bulge over time, particularly if they are exposed to higher blood pressure than normal, or if the vessel develops atherosclerotic plaques. We usually see aneurysms in arteries because these are higher-pressure vessels. An aneurysm weakens the wall of the vessel, which can rupture if the aneurysm reaches a significant size (see Figure 3.14). This leads to rapid blood loss, so a burst aneurysm is often fatal, especially if it occurs in the brain or abdomen.

Figure 3.14 Aneurysms usually form slowly, gradually increasing in size until they eventually become big and thin-walled enough to rupture.

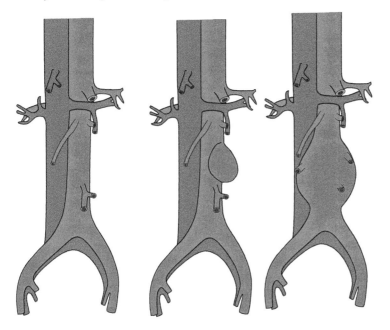

© ilusmedical/Shutterstock.

Aneurysm repair

Aneurysms are often symptomless until they burst. If an aneurysm is detected before it ruptures, then doctors may operate immediately, or they may decide to keep the aneurysm under surveillance. This is usually determined by the size and location of the aneurysm itself, along with whether it is affecting any nearby blood vessels, organs, or structures.

If an aneurysm repair is required, it will often need open surgery. This is a major undertaking, requiring a general anaesthetic. The weakened area of the blood vessel is bypassed, using a graft similar to that described in bypass graft surgery. Usually this graft is synthetic, making it extremely durable. Thanks to advances in medical imaging and 3D modelling, these grafts can be custom-shaped to ensure that they take into account an individual patient's anatomy. They may have multiple branches to preserve the blood supply to any other arteries branching off from the aneurysm.

Sometimes, depending on the size, location, and shape of the aneurysm, an endovascular aneurysm repair may be possible. This is a little like the TAVI described in the section on valve surgery earlier in this chapter: using a guidewire and catheter, a synthetic graft is advanced to the site of the aneurysm, and deployed within the blood vessel itself, anchoring itself above and below the area of disease and allowing the aneurysmal area of blood vessel to become defunct.

An ailing pump

Heart failure is a dramatic term—and many people associate it with a heart attack. But heart failure is actually used to describe a reduced ability of the heart to pump blood to the lungs and the rest of the body. The effectiveness of the heart as a pump may be impaired by any of the conditions you have learned about above—or even by more than one of these problems. Coronary artery disease (in the form of a myocardial infarction) may cause muscle cell death in one part of the heart wall, and therefore prevent that part of the heart from contracting properly. Valve disease or cardiomyopathy may result in thickening of the heart muscle, preventing the heart from contracting effectively. Arrhythmias may simply cause the heart to beat too quickly or too slowly to pump blood efficiently. Even high blood pressure can gradually lead to thickening of the heart muscle, and over time impede the effective contraction of the chambers of the heart.

The only procedure available to treat heart failure is heart transplantation—although treating the underlying cause of the heart failure can sometimes improve the heart's function, too. Correcting an arrhythmia or replacing a damaged valve, for example, can significantly improve an individual's symptoms. Once cardiac muscle has died off, any damage done to the heart's function is usually permanent—although medications can sometimes help to keep the heart pumping as efficiently as possible.

Congenital heart problems

Many of the conditions we have looked at so far in this chapter are mainly problems of middle and old age. Some cardiovascular problems, however, affect babies and children, usually as a result of an inherited condition or because the heart does not form properly as the foetus develops (another book in this series, *Animal Developmental Biology: Embryos, Evolution, and Ageing,* explains how these problems can arise). There are many different congenital conditions, but here we'll look at two of the more common problems: patent ductus arteriosus, and 'hole in the heart'.

When a baby is still in the uterus, its blood is not oxygenated in its lungs. Blood leaves the foetus in the umbilical artery, flows into the placenta, is oxygenated from the mother's blood and flows back into the foetus through the umbilical veins. A small blood vessel, the ductus arteriosus, acts as a shunt so blood simply flows into and out of the heart without going to the lungs. The foetus has to pump its own blood around its body, even if it relies on mum to oxygenate it! Once the baby is born, it has to breathe and oxygenate its own blood using the lungs. Normally, the ductus arteriosus closes off shortly after birth—it is no longer needed and is eventually reabsorbed. Sometimes, however, this elegant system fails and the ductus remains open after birth. This is known as patent ductus arteriosus—see Figure 3.15. The problem is picked up when doctors listen to the baby's heart and hear a murmur from the unusual blood flow. It is much more common in premature babies than in full-term infants. These tiny babies can be anaesthetized

Figure 3.15 The patent ductus arteriosus between the aorta and the pulmonary artery is clear in this diagram—you can see how deoxygenated and oxygenated blood might mix once the baby is born and breathing for itself.

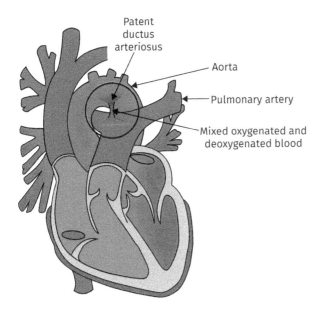

Patent ductus arteriosus

Aorta

Pulmonary artery

Mixed oxygenated and deoxygenated blood

and a metal clip or suture is placed around the blood vessel, closing it off. The operation usually lasts around an hour and is very successful.

Another heart problem which can affect babies and children (and adults) is a hole in the septum between the two sides of the heart—usually known as a hole in the heart. While the baby is in the uterus the septum doesn't need to be complete, because the blood flowing through the heart is all the same. But after birth, the deoxygenated blood from the right side of the heart must not mix with the oxygenated blood on the left, or the tissues risk being deprived of oxygen. Having a hole in the heart is surprisingly common, and if it is very small, doctors usually leave it alone, as it is unlikely to cause any symptoms or problems and may well heal over by itself. Larger holes can be repaired, often in a procedure very similar to that used to repair aneurysms in adults.

Amazing as it may seem, some forms of heart abnormalities can be operated on and repaired before a baby is even born. At the moment, this type of surgery is rare and only carried out when the benefits outweigh the risks to both mother and infant—but as techniques improve, our ability to intervene early and enable healthy babies to be born is only going to increase.

Heart transplants

If an individual develops severe heart disease—through myocardial infarction, valvular disease, cardiomyopathy, or other causes—then there may ultimately be no choice but to consider a heart transplant. This is a huge operation, requiring not only that the individual's heart disease is severe enough to warrant replacement, but that they are also otherwise fit enough to survive the surgery. Additionally, a compatible donor heart must be found, and it must be possible to unite the individual with this donor heart in a timely fashion.

Heart transplants have only been a possibility since the mid-twentieth century, and are still not a commonly performed procedure. You can read more about early heart transplants in Case study 3.1.

Case study 3.1

Barnard and the beating heart donors—the story of early heart transplants

In the late 1960s, a South African surgeon named Christiaan Barnard performed a procedure that many had thought impossible. Over the course of a five-hour operation, Barnard and his team transplanted the heart of a healthy twenty-five-year-old woman tragically killed in a road accident into the body of a fifty-three-year-old diabetic man, who had been bedbound due to severe heart failure. The surgery was successful, and the patient, Louis Washkansky, survived for eighteen days post-operatively before dying from pneumonia.

CS 3.1 Figure A Christiaan Barnard and his surgical team in the 1960s, utilizing a heart–lung machine to bypass cardiac circulation for open-heart surgery.

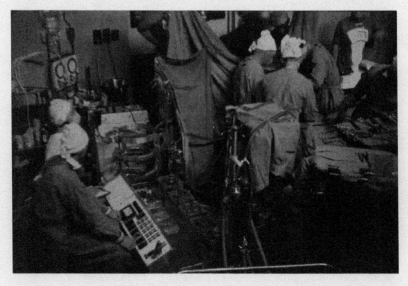

© David Cooper, 'Christiaan Barnard—The surgeon who dared: The story of the first human-to-human heart transplant'. *Global Cardiology Science & Practice* 2018 (2), fig. 5. http://dx.doi.org/10.21542/gcsp. Copyright (c) 2018 David K C Cooper. CC 4.0.

Barnard had spent some time preparing for this operation, studying the relatively new discipline of open-heart surgery in the United States. After thirty months of this secondment, he returned to South Africa with a pump oxygenator, which permitted him and his team to begin performing surgery in his home country. He designed and implemented a prosthetic heart valve, which was successful for its time, and performed various other types of cardiac surgery with considerable success and skill, before deciding to attempt the transplant surgery.

After selecting a suitable patient, Barnard and his team waited for a donor heart to become available. The opportunity came on 2 December 1967. A young woman named Denise Darvall had been involved in a traffic accident and had suffered a severe brain injury as a result. Within hours, the hospital neurosurgeons had certified that she was brain-dead, and her father had given his consent for her heart and kidneys to be used as transplants.

Darvall's heart was allowed to stop beating. It was then removed from her chest and attached to a heart–lung machine, providing the donor heart with cool, oxygenated blood to prevent any further tissue damage whilst it was being transferred to the neighbouring operating theatre. Louis Washkansky's heart was rapidly removed from his chest, and Darvall's heart was sewn into place instead. Barnard recalled later in interviews that, as Washkansky's heart had been enlarged and dilated by heart failure, Darvall's heart had appeared tiny by comparison (see CS 3.1 Figure B).

Once the great vessels supplying and draining the heart had been connected, the surgical team allowed the blood from Washkansky's heart–lung machine to begin perfusing through the donated organ. For the first few agonizing minutes, the donated heart refused to beat—although it did **fibrillate**, demonstrating electrical activity. Eventually Barnard stepped in and delivered an electric shock to the donated heart, which succeeded in stimulating a normal heartbeat. The donated heart beat weakly at first, but eventually the surgical team successfully disconnected the heart–lung machine which was

CS 3.1 Figure B Denise Darvall (left) and Louis Washkansky (right, in bed post-operatively) both lost their lives, but ultimately contributed hugely to modern transplant surgery.

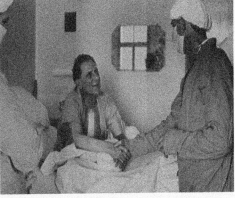

© David Cooper, 'Christiaan Barnard—The surgeon who dared: The story of the first human-to-human heart transplant'. *Global Cardiology Science & Practice* 2018 (2), fig. 11. http://dx.doi.org/10.21542/gcsp.

aiding the new heart's efforts to pump. Washkansky's new heart gradually took up the strain, and the exhausted surgical team could finally begin to close the patient's chest.

Washkansky initially appeared to recover well from the gruelling procedure. However, after the first week, he started to complain of feeling fatigued and less well. After twelve days his condition worsened, and he developed some troubling signs on X-rays of his lungs. Initially these signs were felt to be related to a 'transplant reaction', and the dose of his immunosuppressant drugs was increased. Sadly, the X-ray changes were in fact related to pneumonia—and the increasing of these potent drugs probably contributed to the speed of his demise. Washkansky deteriorated rapidly despite antibiotic therapy and died eighteen days after the procedure. At the **post-mortem**, a pathologist could find no features of tissue rejection of the donor heart, and no evidence that the surgery itself had contributed towards his death.

Although his patient had died, Barnard had conclusively proven that heart transplantation was possible in humans. A month later he transplanted another heart. This time the heart came from twenty-four-year-old Clive Haupt, who had collapsed and died on a Cape Town beach, and it was transplanted into Philip Blaiberg, a fifty-nine-year-old dentist. Blaiberg recovered well and lived almost two years before complications from other diseases along with transplant difficulties ended his life. Initially there was a rash of poorly regulated copycat operations around the world, but the medical establishment learned from these early procedures, and small numbers of highly specialized surgeons gradually emerged, performing the life-saving procedure of heart transplants on many patients who would otherwise have certainly died of their illnesses. Today, around 5,500 heart transplants are carried out around the world each year: 80–90 per cent of the patients will be alive a year later, and around 50 per cent will still be going strong ten years after their surgery. Heart transplants can even, in rare cases, be done on tiny children. Kaylee Ann Davidson-Olley was four months old when she had a heart transplant in 1987. At the time of writing, thirty-three years on, she is still doing well—she has taken part in the World Transplant Games, and is a strong advocate for organ donation.

❓ Pause for thought

- Barnard's surgery was certainly revolutionary, but it also raised some significant ethical questions. His approach would not pass ethical tests today. How would you feel about being the first person to undergo such a radical procedure?

- In the days when these early operations took place, the clinically accepted sign of death was that the heart stopped beating. This definition has changed over time. Investigate how death is determined today before a transplant. What steps need to be taken to ensure that a potential organ donor has undergone brainstem death?

Artificial hearts—buying valuable time

Heart transplantation is still not a common procedure—but by the time someone needs a heart transplant, they cannot usually wait long for a donor. Sometimes a heart becomes available quickly, but a heart transplant requires a donor who has recently died, is a compatible tissue match for the recipient, and has consented to donate their organs. It must also be possible to transport the donor heart rapidly to the patient, or vice versa. If a suitable match is not quickly identified, doctors can now artificially extend the life of the patient's existing heart by using a mechanical heart to assist their circulatory system.

These total artificial hearts (TAHs) require the original diseased heart to be removed, and the TAH to be sutured into its place. However, the power supply for the TAH is kept external to the body, along with a device which forces compressed air into the artificial heart itself, moving the ventricles artificially, and continuing to pump blood around the recipient's body. People who receive this amazing technology must carry the bulky external power supply and air compressor around with them everywhere, with a battery life of only around two-and-a-half hours.

At present, total artificial hearts represent a 'bridge' for people currently awaiting a human heart transplant. But the list of people waiting for a heart transplant far outstrips the supply of donor hearts. As medical technology continues to improve, it is possible that more advanced artificial hearts may one day be used instead of donor hearts for many individuals in end-stage heart failure.

 ## Chapter summary

- The cardiovascular system comprises the heart and blood vessels, which work together to supply the body with oxygenated blood from the lungs.
- Diseases of the cardiovascular system may affect the blood vessels themselves, or affect the valves, electrical system or muscle of the heart.
- Symptoms of cardiovascular diseases are often quite similar—so accurately identifying the cause of breathlessness or angina-like symptoms is very important.
- Surgery is the only management option for some cardiovascular diseases—whereas others can be managed with medication and lifestyle changes alone.

Further reading

British Heart Foundation *The History of Heart Transplant*. https://www.bhf.org.uk/informationsupport/heart-matters-magazine/medical/history-of-uk-heart-transplant/heart-transplant-timeline#1953

A British Heart Foundation timeline of developments in heart transplant surgery, with particular focus on the UK. It goes through to the present day and includes case histories of several patients.

Hoffenberg, Raymond 'Christiaan Barnard: His first transplants and their impact on concepts of death' *British Medical Journal* 2001 323(7327), pp 1478–1480. https://www.ncbi.nlm.nih.gov/pmc/articles/PMC1121917/

An interesting read, detailing how the need for clear and consistent guidelines on when a patient is dead only really evolved once solid organ transplantation had become a reality.

Melly, Ludovic et al. 'Fifty years of coronary artery bypass grafting' *Journal of Thoracic Disease* 10(3) 2018, pp 1960–1967. https://www.ncbi.nlm.nih.gov/pmc/articles/PMC5906252/

A potted history of the evolution of the most commonly performed cardiac surgery in the world today.

 Discussion questions

3.1   Suggest reasons why bioprosthetic artificial heart valves made with bovine or porcine tissue can be used succesfully to replace damaged valves but only donated human hearts are used for a heart transplant in spite of the fact that they are in short supply.

3.2   Consider all the factors (medical, ethical, scientific) facing surgeons before they carry out a pioneering procedure such as the heart transplant carried out by Christiaan Barnard on Lewis Washkansky in the late 1960s.

4 A BREATH OF FRESH AIR

The respiratory system provides the cells of our bodies with oxygen, and removes waste carbon dioxide. Like the cardiovascular system, it functions in a largely automated way throughout our entire lives. Its workload increases and decreases according to our activity levels, disease states—and the quality of the air we breathe in. Our respiratory system is directly open to the outside world, so it must cope with an influx of pathogens and particulates, and changes in environmental conditions, and still continue functioning at peak capacity. There is so much spare capacity that our lungs keep functioning even after sustaining considerable amounts of damage—John Wayne famously continued to work as an actor in the 1960s after having an entire lung removed!

The lungs develop rapidly in a growing foetus. By three weeks a lung bud is evident in the embryo, formed from the developing oesophagus. However, it is many more weeks before the lungs will be capable of sustaining the foetus without its supply of oxygen from the mother. From the fifth week onwards, the lung bud splits into two, and begins to divide into bronchi and bronchioles. By the twenty-sixth week of gestation, the lungs have developed into their full branching structure, and the close network of capillaries required for gas transfer has begun to develop. By around thirty weeks of pregnancy, the lungs are pretty much ready to go, although it doesn't stop there—we don't develop our full complement of alveoli until we are about eight years old!

In this chapter we will summarize the anatomy and physiology of this amazing organ system (see Figure 4.1), focusing on some of the ways that surgery can be used to overcome problems when they arise. We cannot hope to cover them all!

Figure 4.1 A resin cast of the airways and arteries of the lungs.

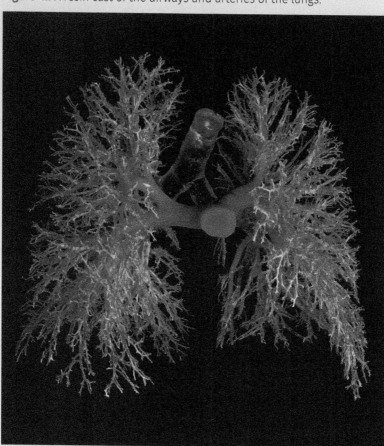

Martin Dohrn/Royal College of Surgeons/Science Photo Library.

From oropharynx to alveolus: the anatomy of the respiratory system
The upper respiratory tract

We divide the anatomy of the respiratory system into two broad segments—the upper and lower respiratory tracts. The upper tract includes the mouth and throat (also known as the oropharynx), the nose and nasal passages, and the portion of the larynx (voice box) which lies above the vocal cords. The upper respiratory tract also includes the paranasal sinuses—four pairs of air-filled spaces around the nasal passageway—see Figure 4.2.

The larynx—speaking and swallowing

The larynx or voice box sits at the junction between the upper and lower respiratory tracts. You can feel your own larynx as a lumpy bit of cartilage about halfway down the front of your throat. When you swallow, it moves up and down and when you speak, it vibrates.

Figure 4.2 The upper respiratory tract stretches from your mouth and nostrils to just above the vocal cords and includes the paranasal sinuses.

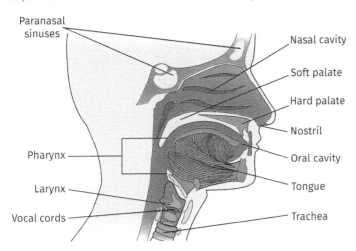

The vocal cords are two membranes, one on each side of the larynx. They are attached to the cartilage at the sides of the airway, but the middle of the membranes is free to oscillate as air flows in and out of the respiratory tract. The oscillation of the cords produces sound—and, by manipulating the vocal cords and changing the shape of portions of the upper respiratory tract, we produce the huge variety of different sounds which make up human speech.

The larynx is important for speech, but there is a structure sitting above the larynx which is also vital when swallowing—the **epiglottis**. This very flexible piece of cartilage temporarily obscures the opening to the trachea when we swallow food or fluid, preventing anything untoward ending up in the lungs. As we swallow, the movements of the pharynx and larynx cause the epiglottis to swing over the trachea—see Figure 4.3. When you are not swallowing, the oesophagus exists more as a potential space than as a distinct tube, just behind the trachea. This region, the junction between the upper and lower respiratory tracts, is the trickiest area for anaesthetists—see Chapter 2.

Figure 4.3 A cross-section of the upper respiratory tract at the level of the larynx, showing the vocal cords and the larynx.

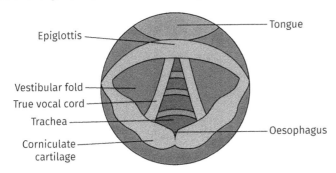

The lower respiratory tract—a branching tree

The lower respiratory tract starts just below the level of the vocal cords, and extends to the base of the lungs themselves. As the lower respiratory tract develops in the womb, the initial lung buds further subdivide, forming bronchi and bronchioles which branch out in a tree-like fashion. There are about twenty-three divisions from the main bronchi to the final alveoli. From about the sixteenth division of the bronchioles, they are lined with alveoli, and after about the twentieth division they are called alveolar ducts, as the walls are entirely composed of alveoli. In total you have over 1 million bronchioles, and many millions of alveoli.

Where the bronchioles end, they form alveoli—small, thin-walled sacs which massively increase the surface area of the lungs, vital for effective gas exchange. The lungs are divided into lobes—three lobes in the right lung, two in the left. Because the left lung shares its space in the chest cavity with the heart, it also has a cardiac notch—space for the heart to sit within the chest—in the centre of the lower lobe (see Figure 4.4).

Supporting structures—collagen and elastin

If the trachea and larger bronchi were made only of soft tissue, they would collapse in on themselves. Support structures have evolved, providing structure to the complex network of tubing—the trachea, for example, is held open by C-shaped rings of cartilage, preventing it from collapsing whilst enabling bulges of food to move down the oesophagus. Cartilage rings are also present in the walls of the bronchi, supporting them and keeping them open.

Figure 4.4 The lower respiratory tract stretches from just below the vocal cords to the alveoli at the very ends of each bronchiole. The tree-like structure maximizes the available surface area for gas exchange.

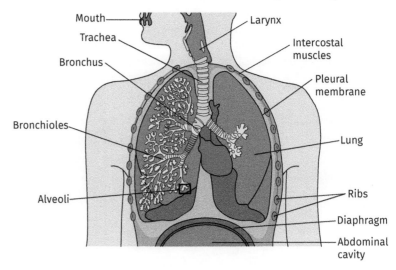

© Ann Fullick, Jo Locke, and Paul Bircher, *A Level Biology for OCR A* (Oxford University Press, 2015), p 157, fig. 1.

The alveoli form a dense network of tissue throughout the lungs, giving them their spongy appearance. Between the alveoli, the lungs contain elastic tissue and collagen fibres, which enable them to stretch and return to their original shape through the breathing cycle. This linked connective tissue is known as the **parenchyma** of the lung.

The pleura are membranes which line the inner chest cavity and surround each lung. The visceral pleura line the outer surface of the lungs, and the parietal pleura line the inner surface of the chest wall. Between them is a potential space, known as the pleural cavity (see Figure 4.5). The membranes secrete a small quantity (10–15cm³) of fluid into this space, reducing friction on the lungs as they move within the chest cavity, and preventing them from sticking to the interior chest wall.

Some diseases affect the pleura, causing a build-up of excess fluid, air, or even blood. Some rare cancers also affect the membranes and the space between them. Pleural effusions occur when fluid builds up in the pleural space between the chest wall and the lungs, often as a result of heart, kidney, or liver failure, certain cancers or infections such as pneumonia. Breathlessness is the most common symptom, although chest pain, and coughing up clear or frothy sputum are also common. Sometimes the problem gets better when the condition which caused it is treated—for example, if kidney function improves. Often the fluid has to be drained either using a syringe (a pleural tap) or a chest drain inserted into the pleural cavity.

If air gets into the pleural cavity via lung or chest wall injury, it is known as a **pneumothorax**. The elastic tissue of the lung parenchyma means the lung collapses, considerably reducing the efficiency of gas exchange. If the amount of air that gets into the pleura is small, it often gets better without treatment beyond rest and pain relief. If, however, there is a large amount of air, it can seriously affect the patient's breathing, and they may have to have a tube inserted between their ribs. This allows air to drain out of the pleural space, and the lung to reinflate. In rare cases, the two layers of the pleura have to be stuck together in a process known as **pleurodesis**.

Figure 4.5 The pleura and the pleural cavity, which is usually filled with a small volume of fluid, lubricating the pleural surfaces and allowing smooth movement of the lungs.

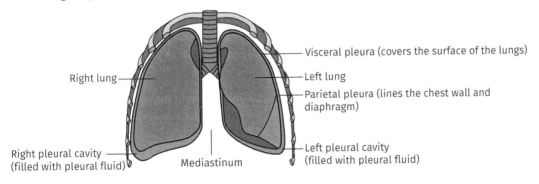

Cilia and mucus—the cellular structure of the respiratory tract

The upper respiratory tract is lined with a mixture of stratified and pseudostratified columnar epithelial cells forming a physical barrier to pathogens, preventing them from entering the rest of the body (see Figure 4.6).

Both types of epithelia also have other ways of reducing the risk of infection.

1. **Mucus-producing goblet cells:** these cells secrete sticky mucus, largely made up of water and specialized glycoproteins (which produce the characteristic stickiness). The mucus traps pathogens and particulate matter (such as smoke particles and dust), so they can be **phagocytosed** (engulfed and broken down) by the cells of the immune system or expelled from the body. Mucus production is increased or decreased, depending on need. When you have an upper respiratory tract infection, your nose may produce more mucus than you are comfortable with!

2. **Ciliated epithelial cells:** mucus must be expelled from the respiratory tract to prevent it pooling in the airways, potentially preventing efficient gas exchange. Most of the epithelia of the airways are lined with cilia—tiny hair-like structures, which beat together in a sine wave pattern to propel mucus away from the lungs. Once the mucus reaches the upper respiratory tract, it may be coughed or sneezed out, physically expelling pathogens and particulates. It may be removed when you blow your nose—or it may be swallowed, where the low pH of stomach acid destroys many pathogens, rendering them harmless.

Figure 4.6 Stratified columnar epithelium and pseudostratified columnar epithelium: can you spot the difference?

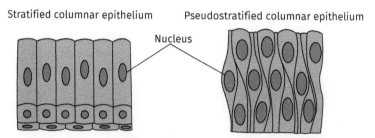

Stratified columnar epithelium   Pseudostratified columnar epithelium

Nucleus

The respiratory zone—for efficient gas exchange

At the lower end of the respiratory tract, the function of the airways fundamentally changes from the movement of air to gas exchange. The bronchioles branch from the bronchi, and then divide further into terminal bronchioles. The bronchioles are not cartilaginous like the bronchi and much of the upper respiratory tract. Instead, each bronchiole is lined with smooth muscle which contracts and relaxes to dilate or constrict the lumen of the tube, which in turn increases or decreases airflow. At the end of the terminal bronchioles, there are even smaller bronchioles—respiratory bronchioles—which divide once more into alveolar ducts. The alveoli are thin-walled sacs essential for efficient gas exchange between the lungs and the bloodstream. They sit in clusters at the ends of the alveolar ducts, rather like microscopic bunches of grapes. The area from the terminal bronchi to the alveoli is termed the **respiratory zone**, as it is directly involved with gas exchange.

The alveoli within each cluster are connected to each other via alveolar pores, which help to maintain the same air pressure throughout the cluster. Each alveolus has a highly elastic wall, allowing it to stretch significantly during inhalation and then return to its original size. The walls of each alveolus are made up of three different cell types. Type I alveolar cells make up about 97 per cent of each alveolar wall. They are squamous epithelial cells, about 25 nanometres (nm) thick and are highly permeable to gases. Type II alveolar cells are interspersed between the type I cells. They secrete pulmonary (lung) surfactant, a substance made up of phospholipids and proteins, which decreases the surface tension in the alveoli. This prevents the alveolar walls from sticking together, allowing them to fill with air during inhalation and stay open during exhalation (see Case study 4.1). Finally, alveolar macrophages—a specialized phagocytic cell of the innate immune system—circulate around the alveolar wall. These cells identify and destroy any pathogens and foreign matter which enter the alveoli from the upper airways. The type I alveolar cells are attached to a thin, elastic basement membrane. This basement membrane borders the endothelial membranes of surrounding capillaries, forming a respiratory membrane around 0.5mm thick (see Figure 4.7).

Figure 4.7 The top image demonstrates alveolar clusters, with a surrounding network of capillaries to facilitate gas exchange with the blood. The bottom image shows a cross-section of a single alveolus with its adaptations for gas exchange.

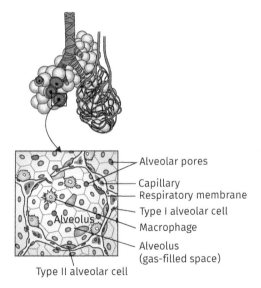

Alveolar pores

Capillary
Respiratory membrane
Type I alveolar cell
Macrophage

Alveolus

Alveolus
(gas-filled space)

Type II alveolar cell

Case study 4.1
Lung surfactant: miracle molecule

During pregnancy, a foetus develops inside its mother's womb. All of its oxygen and food needs are supplied by the mother through the placenta, which also removes carbon dioxide and urea, the waste products of metabolism. The lungs of the foetus are not used for breathing—they are filled with fluid, and take up a relatively small volume in the chest cavity. Although the developing foetus practises breathing movements of the diaphragm and ribs while it is in the uterus—even sometimes getting hiccups!—no air is taken in and no gases are exchanged. As soon as the baby is born, all that has to change. It must take its first breath or die.

That first breath is a real achievement. The force required to inflate the lungs of a newborn baby for the first time is 15–20 times greater than the force needed for every normal inhalation that follows. This first, forceful inhalation stretches the lungs enormously, and the elastic tissue within the alveoli never returns to its original, foetal length.

How does this happen? You might expect the alveoli of the lungs to collapse again as air is breathed out, and the damp walls of the microscopic air sacs to stick together. The reason that they don't is the presence of the pulmonary surfactant produced by type II alveolar cells (see Figure 4.7). Surfactant lowers surface tension between the molecules at the surfaces of the alveoli, making it much easier to separate them when air moves into the lungs. But how does this work? Surfactant molecules have a polar (charged) end. As the alveolus shrinks, the charged sections of the surfactant molecule come closer together and, like north poles of two magnets, repel each other. This forces the alveolus open in inverse proportion to how small it is, overcoming the effect of surface tension!

The lungs of the developing foetus begin making pulmonary surfactant at around the twenty-eighth week of gestation (pregnancy), and so a healthy full-term baby draws its first breath and then breathes easily as it begins the great adventure of life (see CS 4.1 Figure A).

Born too soon

For all sorts of reasons, some babies are born too soon, before the end of a normal forty-week pregnancy. Babies born at twenty-eight weeks or earlier do not have the lung surfactant they need to inflate their lungs and breathe properly. For hundreds of years, this struggle to breathe was one of the main causes of death in very premature babies, and if they survived, their lungs were often permanently damaged. The importance of lung surfactant was only discovered in the 1950s, and amazingly, by the 1970s scientists had developed an artificial version. A tiny amount, introduced into the lungs of a preterm baby, has an amazing effect on long-term survival and the health of the lungs (see CS 4.1 Figure B). The introduced surfactant coats the alveoli just like the natural product, making breathing so much easier and

CS 4.1 Figure A The first cries of a newborn full-term baby are a miracle of biology—the surfaces of the alveoli of the lungs are coated with pulmonary surfactant, which makes normal breathing possible.

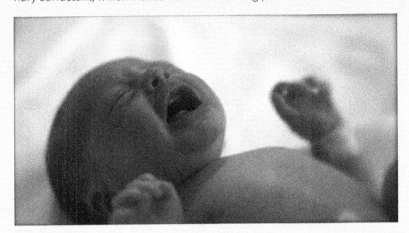

© Bricolage/Shutterstock.

CS4.1 Figure B The ability to give tiny premature babies the lung surfactant they need has given thousands of children the chance of life with healthy, undamaged lungs.

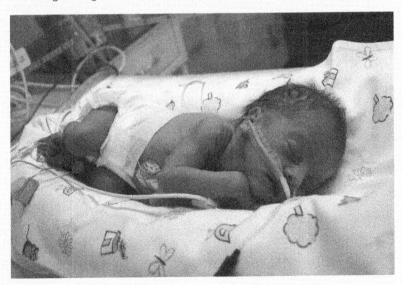

© Gert Vrey/Shutterstock.

preventing lung damage. This amazing development has also helped full-term babies who have inhaled fluid and meconium (poo!) during the birth process. Even more recently, scientists have managed to extract and use natural surfactants, both from humans and from other mammals. The evidence is now building that natural surfactants have even better long-term outcomes for premature babies than the early synthetic ones—but all have been, and remain, life savers.

? Pause for thought

Premature babies usually have multiple needs and require a lot of medical support and intervention. Discuss the ethical and practical issues which must be considered by paediatricians and nurses before any treatment is begun.

The mechanics of ventilation

For the specialized structures of the respiratory tract to do their jobs, air must move in and out of them in the process we call breathing. Breathing is an almost entirely automated process, controlled by the brainstem. Our breathing depth and rate change automatically, depending on our oxygen demand, activity levels, altitude, and many other factors. The mechanical process of breathing uses both the diaphragm, and the intercostal muscles of the ribcage. During inhalation, the diaphragm contracts and flattens, and the external intercostal muscles contract, lifting the ribs outwards and upwards, increasing the volume of the cavity. This results in a drop in pressure throughout the cavity, including the lungs. Once the pressure in the chest falls below the pressure of the surrounding atmosphere, air moves into the lungs, equalizing the pressure differential. When it reaches the alveoli, gas exchange occurs.

The air is then exhaled, by a reversal of the same principle. The diaphragm relaxes and resumes its resting domed shape. The external intercostal muscles relax, so the ribs drop down and in, decreasing the volume of the thoracic cavity. The elastic interstitial tissue of the lungs allows them to spring back to their original shape. As a result of all these factors, the pressure inside the lungs rises above atmospheric pressure, forcing carbon-dioxide-rich air out of the body (see Figure 4.8). Inhalation is an active process, using ATP as the muscles contract, but basic exhalation is passive, involving only the relaxation of muscles and elastic recoil of the lungs.

When we need more oxygen—when we are exercising, when we have certain illnesses, or when we are at high altitude—other muscles, known as accessory muscles, come into play. They help increase and decrease the volume of the thoracic cavity in a process called forced breathing.

Gas exchange—a question of diffusion

The body needs oxygen from the atmospheric air to carry out cellular respiration, and it needs the toxic carbon dioxide waste product to be removed. Oxygen from the air moves into the bloodstream in the complex networks of capillaries surrounding each alveolar cluster. Whilst the uptake of oxygen is obviously vital to the body, so too is the removal of the toxic carbon dioxide produced during cellular respiration. Carbon dioxide diffuses down

Figure 4.8 The diaphragm and external intercostal muscles contract and relax, expanding or reducing the volume of the chest and moving air into and out of the lungs down the pressure gradients which result.

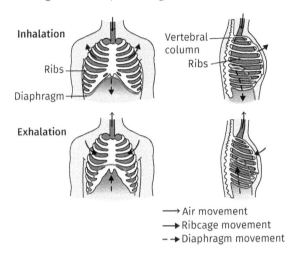

© Ann Fullick, Jo Locke, and Paul Bircher, *A Level Biology for OCR A* (Oxford University Press, 2015), p 61, fig. 6.

a concentration gradient from the blood into the air in the alveoli. This process is known as **pulmonary excretion**. In addition to carbon dioxide, water molecules leave the lungs as water vapour, making up approximately 300–400ml of the total water lost from the body each day. Other gases, including volatile compounds such as ethanol, are also removed via the lungs by diffusion from the blood to the air.

When things go wrong

The diseases of the respiratory tract are many and varied—not least because the respiratory tract itself is so varied, leading from the mouth and nose right down to the alveoli. Some of these conditions are nothing more than a minor irritation—but others may be life-threatening. There simply isn't space here to explore all of them, so we are focusing mainly on some of the conditions that require surgery to treat them.

The top of the tract

The medical speciality of otorhinolaryngology refers to the study of diseases of the ears, nose, and throat—sometimes also known as ENT. Like the rest of the respiratory tract, the ears, nose, and throat are all susceptible to a vast number of different diseases. Here, we are going to take a lightning tour of some of the most common surgeries associated with this part of your body—and some of the rarest. Problems in these areas are particularly common in young children. You may have experienced some of these surgeries yourself!

The ears

Although the ears don't actually form part of the respiratory tract, they are linked to the back of the oropharynx by the Eustachian tubes. Because of this, conditions which affect your ears may also affect your nose, or throat.

Ear infections may affect the external auditory canal—when they are called infective **otitis externa**, or the middle ear (behind the eardrum)—when they are termed **otitis media**. Both infections may cause pain, itching, or discharge from the ear. They can also cause a temporary loss in hearing. Otitis media also often results in a perforated eardrum, as the pressure in the middle ear rises until the tympanic membrane ruptures. This usually heals spontaneously, although it sometimes requires surgical repair.

When a perforated eardrum does not heal itself, surgeons may intervene and repair the membrane. This is especially likely if a person is suffering with repeated infections, or if their hearing has been adversely affected. A tympanic membrane repair usually takes the form of a small patch—often made of cartilage or connective tissue, but sometimes made of artificial materials—which is placed over the hole in the eardrum during a day-case procedure.

Chronic suppurative otitis media—'glue ear'

Sometimes, after a cold or otitis media infection, or sometimes due to problems with the glands, the middle ear becomes filled with a sticky, clear fluid. The medical name for this condition is chronic suppurative otitis media, but it is often known as glue ear—and it is much more common in children than in adults. It does not usually cause pain, but often results in hearing loss due to the thick fluid filling the middle ear. Glue ear often resolves spontaneously, but this isn't always a quick process—it may be three months or more before the fluid completely drains through the Eustachian tube into the throat.

Grommets—draining the glue

When glue ear does not resolve spontaneously, or if the loss of hearing is interfering with a child's schooling, specialists may make the decision to artificially drain the fluid by making a hole in the eardrum and inserting a small plastic tube, called a grommet (see Figure 4.9). The grommet is necessary as the tympanic membrane would otherwise heal quickly, preventing the fluid from draining properly. Once inserted, the grommet is gradually pushed out as the tympanic membrane heals itself and naturally expelled from the body.

The nose

Human noses are unusual in the mammalian world for the way they stick out from our faces. The internal structure of the nose has a huge surface area, rich in blood vessels, it has hairs and its epithelia contains many mucus-secreting cells. As air moves into our lungs through our noses, it is warmed up and humidified. At the same time, particles and pathogens are trapped by the hairs and the mucus, and are removed. Breathing in through

Figure 4.9 A grommet correctly inserted into the tympanic membrane, to allow the drainage of fluid from the middle ear.

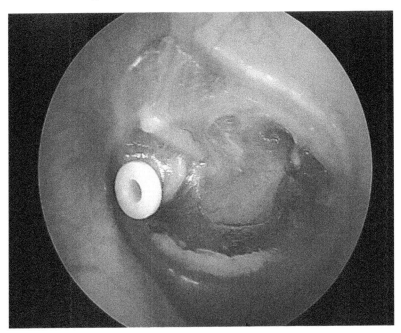

Professor Tony Wright, Institute of Laryngology and Otology/Science Photo Library.

our noses is important—and whilst problems with the nose might seem rather trivial, they can have a major impact on our health and wellbeing.

Rhinitis and sinusitis—infection and inflammation

The mucus-producing tissue of the nose and sinuses is vulnerable to both infection and inflammation. Whilst inflammation may occur as a direct result of infection, it can also be caused by allergies, smoking, or even atmospheric pollutants. Regardless of the cause, inflammation of the nasal passages or sinuses usually results in congestion (a blocked nose) and rhinorrhoea (mucus draining from the nose, either out of the nostrils or dripping into the throat—this is known as post-nasal drip). Other symptoms such as headaches, facial pain, sore throat, **anosmia**, fevers, or fatigue also occur, depending on the cause and severity of the inflammation. Symptoms primarily affecting the nose are called rhinitis, whereas symptoms involving the sinuses are known as sinusitis.

Infective rhinitis is usually viral and gets better on its own with some simple pain relief and rest. Infective sinusitis is also often viral—but, occasionally, bacteria take over as well, in which case we use oral antibiotics to wipe out the bacteria present. Sometimes we also use steroid-based medications to reduce inflammation after an infection has cleared.

Chronic sinusitis sometimes requires surgical treatment, particularly if the mucus-secreting tissue within the sinuses becomes significantly thickened and inflamed. This can lead to symptoms such as constant facial pain and nasal congestion. Modern sinus surgery is usually carried out endoscopically to remove diseased sinus tissue, allowing healthy tissue to grow back in its place. This reduces scarring, improves recovery time, and reduces some of the risk involved in the procedure. Sinus surgery is often combined with surgery to correct airflow in other parts of the nose, such as a deviated septum, or nasal polyps. Polyps are areas of over-growth in the mucosal lining of the nasal passages and they reduce airflow through the nose by decreasing the size of the nasal cavity and secreting excess mucus. Symptoms of nasal polyps usually include nasal congestion, post-nasal drip symptoms, and sometimes a change in the sufferer's voice. Snoring is also sometimes an issue for people with polyps—or the person who shares their bed at night! Polyps are usually removed endoscopically, using small tools to destroy and remove the polypoid tissue but sadly, even following surgery, polyps may grow back.

The throat

Like the rest of the respiratory tract, our throats are vulnerable to infection. The tonsils or back of the throat are commonly affected, causing tonsilli-tis or pharyngitis—which may be bacterial or viral. Tonsillitis is common in small children—it is painful and distressing but not usually dangerous. Surgery, like most things in society, has fashions. It used to be common for children to have their tonsils out—sometimes siblings would all be done together as a 'job lot'! Now, tonsillectomies are relatively rare—although evidence of a rise in other associated infections means doctors are looking at the evidence again (see Figure 4.10).

Figure 4.10 Swings and roundabouts—a reduction in tonsillectomies may be leading to an increase in Group A *Streptococcus* (GAS) infections.

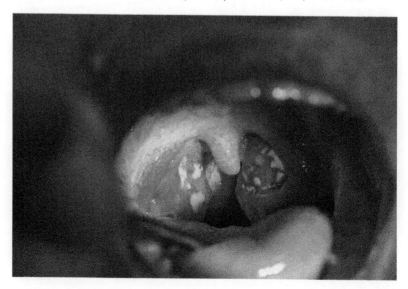

© yuriy23/Shutterstock.

Occasionally a more serious complication from throat infections may occur, such as a quinsy. This is an abscess which forms near the tonsils, caused by a bacterial throat infection. Left untreated, the abscess just gets bigger and in the worst cases it may even erode through into the circulatory system and cause septic emboli in the lungs. Surgical treatment for quinsy involves draining the abscess—often performed under local anaesthetic. This is usually accompanied by intravenous antibiotics and a hospital stay.

Benign laryngeal growths

Benign growths of the vocal cords are relatively common, occurring due to chronic irritation of the larynx. This may be due to overuse of the voice, acid reflux from the oesophagus spilling over into the larynx, damage from smoking or alcohol, or even atmospheric pollutants. Regardless of the cause, the commonest symptom is a hoarse voice, which gets progressively worse with time. Pain or discomfort is rarely a feature. Benign laryngeal lesions include polyps, nodules, and granulomas—all of which look slightly different when we look at them through a flexible naso-endoscope. This is a thin fibre-optic cable with a viewing lens at one end, and a torch at the other. A specialist passes this through the nose and into the pharynx, moving the fibre-optic cable around to observe the larynx and nearby structures.

Cancers of the respiratory tract

Perhaps the best known and most feared diseases which affect the gas exchange system are cancers. Cancers involve uncontrolled cell growth in different tissues. (Discover more about how cancer develops and how we treat it in another title in this series, *Cancer: Biology, Causes, and Treatments*.)

Cancerous changes can occur at any level of the respiratory tract, from the oral cavity (mouth) and nasal passages right down to the bases of the lungs themselves. Here we focus on some of the most common.

Malignancies of the upper respiratory tract

Cancers of the lip and tongue, larynx, oropharynx, hypopharynx, and salivary glands are respectively the 16th, 21st, 24th, 25th, and 28th most common cancers worldwide. Cancers of the nasal passages and sinuses are, by comparison, relatively rare. In the upper respiratory tract, the most common type of malignant growth is a squamous cell carcinoma—although many other types of malignancy also affect these tissues.

The biggest risk factors for upper respiratory tract cancers are, perhaps unsurprisingly, smoking and alcohol. The carcinogens produced by tobacco smoke directly damage the cells of the respiratory tract, and alcohol also acts as a potent carcinogen. The effects of tobacco and alcohol on the upper respiratory tract are synergistic—individuals who both smoke and drink have a much higher risk than those who only smoke or only drink alcohol. The combination makes an individual three hundred times more likely to develop oropharyngeal cancers than those who neither drink nor smoke! Tobacco which is taken orally (such as chewing tobacco), or tobacco which is smoked but not inhaled (like pipe smoking or cigars) specifically increase the risk of oral cancers, rather than pharyngeal (throat) cancers. Other atmospheric pollutants—such as fumes from vehicle engines or industry—also increase the risk of upper respiratory tract malignancies, along with some occupational hazards—carpenters and woodworkers, for example, have a higher risk of nasal malignancies, due to their exposure to sawdust and wood preservatives.

There is a third significant risk factor for upper respiratory tract malignancies which has only been confirmed in the past two decades—see The bigger picture 4.1.

The bigger picture 4.1
Human papillomaviruses—warts and all

Throughout the Western world, rates of tobacco use have consistently fallen for several decades. Alcohol use has declined, too, albeit more slowly. However, the incidence of head and neck cancers has not followed the same downward trend. In fact, according to Cancer Research UK, head and neck cancers in the UK have risen by more than 33 per cent since the early 1990s. The culprit behind this rise in ENT cancers was identified more than half a century ago—but it has taken many years of dedicated research to clarify the link between genital warts, cervical cancers, and the rise in head and neck cancer rates.

In the 1950s and 1960s, scientists studying cancer of the cervix discovered the risk of developing the disease was highest in women who had started having sex relatively young, and women who had multiple sexual partners. This seemed odd to the researchers—cancer was not considered a contagious disease, yet cervical cancer cases appeared to follow an infectious pattern. A German virologist named Harald zur Hausen took note of these results—he had already performed research into a cancer-causing virus called Epstein–Barr virus (EBV). He read about women with genital warts also developing cervical cancers, and also studied data from an American researcher in the 1930s showing that rabbits infected with a papillomavirus went on to develop warts and cancers (see BP 4.1 Figure A). He set out to determine whether a similar virus could be responsible for cervical cancer in humans.

Zur Hausen's research into HPV started with genital warts, identifying a strain of HPV named HPV-6. However, although HPV-6 is a cause of genital warts, it was not detectable in any of the cervical cancer samples studied—but zur Hausen and his team kept going. They discovered that there were many more strains of HPV than originally thought, and that some—most notably HPV-16 and HPV-18—were present in significant numbers of cervical cancer cases. They published their research in the 1980s, and over the following decade more evidence poured in, linking these particular strains of HPV to more than 93 per cent of all cervical cancer cases worldwide.

BP 4.1 Figure A There are more than a hundred confirmed strains of human papillomaviruses (HPVs)—small, non-enveloped DNA viruses. Most do not cause diseases and are easily eradicated by the immune system.

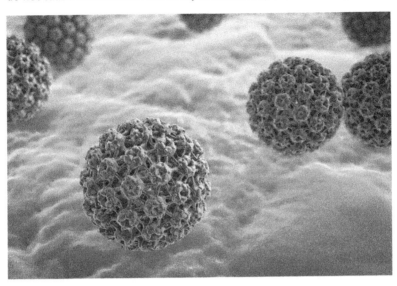

© Kateryna Kon/Shutterstock.

BP 4.1 Figure B Graph to show the impact of the HPV vaccine on cervical changes in young women. Over time, it is hoped a similar impact will be seen in the development of oropharyngeal cancers in both men and women.

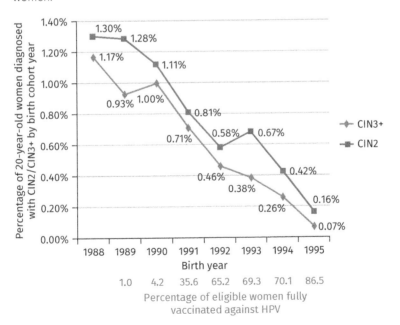

© https://vk.ovg.ox.ac.uk/vk/hpv-vaccine.

In 1999, a group of scientists diligently re-tested many of the cervical cancer samples gathered throughout the previous decades of research. Their discovery was shocking—their data suggested that over 99 per cent of cervical cancer cases worldwide were caused by HPV. This realization led to the development of cervical cancer screening programmes in many countries, and ultimately to the development of HPV vaccines protecting against the forms of HPV which commonly lead to cancer, and some of the strains which cause genital warts.

What does this fascinating story have to do with the respiratory system? Whilst the links between HPV and cervical cancer were being established, so too were suspicions that HPV could be linked to other forms of cancer. HPV infects both skin cells and the cells of the mucous membranes, so it is easily transmitted sexually. Studies showed the virus was also closely linked to penile and anal cancers. Transmission of warty lesions from the genitals to the mouth was actually confirmed at the beginning of the twentieth century—but the significance was not fully realized until the end of the same century.

From the late 1980s onwards, scientists looked in greater detail at the role HPV might play in the development of head and neck cancers. They discovered that, whilst not quite as high as cervical cancer, over 70 per cent of head and neck cancers in Europe are positive for HPV-16 or HPV-18. Oropharyngeal cancer is the most common HPV-positive head and neck cancer, and smoking and alcohol increase the risk of HPV-infected individuals developing cancer even further.

The HPV vaccination programme in the UK originally only targeted girls, aiming to significantly reduce the rates of cervical cancer (see BP 4.1 Figure B). However, the evidence for HPV in other types of cancer (including head and neck cancers) is so overwhelming that both girls and boys are now offered vaccination. Since the vaccination programme was introduced in 2008, rates of precancerous changes and cervical cancer have fallen in the vaccinated age groups by up to 88 per cent. As head and neck cancers tend to occur later in life than cervical cancers, it will take several decades before we see a hoped-for similar drop in the cases of head and neck cancers—watch this space.

Lumps, bumps, and blockages

The symptoms of upper respiratory tract cancers vary depending on their location. Sometimes a new lump appears, either directly over the affected area, or in the lymph nodes found throughout the head and neck. Some people notice a non-healing ulcer on their tongue, in their mouth, or in their throat. In pharyngeal and laryngeal malignancies, sufferers may experience a persistently sore throat or hoarse voice. Sometimes people also experience difficulty or pain on swallowing. If the tumour begins to cause problems with airflow through the upper respiratory tract, **stridor** may occur.

This unpleasant sound is a sign that a tumour is leaving only a narrow passageway in the upper respiratory tract, and urgent medical attention is needed, before the airway blocks entirely. Diagnosis of upper respiratory malignancies is usually from a **biopsy** of the affected tissue combined with imaging to help 'stage' the cancer—to work out whether it has spread to any nearby lymph nodes, or other areas of the body.

Treatment for upper respiratory cancers depends on the stage when they are diagnosed. It may be possible to simply excise (cut out) the tumour without any additional treatment but, because of the risk of **metastasis**, people are often treated with **adjuvant** chemotherapy, radiotherapy—or both. These additional therapies aim to reduce the likelihood of the cancer spreading to the rest of the body, or from recurring in the same place at a later date.

The risks of surgery and anaesthesia are the same when removing a tumour as for any operation—potential bleeding, infection, and even death or injury from anaesthesia (see Chapter 2). If nerves around the operation site are damaged, there may be facial paralysis, numbness, chronic pain, and possibly a permanently hoarse voice. In addition to the risks of surgery, chemotherapy and radiotherapy may also cause significant side effects, even though they help to reduce the risk of **recurrence**. Chemotherapy is usually **cytotoxic**, meaning that it destroys cancer cells—but it will often also affect other cells of the body, leading to a temporary immunosuppression, inflammation of mucous membranes, nausea, vomiting, diarrhoea, and sometimes symptoms such as hair loss or neurological damage. Radiotherapy is designed to destroy cells around the cancer site. Modern radiotherapy is extremely precise, to minimize the damage to healthy tissue—but it will still often cause localized skin reactions, inflammation to soft tissues, and pain.

The survival rates for head and neck cancer depend on the location of the tumour, and how advanced the disease is when it is diagnosed. Survival rates are highest in salivary gland tumours, and lowest in those with hypopharyngeal cancers. Looking at head and neck cancers in general, between 60 per cent to 85 per cent of patients survive for one year after diagnosis. Sadly, this number drops rapidly when five-year survival rates are examined—with only between 27 per cent and 65 per cent of individuals surviving to five years, after which survival rates continue to fall. How do we explain these low survival rates?

- Upper respiratory malignancies are often aggressive cancers, growing and metastasizing rapidly.
- The lymphatic and blood supply to the head and neck is exceptionally good, enabling the disease to spread easily.
- Head and neck cancers are often diagnosed at a relatively late stage, making treatment significantly more challenging, and increasing the likelihood of metastatic spread or recurrence after treatment.

Individuals who are diagnosed at early stages of head and neck cancers often have good outcomes—and so the early detection and treatment of these diseases is absolutely crucial, as are preventative measures such as

HPV vaccination, stopping smoking, and education on the harmful effects of alcohol.

Reconstructive surgery may also be an option for people suffering from significant complications as a result of the treatment of upper respiratory tract malignancies. Significant scarring or deformities of the face can be corrected through careful reconstructive surgery, as can deformities to the oropharynx, teeth, and tongue. This reconstructive surgery enables people to eat and drink more easily, restores speech and other social functions, and helps to reduce the psychological problems which can accompany major changes to the head and neck post-operatively—this is why it is often a planned part of treatment for head and neck malignancies.

Malignancy of the lower respiratory tract: lung cancer

The most common cancer of the respiratory tract is lung cancer, and the overwhelming majority of primary lung cancers—more than 85 per cent—are due to smoking (see Figure 4.11). The term *primary lung cancer* refers to cancers which originate within the lungs, as opposed to secondary or metastatic tumours, which spread to the lungs from other areas of the body—such as the breast, prostate, kidney, or bones. Both primary and secondary tumours cause similar symptoms, but, because the lungs are large organs, people may not experience any symptoms at all until the tumour is relatively large. Symptoms often include progressive breathlessness, **haemoptysis**, coughing, wheezing, fatigue, and weight loss.

Figure 4.11 Lung cancers can be surgically removed, if they are detected before they have metastasized to other areas of the body.

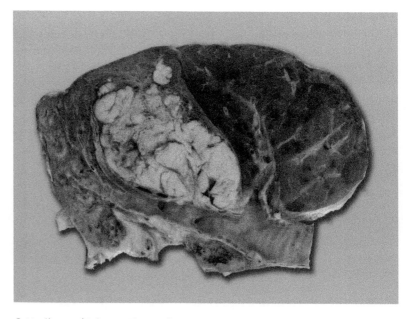

© Medimage/Science Photo Library.

Lung cancer is usually diagnosed through a combination of radiology (X-rays and CT scans) and biopsy, which may be obtained by **bronchoscopy** or performing a CT-guided biopsy. The two commonest types of lung cancer are small cell lung cancer (SCLC)—arising from neuroendocrine cells in the bronchus—and non-small cell lung cancer (NSCLC)—which may arise from squamous cells, type II pneumocytes, or epithelial cells within the lungs. Small cell lung cancers are often very aggressive, growing fast and metastasizing early. They often respond well to chemotherapy initially, but there is a high risk of relapse, and the five-year survival rate remains low. Non-small cell lung cancers are significantly more variable—but, as a rule, they grow more slowly, and metastasize later in the course of disease.

Treatments for lung cancer depend on the stage of the disease, as well as the type of tumour involved. Doctors must determine whether the cancer is a primary lung tumour or not, as well as the cell type of the tumour. This is vital for determining the treatment chosen. A full-body CT scan will usually be performed to determine whether the cancer has metastasized locally (within the lung and nearby lymph nodes) or distantly (to other sites in the body, such as the bones). If the disease appears to be localized, surgery may be an option to physically remove the tumour. This is often combined with chemotherapy or radiotherapy, to shrink the tumour before surgery and reduce the rate of recurrence. Surgery may aim to remove only the diseased area of lung (a wedge resection), one or multiple lobes of a lung (lobectomy surgery), or even an entire lung (a pneumonectomy). The type of surgery required depends on the location of the tumour, along with what other structures lie nearby. If the tumour is growing very close to a blood vessel, the oesophagus, or the trachea, then surgery may not be possible. Surgeons will often remove several lymph nodes from the area around the tumour, to check for evidence of any metastasis. This helps to determine the need for ongoing chemotherapy after the operation. Whilst primary lung cancer has a relatively low survival rate, it is also one of the easiest cancers to avoid—don't smoke!

Respiratory medicine: diseases of the lower respiratory tract

Below the level of the larynx, the lower respiratory tract—from the trachea to the parenchyma of the lungs—is the domain of respiratory medicine. Diseases affecting the respiratory tract often present with similar symptoms, such as coughing, breathlessness, and sputum production, but the underlying causes of—and treatments for—these conditions are hugely varied.

One of the most common problems is asthma. Often thought of as a disease of childhood, asthma persists in many adults—and can even occur for the first time in adult life. It is treated with medicines both to relieve the symptoms and reduce the likelihood of attacks. Infections of the lower respiratory tract such as bronchitis and pneumonia are also major health issues, affecting hundreds of thousands of patients every year. If bacterial, they are usually treated with antibiotics.

In spite of the importance of both asthma and infections in respiratory medicine, they are not treated by surgery, and so we will only mention them briefly here.

Chronic obstructive pulmonary disease

Chronic obstructive pulmonary disease (or COPD) refers to a group of lung diseases which are primarily smoking-related. These conditions—mainly chronic bronchitis and emphysema—affect the ease of air flow in and out of the lungs, leading to breathlessness, coughing, and wheezing. In COPD sufferers, the bronchi and bronchioles become progressively narrower due to chronic inflammatory changes. In addition, the walls of the alveoli gradually break down, leading to larger 'blister-like' structures called **bullae**. These bullae reduce the surface area of the lungs, so gas exchange with the blood becomes much less efficient.

These two processes lead to reduced airflow throughout the lungs, with significant volumes of air trapped in the lungs with each breath. You can see both of these processes at work in Figure 4.12. COPD is a progressive disease, meaning that it will continue to worsen over time, even with treatment. Continuing to smoke after diagnosis, however, contributes to more rapid progression of COPD.

There is no cure for COPD—once the lungs have been sufficiently damaged, they cannot repair themselves. Most treatment for COPD sufferers is based on improving symptoms and day-to-day ability to function. Inhalers—including the short- and long-acting bronchodilators used in asthma, as well as inhaled corticosteroids—help to reduce wheezing and breathlessness. Oral medications such as carbocysteine act as **mucolytics**,

Figure 4.12 Chronic bronchitis causes narrowing of the bronchi and bronchioles, along with excess mucus secretion. Emphysema damages the walls of the alveoli, leading to larger alveolar sacs and less efficient oxygen transfer. These two conditions together are known as COPD.

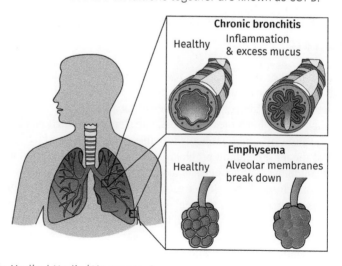

thinning the large amounts of sticky sputum produced in COPD and making it easier to cough up and clear.

Oxygen therapy often becomes necessary for later-stage COPD patients. It does not improve the outcome, but can be useful to treat the symptoms, helping people feel less breathless. Occasionally, in extremely severe COPD, higher-pressure ventilation systems may be needed to help force air in and out of the lungs.

Sometimes the bullae present in COPD can become extremely large, compressing surrounding lung tissue and reducing the effectiveness of the compressed regions (see Figure 4.13). In these cases, **bullectomy** surgery may help relieve the breathlessness. Bullectomy aims to remove the largest of the bullae, allowing surrounding less diseased areas of lung to expand, improving their function.

Figure 4.13 A CT image of a giant bulla (on the left of the images). The healthy lung tissue is being compressed by the size of the air-filled bulla.

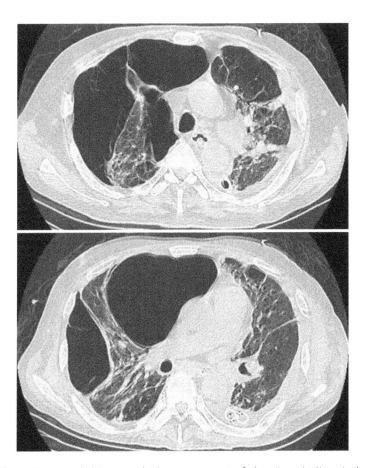

© Sheng-Yuan et al., 'Non-surgical management of giant lung bullae during mechanical ventilation'. *Respiratory Care* 2011 56(10), pp 1614–1616, fig. 2. https://doi.org/10.4187/respcare.

Some COPD patients may be candidates for lung transplantation. These cases are usually younger people with severe COPD, as they will benefit the most from the procedure. Lung transplants in COPD are relatively uncommon, but can give sufferers a significant improvement in their quality of life.

Pulmonary fibrosis

Pulmonary fibrosis is a blanket term used to refer to diseases of the lung parenchyma. There are many potential causes of pulmonary fibrosis, including connective tissue disorders, certain medications, exposure to atmospheric or work-related pollutants or, most often, no obvious cause at all, when it is said to be **idiopathic**. Whatever the cause, pulmonary fibrosis produces scarring of the interstitial tissue of the lungs, reducing the elasticity of the lungs and leading to progressive breathlessness (see Figure 4.14). Sufferers may also experience a dry cough, fatigue, and chest pain. Pulmonary fibrosis usually progresses rapidly, and there is no cure, although sometimes immunosuppressive medications such as oral steroids slow progress of the condition. A lung transplant is the only long-term option—without a transplant, most individuals with pulmonary fibrosis only live for five years after diagnosis.

Lung transplantation

Lung transplants may be considered for patients with severe COPD or pulmonary fibrosis. They may also be an option for patients with other conditions, such as **cystic fibrosis**, **pulmonary hypertension**, **sarcoidosis**,

Figure 4.14 A normal chest X-ray (on the left) compared to the chest X-ray of someone with severe pulmonary fibrosis (on the right). The fluffy white appearance on the pulmonary fibrosis X-ray is the thickened, scarred lung parenchyma.

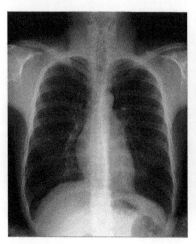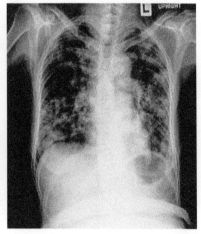

© ChooChin/Shutterstock.

or **bronchiectasis**. Because lung transplantation is a major operation, and because donor lungs are relatively difficult to obtain, lung transplantation is only performed as a last resort, in severe disease that has proven resistant to other, more conservative forms of treatment.

Lung transplants may involve part of a lung (a lobar transplant), a single lung transplant, a double lung transplant, or even a heart and lung transplant. All of these procedures, apart from lobar transplantation, require a cadaveric donor—someone who has been pronounced brain-dead, who is a suitable tissue match for the donation, and who has appropriately healthy lungs for a transplantation. To be considered suitable for a lung transplant, an individual must be in relatively good health (apart from their lung disease), compliant with all previous treatment, not significantly over- or under-weight, and usually under the age of sixty-five. These criteria provide the best possible chance of success for lung transplants, but even so there are significant risks involved with the surgery and the process of transplantation. During and immediately after the surgery, sepsis and bleeding are significant risks. Transplant rejection is always a possibility, and transplant recipients will have to take immunosuppressive drugs for the rest of their lives. These drugs reduce the likelihood of transplant rejection, but increase the risk of infection, as well as of developing a form of lymphoma called post-transplant lymphoproliferative disorder. In spite of the risks, lung transplants often give patients many more years of active life.

 Chapter summary

- The respiratory system can be divided into the upper and lower respiratory tracts, each of which have their own specific diseases.
- Upper respiratory tract symptoms are varied, from excess nasal mucus to vocal hoarseness.
- Upper respiratory tract cancers are often associated with HPV infection, and it is hoped that the rates of these cancers will significantly reduce with the uptake of the HPV vaccine.
- Lower respiratory tract diseases often cause breathlessness, cough, and increased sputum.
- Both the upper and lower respiratory tract are very vulnerable to smoking-related damage, as they directly receive inhaled smoke from cigarettes and other tobacco products.
- Surgery can aim to improve quality of life—such as with tonsillectomies or nasal surgery for polyps—or can be life-saving, such as lobectomies or lung transplants.

Further reading

Bartrip, Peter J W 'History of asbestos related disease' *Postgraduate Medical Journal* 2004 80, pp 72–76. http://dx.doi.org/10.1136/pmj.2003.012526

An interesting look at how researchers proved the link between asbestos exposure and lung disease, including mesothelioma.

Cummings, Michael K, Brown, Anthony, and O'Connor, Richard 'The cigarette controversy' *Cancer Epidemiology, Biomarkers & Prevention* 2007 16(6), pp 1070–1076. https://doi.org/10.1158/1055-9965.EPI-06-0912

A history of cigarette smoking in relation to cancer, plus an examination of how tobacco companies actively worked to suppress information that cigarettes were a cause of cancer.

 Discussion questions

4.1   The scientific process is supposed to be as transparent as possible, and to produce results which are free from bias. Yet scientists are sometimes persuaded to take part in research which is seriously flawed. Why do you think some scientists (such as those working for the tobacco companies in the twentieth century) are prepared to compromise the scientific process? Suggest ways of avoiding this type of bias in future research.

4.2   Given the success of the HPV vaccine at reducing cervical cancer rates, do you think that mandatory vaccination can ever be acceptable in modern society? Explain your reasoning.

5 FROM FOOD TO FAECES

The gastrointestinal tract (GI tract) is a formidably complicated collection of interdependent organs. The processes of digestion are handled automatically, using a complex series of feedback loops. We aren't usually aware of just how efficiently these processes work—we simply feel hungry, eat to fill our stomachs, and then use the toilet to get rid of any undigested material at the end of the process! (see Figure 5.1).

When any of the processes of digestion are affected by disease, we suffer from symptoms—pain, an altered bowel habit, nausea, vomiting . . . There are too many different diseases of the digestive tract to cover in detail in this book. In this section, we will focus on just some of the most common conditions which require surgical treatments.

The mighty digestive tract

Your digestive system is a hollow tube up to 10 metres in length that runs all the way through your body from your mouth to your anus. It has many associated organs and glands, and it is folded to fit mainly within your abdomen. In your lifetime it will process, break down and distribute around 35 tonnes of food, and produce almost 12,000kg of faeces. Figure 5.2 summarizes the main structures in this impressive organ system.

This section will introduce you to the main structures associated with the gastrointestinal tract, along with their functions.

Figure 5.1 'Cloaca' is a digestive machine created by Belgian artist Wim Delvoye. This complex series of tubes and chambers aims to mimic the human digestive process, taking in food at one end and producing solid and liquid waste at the other end. The process of developing this art installation took Wim Delvoye over eight years. It required consultation with both medical professionals and plumbers to achieve an effect similar to that managed by our own digestive systems every day of our lives.

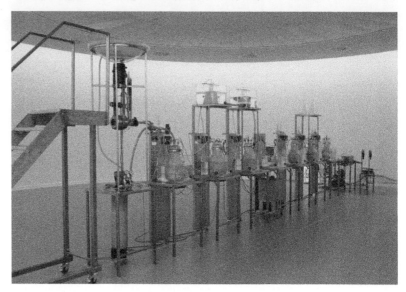

© https://wimdelvoye.be/work/cloaca/cloaca-original.

Figure 5.2 The main organs of the human digestive system.

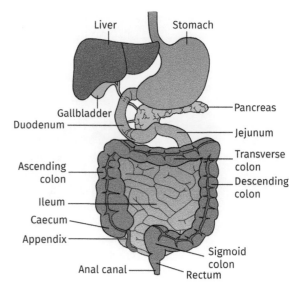

The mouth, teeth, tongue, and salivary glands: the entrance hall of the gut

The teeth break down food mechanically. Salivary glands in the cheeks and under the tongue produce saliva that contains the enzymes lysozyme (destroys potentially harmful microbes in the mouth) and salivary amylase (begins the breakdown of complex carbohydrates). The tongue shapes the food for swallowing and secretes another enzyme—**lingual lipase**—involved in the breakdown of lipids.

The pharynx and oesophagus—down the hatch

In a process taking around a second, muscles in the pharynx constrict in sequence from top to bottom, pushing the food bolus down towards the oesophagus. The **soft palate** closes off the nasal cavity, the vocal cords (see Chapter 4) close to seal the glottis, and muscles around the hyoid bone tilt the epiglottis, covering the entrance to the larynx stopping food reaching the lungs. Now, the muscular tube of the oesophagus relaxes and contracts in peristaltic waves to push the bolus down towards the stomach.

The stomach—breaking down the bolus

Once the oesophagus passes through the diaphragm, it joins the stomach—a hollow, muscular organ responsible for the second stage of digestion. The gastric juices of the stomach are made up of a number of different enzymes, along with hydrochloric acid—all of which are secreted from the gastric glands. Various hormones are also secreted by different areas of the stomach and they act in different ways throughout the digestive process—even regulating how hungry we are, and how full we feel!

The muscles of the stomach churn the food, with waves of contraction approximately every twenty seconds. This physically breaks down the food, and mixes it with gastric juices to produce **chyme**. The pyloric sphincter permits very small amounts of chyme (around $3cm^3$ at a time) to pass through into the duodenum. The process usually takes between two and four hours, but can be longer depending on the type of food eaten.

The small intestine—digesting and absorbing

The small intestine is the longest part of the alimentary canal, and it is where the great majority of digestive and absorptive processes occur. It is made up of the following parts.

- **The duodenum** is the shortest part (25cm) of the small intestine. It regulates the flow of bile (which emulsifies lipids and reduces the acidity of the chyme) and pancreatic enzymes (which further break down the products of digestion) into the small intestine.
- **The jejunum** stretches for around 90cm. It absorbs electrolytes and the small, soluble molecules which are the products of digestion in the duodenum.

Figure 5.3 A cross-section of the intestinal mucosa showing villi and microvilli.

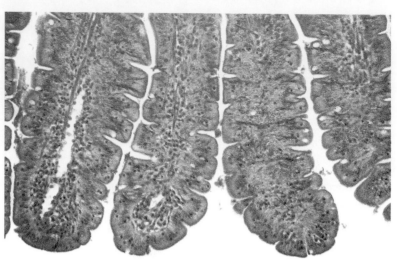

© Kateryna Kon/Shutterstock.

- **The ileum**, the longest portion of the small intestine, has folds of lining studded with thousands of finger-like projections called villi, around 0.5–1mm long. Each villus is covered in tiny microvilli, around 1μm in size (see Figure 5.3). They increase the surface area, allowing the products of digestion to be absorbed more efficiently.

Waves of smooth muscle contraction push the chyme back and forth, mixing it with the digestive juices. Once most of the chyme is absorbed, peristaltic waves move the remaining products through to the caecum—the first part of the colon. It takes around three to five hours for a meal to pass right through the small intestine and into the colon.

The colon—from food to faeces

The last part of the gut deals with final nutrient and fluid absorption, along with formation of faeces and the removal of these unwanted products from the body through the anus. The rectum is very similar to the rest of the colon but the inner layer of smooth muscle forms the first anal sphincter, under involuntary control. The second anal sphincter is made of skeletal muscle, and is (usually!) under voluntary control. Both anal sphincters usually remain closed unless defaecation is taking place.

Bacterial flora—the microbiome of the gut

Whereas most of the digestive processes taking place in the stomach and small intestine have focused on eliminating pathogenic micro-organisms, the colon needs its own collection of billions of bacteria to function properly. There are around 700 identified species of non-pathogenic bacteria living in an adult colon, known as the gut flora. Many of them facilitate chemical digestion within the colon, as well as synthesizing and secreting some substances important for the health of the rest of the body, including vitamin K, pantothenic acid (vitamin B5) and biotin (vitamin B7). A complex interplay between these **commensal** organisms and the immune tissue within the gut prevents these bacteria from entering the bloodstream, where they could potentially cause harm. It is becoming increasingly clear that the delicate symbiosis between our intestines and their bacteria is crucial, not only for gut health, but for the wellbeing of the rest of the body too.

Final absorption and excretion

Ninety per cent of the original water in food is absorbed by the small intestine. Over a period of twelve to twenty-four hours, the leftover products of digestion pass slowly through the large intestine. Most of the remaining water is absorbed, making the chyme firmer. The gut flora break down the last carbohydrate molecules into sugars, absorbed by the walls of the colon. This process produces gases such as methane and carbon dioxide, passed rectally as wind or 'flatus'. The undigested chyme is bulked out by millions of bacteria, shed endothelial cells from the intestinal lining, and enough water to keep it from becoming too hard to pass. As the rectum fills, the walls stretch, and the defaecation reflex is triggered.

The accessory organs of digestion

The liver, pancreas, and gallbladder are considered 'accessory' organs of the digestive tract—but without them, digestion would be a significantly less efficient process (see Figure 5.4).

Figure 5.4 The liver, gallbladder, and pancreas all sit within the upper half of the abdomen.

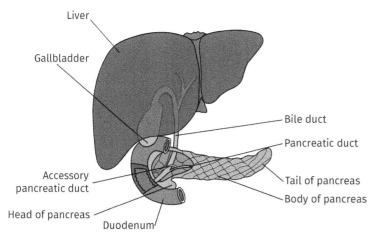

The liver—secreting and detoxifying

The liver is the largest gland in the body. It is vital for digestion, to break down the (often toxic) by-products of bodily processes, and to regulate various homeostatic mechanisms within the body. The hepatic artery supplies the liver with oxygenated blood from the aorta, and the hepatic portal vein delivers partially deoxygenated blood, rich with nutrients and other substances absorbed from the small intestine. The liver processes these nutrients, splitting amino acids to form ammonia and then urea in the ornithine cycle, and storing or breaking down fatty acids. The liver also breaks down toxins and metabolizes many medicinal drugs.

The liver cells secrete about a litre of bile—an alkaline mixture of bile salts, water, bile pigments, electrolytes, phospholipids, triglycerides, and cholesterol—daily. Most of it arrives directly in the small intestine. The main bile pigment is bilirubin, which gives bile its characteristic green colour. It is sourced from the breakdown of red blood cells in the spleen. Bile emulsifies lipids in the small intestine, increasing the available surface area for lipases to act. Most of the constituents of bile are excreted in the faeces—but bile salts are reabsorbed in the colon and recycled into newly formed bile.

The gallbladder—storing and squeezing

The gallbladder is a thin-walled structure, sitting behind most of the liver. It stores extra bile, squeezing it out into the duodenum only when more bile is needed after a high-fat meal.

The pancreas—exocrine and endocrine

The **exocrine pancreas** secretes clear pancreatic juice, mainly made up of water, sodium hydrogen carbonate, and various enzymes. The slightly alkaline nature of pancreatic juice helps to **buffer** the acidic chyme in the small intestine, deactivating pepsin from the stomach and creating a perfect environment for pH-sensitive enzymes in the small intestine. Many of these enzymes are produced in an inactive form, to prevent the enzymes from digesting the pancreas itself!

The endocrine pancreas involves the islet cells which secrete the hormones insulin, pancreatic polypeptide, glucagon, and somatostatin directly into the bloodstream. These hormones are then carried to target organs all around the body, to play a vital role in the homeostatic control of blood glucose levels.

Blood supply and support—the mesentery and omentum

Without structural support, the organs of the digestive tract would quickly end up tangled together in the lower abdomen. The mesentery is a double fold of peritoneal tissue, which anchors the small and large intestines to the

Figure 5.5 The mesentery anchoring the intestines inside the abdomen.

© Kaushik_Ghosh/iStock.

posterior abdominal wall. The mesentery is made up of connective tissue, and provides a framework for the blood vessels, nerves, and lymphatics which supply the bowels (see Figure 5.5).

Other folds of connective tissue are needed to help support the stomach and solid organs in the abdomen, such as the liver. In front of these structures lies the **greater omentum**—a large, apron-like structure, which is the site of large fat deposits in people who are very overweight.

Blood supply

The blood supply for the gastrointestinal tract serves two functions.

- It supplies the digestive organs with sufficient oxygenated blood and nutrients to allow the cells to function.
- It transports deoxygenated blood and nutrients absorbed from the digestive tract and moves these nutrients to where they can be absorbed or further processed within the body.

The majority of the digestive organs are supplied from arteries branching off from the abdominal aorta. The veins which absorb nutrients and water from both the small and large intestines drain into the hepatic portal vein—the large vein delivering partially deoxygenated blood to the liver. This allows the liver to absorb and process nutrients and any toxic substances absorbed from the intestines, before releasing required nutrients back into the bloodstream for transport to where they are required.

Looking into the gut

To understand the gastrointestinal tract (GI tract), and to investigate the diseases which affect it, we have to find ways of seeing inside the body. Apart from the wonders of X-rays, the CT scan, and the MRI scan (see Chapter 1), we can look at the gut using a technique called **endoscopy**. Endoscopy of the GI tract involves inserting an endoscope into the mouth (**gastroscopy**) or anus (**colonoscopy**) of a patient. An endoscope is a long, thin tube with a camera and a light on one end, so doctors can see and film the living, moving gut. An endoscope may also have tools attached, so biopsies of tissue can be taken when problems are seen (see Figure 5.6). **Laparoscopy** is also used, which is when a laparoscope, very similar to an endoscope, is inserted into the body cavity through a small incision in the abdominal wall to examine the different abdominal organs. This requires general anaesthesia, whereas endoscopy is usually performed under sedation.

Figure 5.6 Endoscopy makes the inside of the GI tract visible to doctors in real time.

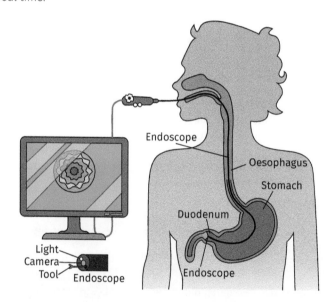

© VectorMine/Shutterstock.

From mouth to stomach: stones, acid, and bacteria

A huge number of conditions affect the oral cavity, but diseases of the salivary glands are of particular interest when discussing the GI tract. The salivary glands, and the ducts which feed saliva into the mouth, are vulnerable to infection tracking back up from the oral cavity. These infections, called sialadenitis, may be bacterial or viral, but the symptoms are usually similar—painful swelling of the face (usually unilaterally, as it is uncommon for salivary glands on both sides of the mouth to be infected at the same time), fevers, rigors, and feeling unwell. The facial skin over the infected gland may become reddened and inflamed. Sometimes, pus may squirt or drain from the infected gland into the mouth, producing a foul taste.

Sialadenitis may be caused by a chronically dry mouth, by acute dehydration, or by salivary stones. These stones form in a similar way to kidney stones, or gallstones—precipitation of normally soluble salts of calcium, magnesium, and potassium. We don't fully understand what triggers this precipitation, but once they do, they accrete into a stone, which gradually increases in size. It is estimated that around 1 per cent of the population have some salivary stones—but only the larger stones block a salivary gland. Initially this causes pain on salivation—before food, or at the thought of food—and sometimes temporary facial swelling, as saliva becomes backed up behind the stone. Ultrasound scans or CT imaging are often helpful for diagnosing salivary stones. Once identified, the stone is usually removed surgically—either by opening the salivary gland up from within the mouth, or by passing a small endoscopic probe into the salivary gland to cut the stone into fragments, or remove it in one piece.

Disorders of the oesophagus—inflammation and dysmotility

Despite its simple structure, the oesophagus is still prone to a number of significant problems. Hernial pouches, known as diverticulae, can form in the wall of the oesophagus over long periods of time. These can cause difficulty swallowing, and even result in the aspiration of food or drink into the lungs, causing an aspiration pneumonia. Food often becomes trapped in these diverticulae, leading to very bad breath (halitosis). Extremely large oesophageal pouches can occasionally cause such severe blockages that the oesophagus ruptures—a condition which requires immediate surgery to save the life of the sufferer.

Oesophageal diverticulae are usually diagnosed either by passing an endoscope into the oesophagus and directly seeing the diverticulum, or by performing a barium swallow. During the latter investigation, a patient is asked to drink a liquid containing radio-opaque dye, and their swallowing is then captured using video fluoroscopy. If a pharyngeal pouch is present, it will fill with the radio-opaque dye during the swallowing process (see Figure 5.7).

Once diagnosed, oesophageal diverticulae are usually surgically corrected to improve swallowing and reduce the risk of aspiration pneumonia. This can be done either via open surgery, or via endoscope or laparoscope, depending on the size and location of the diverticulum. The open surgical approach involves making an incision in the patient's body as close to the diverticulum as possible, and then dissecting down through the overlying tissues until the diverticulum is reached. At this point, depending on the size and location of the diverticulum, the surgeon may choose to fully remove the pouch, or may invert it and staple it to the rest of the oesophagus,

Figure 5.7 This video fluoroscopy image of a barium swallow shows a large diverticulum on the left-hand side of the image, at the end of the oesophagus.

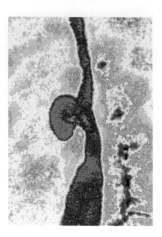

BSIP SA/Alamy Stock Photo.

to prevent it from filling any further. In some cases, the surgeon may choose to just divide the septum between the pouch and the oesophagus, allowing any food which passes into the pouch to easily drain back into the oesophagus.

Open surgery is risky, however. Large blood vessels (such as the carotid arteries and the jugular veins) run close to the oesophagus, as do several important nerves involved in speaking and swallowing. Nowadays, oesophageal diverticulae are more often operated on using either an endoscope inserted into the patient's mouth, or by laparoscopic surgery if the diverticulum is situated further down the oesophagus. This reduces the risk of causing damage to any overlying structures, and results in smaller surgical wounds—reducing the risk of infection, and improving the rate of healing.

Gastro-oesophageal reflux disease

More commonly shortened to just acid reflux or GORD, this condition is a blanket term for the movement of stomach contents—food, acid, and gastric juices—back up into the oesophagus. This commonly causes symptoms such as heartburn, nausea, an acidic taste in the mouth, and halitosis (bad breath). Less commonly, reflux can lead to an altered voice (as the acidic contents reflux up the oesophagus and down the trachea, irritating the vocal cords), difficulty or pain on swallowing, and sometimes even nausea and vomiting.

GORD has a number of causes. An incompetent lower oesophageal sphincter (see Figure 5.8), obesity, smoking, gallstones, and hiatus hernias (see Figure 5.10) all increase the risk of stomach contents refluxing back up into the oesophagus. Infection with the bacteria *Helicobacter pylori* is also an important consideration for people suffering from GORD. Diagnosis of

GORD is usually made clinically. Further investigations such as endoscopy are usually only performed if someone has very atypical or severe symptoms, or they do not respond to treatment. Sometimes a blood or stool test for the presence of *H. pylori* is performed, particularly if an individual suffers from recurrent bouts of GORD.

Once diagnosed, treatment is usually a combination of lifestyle modification and medication. Weight loss, smoking cessation, and dietary changes are all important ways to improve many people's symptoms. Medications called proton pump inhibitors (PPIs) help to reduce the amount of acid produced by the stomach, and other medication such as raft-forming alginates help to create a foamy 'raft' on the surface of the stomach contents, making it harder for them to reflux back up into the oesophagus.

If these attempts at treatment are unsuccessful, surgeons may perform a fundoplication endoscopically, wrapping all or part of the **fundus** around the lower oesophagus, and fastening it in place (see Figure 5.8). This increases the pressure on the lower oesophagus, making it much harder for gastric contents to reflux back up from the stomach. Increasingly the evidence suggests that longer-term benefits may be smaller than treatment with medication.

Barrett's oesophagus

If GORD is left untreated, the effects of the acidic stomach contents on the wall of the oesophagus can lead to a condition called Barrett's oesophagus. When repeatedly damaged by acid, the cells lining the oesophagus divide more and more haphazardly. Over time, the cells become increasingly abnormal, eventually resulting in **neoplasia**—a malignant process. The presence of Barrett's oesophagus significantly increases the risk of oesophageal cancer. You can discover more about neoplasia in *Cancer: Biology, Causes, and Treatments*, another title in this series.

Barrett's oesophagus is diagnosed via endoscopy, and a biopsy of the affected area allows us to see the severity of the disease by looking at the cells under the microscope. Early stages may just require treating the reflux and careful monitoring. Higher degrees of metaplasia (and even early neoplasia) may be treated endoscopically, by **resection** or **radiofrequency ablation**. More severe neoplasia may need the surgical removal of part of the oesophagus, or a combination of surgery, chemotherapy, and radiotherapy. Advanced neoplasia, particularly if the cancer has metastasized, may only be treated palliatively, with radiotherapy, chemotherapy, or occasionally palliative surgery—such as the insertion of an oesophageal stent to allow the patient to continue swallowing food and drink.

Diseases of the stomach: ulcers, polyps, and *Helicobacter*

Conditions such as GORD affect both the stomach and oesophagus, but there are some pathologies which are relatively unique to the stomach itself. The stomach (Figure 5.8) sits in the upper left of the abdominal cavity, with its fundus against the diaphragm.

Figure 5.8 The anatomy of the stomach.

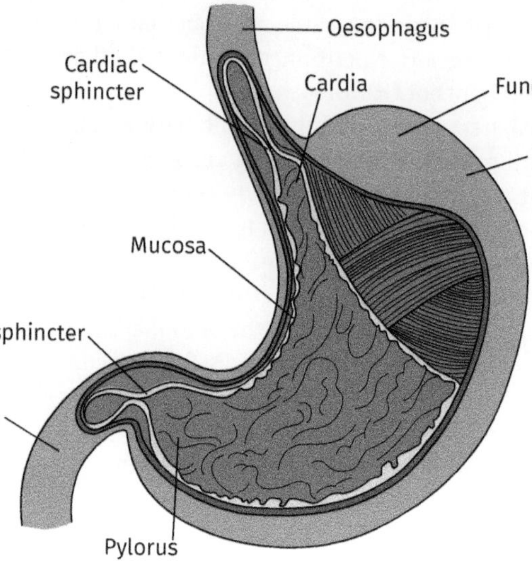

Stomach ulcers

Although the mucous lining of the stomach is resistant to the acidic gastric juices, sometimes this protective layer is eroded, causing an ulcer. Cigarette smoking and non-steroidal anti-inflammatory drugs (NSAIDs) such as ibuprofen make the gastric mucosa less able to repair itself. Colonization of the stomach with the bacterium *Helicobacter pylori* reduces the mucosa's ability to protect itself from the acidic environment within the stomach. The bacterium produces urease, which goes on to produce ammonia—this both damages the gastric mucosa and reduces the pH of the gastric juices, improving the survival of the bacteria. In fact, it is estimated that up to 70 per cent of patients with gastric ulcers (in the stomach) or duodenal ulcers are infected with *H. pylori*. Eradicating this bacterium significantly reduces the risk of ulcer recurrence after treatment. You can see an endoscopic image of a stomach ulcer in Figure 5.9. Stomach ulcers may cause symptoms such as epigastric pain, nausea, bloating, and reflux symptoms. Some individuals experience very few symptoms at all. Left untreated, stomach ulcers may cause localized bleeding or they may perforate into the abdominal cavity, causing **peritonitis**, sepsis, and even death.

If a stomach ulcer is suspected, an endoscopy will confirm its presence. A biopsy can be taken of the stomach ulcer itself, or of the lining of the stomach, to look for the presence of *H. pylori*. If an endoscopy is not required, testing for *H. pylori* can still be done by looking for the presence of antigens in the stool or in the bloodstream, or by performing a urea breath test—checking for the presence of urea, produced by *H. pylori*, in the breath of the patient.

Figure 5.9 This endoscopic image shows a gastric ulcer—it may cause few symptoms, but can also be life-threatening.

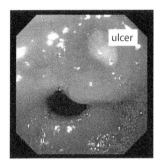

© David M Martin, MD/Science Photo Library.

Treatment for gastric ulcers involves the use of acid suppression therapy such as PPIs and alginates, as well as eradicating *H. pylori* if it is found to be present. A combination of two antibiotics, plus high-dose PPI therapy, is usually used to eradicate the bacteria—confirmation of which can be achieved by using a urea breath test after completing the course of antibiotics.

Surgery for treatment of stomach ulcers used to be very common—before PPIs, surgery was the only long-term treatment for many people with gastric ulcers, and until the role of *H. pylori* in gastric ulcers was proven, ulcers would commonly recur. Occasionally surgery for gastric ulcers is still required—particularly if there has been a large haemorrhage, or perforation of the ulcer. The area of perforation or bleeding is removed, sometimes by removing the diseased area of stomach. This is often combined with a vagotomy—a procedure severing one or more branches of the vagus nerve, to reduce gastric secretions and reduce the risk of ulcer recurrence.

Hiatus hernia

Ordinarily, the muscular sheet called the diaphragm prevents the stomach from moving up into the chest cavity. Sometimes, a weakness in the diaphragm allows part or all of the stomach to move up into the chest cavity. Hiatus hernias may cause no symptoms at all, or they may cause symptoms of GORD, and even Barrett's oesophagus.

There are two main types of hiatus hernia—sliding and rolling (also called paraoesophageal hernias). Sliding hiatus hernias are more common, and do not tend to be associated with any severe problems. Rolling hiatus hernias may also involve other parts of the digestive tract, such as parts of the small intestine or the pancreas. This can rarely lead to obstruction of the small intestines, or of the blood supply to any of these organs, which requires urgent surgical correction to avoid irreversible tissue damage. Many people with hiatus hernias require no treatment at all, particularly if the hernia is completely asymptomatic. Those who suffer from GORD symptoms or Barrett's oesophagus as a result of a hernia are treated for their symptoms.

Figure 5.10 A normal stomach and diaphragm alongside a sliding hiatus and a more serious rolling hiatus hernia.

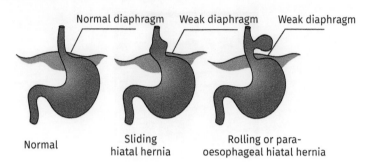

© Annakek/Shutterstock.

In people who do not respond to conservative treatment, who have very large hernias, or who have a rolling hiatus hernia, we may consider surgery. This is usually done laparoscopically, although occasionally open surgery is performed. Surgery usually involves a degree of fundoplication. Sometimes the hiatus—the hole in the diaphragm which the oesophagus passes through—may also be tightened surgically, to reduce the risk of further hiatus hernias in the future (see Figure 5.10).

The small and large intestines

Ulceration also occurs in the small intestine—chiefly the duodenum. The pathological process mirrors that of gastric ulceration, with similar symptoms. The causes, too, are the same—*H. pylori* infection, NSAIDs, and smoking. Significant, severe stress can also play a role in the development of duodenal ulcers—and the development of these 'stress ulcers' in intensive care patients is well documented. Occasionally, severe stress outside a hospital setting can also cause duodenal ulcers—but this is rare. The treatment for duodenal ulcers is identical to that of gastric ulcers. In fact, the two are often grouped together under the term 'peptic ulcer disease'. There are, however, many more conditions which affect the small and large intestines more exclusively.

Inflammatory bowel diseases

There are two main types of inflammatory bowel disease—conditions which cause inflammation to the mucosa of the GI tract. One is **Crohn's disease** and the other is **ulcerative colitis (UC)**.

Crohn's disease

The inflammation caused by Crohn's disease can occur anywhere from mouth to anus. This can result in symptoms including abdominal pain, diarrhoea (sometimes bloody), weight loss, mouth ulcers, and even symptoms outside the GI tract—inflammation of the eyes or the joints. Crohn's can even increase the risk of gallstones. It often takes a long time to diagnose Crohn's, because it presents in so many different ways.

The exact causes of Crohn's are not completely understood—but we think it is the result of a combination of genetic, environmental, and possibly infective factors including:

- smoking
- some drugs, e.g., the antibiotic doxycycline
- infection by certain bacteria and viruses
- stress.

Diagnosis of Crohn's disease is usually through a combination of history-taking and blood tests (looking for signs of anaemia, and raised inflammatory markers) followed by endoscopies (often of both the upper and lower GI tracts). Biopsies are usually taken during these procedures, and the histology of these biopsies is very helpful in aiding diagnosis. The inflammation seen in Crohn's disease affects the whole intestinal wall, and often starts and ends very abruptly. Severe Crohn's disease causes ulceration of the affected tissues—and all of these signs can help specialists come to a decision about the diagnosis.

Once diagnosed, Crohn's disease can be treated—but it cannot be cured. Steroids are often used to reduce the severity of disease initially and, once the inflammation is under control, immunosuppressant medication may be used to prevent relapses. This is helpful, but many individuals will have significant flares of disease during their lifetimes.

In severe Crohn's disease—where the intestines become blocked or have ulcerated through into the peritoneum—life-saving surgery may be needed. Surgeons often have to remove significant sections of intestine—both small and large. Unfortunately, Crohn's disease usually returns despite surgery— and will often recur along the sites of previous operations. **Stomas** (such as **colostomies** and **ileostomies**) are formed by attaching the end of a healthy portion of bowel to the skin. This is generally only performed if a significant amount of diseased bowel has to be removed, as it is a life-changing procedure. Rather than the bowels emptying normally, the faeces empty into a bag attached to the outside of the stoma (see Figure 5.11)—a bag which is completely invisible under clothes.

Ulcerative colitis

The second of the inflammatory bowel diseases, ulcerative colitis (UC) causes painful inflammation and ulceration of the colon, and very rarely affects any other part of the GI tract. Like Crohn's disease, UC may also cause symptoms outside the GI tract—affecting the eyes and joints, and sometimes the liver, the gallbladder, or the skin. People suffering from UC often complain of similar symptoms to those with Crohn's disease and, as in Crohn's, the cause of UC is not fully understood. It is thought to be caused by a combination of genetic and environmental factors, and possibly by changes within the gut flora as well.

Diagnosis is usually through a combination of history-taking, blood tests, and endoscopic biopsy. Although the history and blood test results may be

Figure 5.11 Surgery to remove large sections of bowel affected by Crohn's disease may mean a patient needs a stoma.

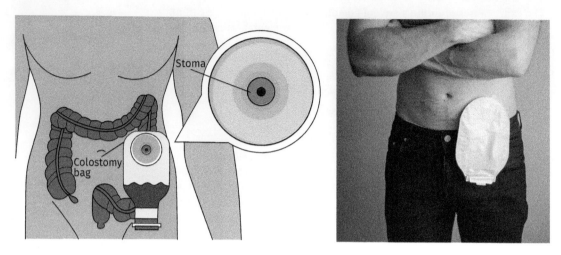

Diagram: © rumruay/Shutterstock. Photograph: © matuska/Shutterstock.

similar to Crohn's, the histology of UC is different. The inflammation and ulceration are confined to the mucosa of the intestine, rather than the whole intestine wall as seen in Crohn's. UC tends to affect significant portions of the bowel wall, too, rather than the abrupt stopping and starting of Crohn's lesions.

Treatment for UC is similar to that of Crohn's—initially steroid therapy, followed by immunosuppressants to prevent relapses. Surgery can cure the bowel symptoms of UC, although removal of the colon (a procedure called colectomy) is only performed in cases of perforation, catastrophic haemorrhage, or severe intractable disease. It is a major procedure, carrying significant risks, and may also require the formation of an ileostomy. Sometimes, however, surgeons manage to connect the small intestine to the anus, using a portion of the small intestine to form a pouch which functions as a rectum.

Diverticular disease

Whilst Crohn's and UC are relatively rare and severe diseases of the intestines, diverticular disease is very common—affecting up to 50 per cent of people over the age of sixty. Many of these people will never have any symptoms from their condition, and it is often only diagnosed incidentally, when investigations for other conditions are performed. It occurs when the walls of the colon become weaker—usually due to the changes associated with ageing in the body. Areas of the colon between the taeniae coli form small pockets or bulges, called diverticulae. They do not tend to cause symptoms themselves—but if they become inflamed or infected, they can cause pain, diarrhoea, and sometimes bleeding. If an infected diverticulum is left untreated, it can perforate or form an abscess—which can lead to **sepsis**. When diverticulae become inflamed, the condition is known as diverticulitis. You can see the difference between diverticular disease and diverticulitis in Figure 5.12.

Figure 5.12 Diverticular disease implies the presence of diverticulae, with or without inflammation—here you can see both diverticulosis (no inflammation) and diverticulitis (infection and/or inflammation).

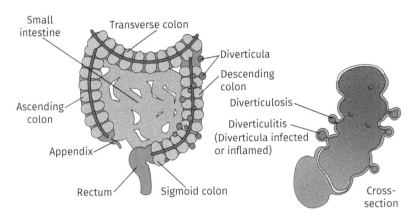

People with diverticular disease are often encouraged to eat a diet high in fibre, fruits, and vegetables, as this appears to reduce the risk of inflammation and infection in the diverticulae. Infections of the diverticulae do not always require surgery. They may be managed with antibiotics—usually taken orally, although sometimes intravenous antibiotics are required. If an infected diverticulum forms an abscess, or perforates into the abdominal cavity, then surgery may be required to remove the diseased section of bowel. Sometimes, if an abscess or area of inflammation is particularly severe or prolonged, a **fistula** may form between the bowel and other organs in the abdomen, such as the bladder or the vagina. This can lead to bowel contents being passed through the fistula and lead to recurrent bladder or vaginal infections. Fistulae have to be corrected by surgery—they are not life-threatening but have a huge impact on quality of life.

Obstruction

Because the intestines are basically a long series of tubes, they can become blocked, or obstructed. This can happen for many different reasons—cancers, large gallstones, hernias, or even twisting of the bowels—a condition known as volvulus. Obstructions can occur at any point in the small or large intestine, and may cause slightly different symptoms, depending on which area they affect.

Obstructions usually present with pain and swelling in the abdomen. Obstructions of the small intestine may quickly result in vomiting, whilst the sufferer may continue to open their bowels until the colon has been emptied. Obstructions of the colon, however, may present with an inability to open the bowels, with vomiting occurring only as a later sign.

If it is not diagnosed quickly, obstruction of any part of the bowels can lead to ischaemia (oxygen starvation) of the affected part of the bowel, which may lead to **necrosis** (death) of that part of the bowel, followed by perforation. Left untreated, bowel obstruction is frequently fatal—but many bowel obstructions (particularly small bowel obstructions) can be treated without the need for surgery. Cancers or structural abnormalities such as narrowing of part of the bowel usually need surgical correction, or even removal of the affected part of the bowel. This is particularly true if ischaemia or necrosis has occurred. On the other hand, many obstructions caused by inflammatory bowel disease self-resolve over time. Most patients who present with an obstruction have a nasogastric tube inserted through the nose and down into the small intestine. To relieve the pressure building up in the intestines, they are given intravenous fluids to relieve dehydration and they are labelled 'nil by mouth'—they are not allowed to eat until the obstruction has resolved.

Perforation

Perforation (a hole in the gut wall) can occur anywhere in the GI tract, from the oesophagus right through to the rectum. They result from conditions ranging from untreated bowel obstructions and diverticular abscesses, through ulceration of the stomach or intestines, to trauma, and untreated GI tract cancers. When the gut perforates, the contents of the GI tract spill into the thorax or the abdomen, depending on the location of the perforation. This is a medical emergency, as the mixture of digestive products and bacteria irritate the body cavities (peritonitis), and may rapidly lead to overwhelming sepsis. Perforation of the GI tract and the subsequent inflammation and irritation of the abdominal cavity—called peritonitis—are almost always treated with surgery to repair the perforation and remove any foreign material from the abdominal cavity. Antibiotics are usually necessary to prevent infection from overwhelming the body. Even with rapid treatment of perforation, there is still a significant mortality rate.

GI cancers: hidden killers

Malignancy (cancer) of the gastrointestinal tract is a major killer worldwide, and is responsible for more deaths than cancers of any other organ system if the accessory organs such as the pancreas, liver, and gallbladder are included.

Survival rates for the different types of GI cancers are very varied, and the symptoms depend on the site of the malignancy.

The symptoms of GI cancers are also very variable—from increased GORD symptoms, to early feelings of fullness while eating, to changes in bowel habits including stools becoming looser and more frequent than usual, or dark, sticky stools called melaena from bleeding tumours. Some GI cancers present with weight loss, while others may present for the first time with bowel obstructions or perforations. Unfortunately, because the GI tract is long, and the abdomen provides a lot of space for cancers to grow, symptoms often do not present until the disease is quite advanced and has metastasized to other sites in the body.

Many health organizations around the world screen for GI cancers, aiming to pick up malignancies early in people with either no or very mild symptoms. By examining the stools of people in the highest-risk age group and looking for traces of blood, GI cancers can sometimes be detected early. People with a positive stool test will undergo endoscopy to look for the source and cause of the bleeding.

Once a GI tract cancer is found, the next step is to stage it to determine whether or not it has spread, either locally (such as invading through the bowel wall) or distally (via the lymphatics, to other organs such as the lungs or brain). Localized cancers may be removed surgically—but more advanced and metastatic cancers may not be surgically curable. In these cases, a combination of chemotherapy and radiotherapy can be offered, to shrink both the primary site of malignancy and any metastases. Sometimes this effectively cures the cancer, but in other cases it may simply shrink the tumours to improve symptoms for a while. People treated by surgery, chemotherapy, or radiotherapy are usually followed up and scanned frequently, because it is difficult to tell if any microscopic fragments of malignancy remain. These scans help determine if any new areas of malignancy are developing, and whether further treatment may be needed.

Surgery for GI tract cancer may be relatively minimal, in the case of a small tumour which has not spread deeply into local tissue. However, many GI tract cancers are only treatable with relatively radical surgery, and it is common for people who undergo cancer surgery on the GI tract to require colostomies or ileostomies. These are sometimes reversible once the cancer has been successfully treated.

Although the diseases we have discussed above are not the only ones which affect the GI tract, we have covered many of the more common problems which people may suffer with throughout their lives—and especially those which can be helped by surgery.

The bigger picture 5.1

Cause and effect?—the risks for gastrointestinal cancers

As you have seen, there are many types of GI cancers, developing in all the different regions of the digestive tract and the organs that feed into it. Yet many of these cancers have very similar risk factors. Why is this?

Your gut is exposed to everything you take into your body through your mouth—and some, perhaps many, of these things affect your risk of developing particular cancers. One of the biggest risk factors for GI tract cancers—and, indeed, cancers throughout the body—is smoking. Despite the knowledge that smoking causes around 8 million deaths around the world every year, the WHO estimates that 1.3 billion people continue to smoke.

Alongside smoking, alcohol use and diet are both significant risk factors for many of the different types of GI tract cancers. The risks for oral cancers, oesophageal and stomach cancers, and cancers of the pancreas, liver, and gallbladder, are significantly increased by alcohol usage.

BP 5.1 Figure A An excessive amount of red meat or processed meat products in the diet increases the risk of GI cancers developing.

© Anthony Short.

Diet is a more contentious issue. Some foods have been definitively shown to increase the risk of GI cancer, such as a diet high in red meat (which increases the risk of colon cancer), or processed meats (which increase the risk of cancer throughout the GI tract) (see BP 5.1 Figure A). However, it is difficult to find true correlation between individual foods and increased incidence of a particular type of cancer.

The risk of significant bias is high, and the difficulty in finding and monitoring a 'control' population can make results difficult to interpret in real-world terms (see BP 5.1 Figure B). For example, there is reasonably good evidence that regular consumption of *mate*, a herbal tea commonly consumed in South America, is associated with oesophageal cancers. *Mate* is usually drunk at a scalding hot temperature. It would be reasonable to assume, then, that drinking hot tea or coffee would have a similar effect—but other international studies have not conclusively proven a link between hot drink consumption and upper GI tract malignancy. So, it may be chemicals in *mate*, rather than the temperature of the drink, that increase risk.

On the other hand, some foods appear to have a protective effect against GI cancers. Diets rich in fruit and vegetables and high in fibre appear to reduce the lifelong risk of many different malignancies, including those of the GI tract. The reasons behind this are not entirely clear. Our best current theory is that the micronutrients present in most fruit and vegetables play a

BP 5.1 Figure B The incidence of GI cancers—including colorectal cancers—appears to have strong lifestyle links, as this data from the AICR shows.

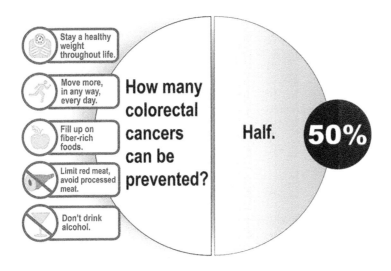

American Institute for Cancer Research.

role—antioxidants, in particular, may help to prevent some of the DNA damage which often leads to malignancy over time.

Genetics play a significant role in the development of some GI tract malignancies—particularly those of the lower GI tract. One group of genes—including the APC and MUTYH genes—appears to increase the risk of polyps forming within the colon, and the greater the number of polyps, the higher the risk of malignancy over time. Other genes appear to directly increase the risk of malignancy itself, by interfering with a process known as DNA mismatch repair (MMR)—a system for recognizing the errors during DNA replication. If the body loses this important way of recognizing abnormal DNA changes, the lifelong risk of malignancy increases significantly.

Even without genetic risks, smoking, and diet-related factors, some people go on to develop gastrointestinal tract cancers. They are hard to predict, hard to find, and hard to treat.

? Pause for thought

Smoking and eating a lot of red or processed meats are known to increase your risk of developing GI cancers. On the other hand, eating a fibre-rich diet is known to lower your risk of developing certain GI cancers.

Suggest reasons why the incidence of these cancers has not plummeted.

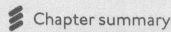

Chapter summary

- The organs of the gastrointestinal tract work from the mouth to the anus to break down and absorb the nutrients found in the food we eat.
- The mouth, oesophagus, stomach, and intestines are aided in this process by the substances secreted from the gallbladder and the pancreas, and the actions of the liver.
- Diseases affecting any part of the GI tract can have significant effects on our nutritional state, and can lead to issues with anaemia, vitamin deficiencies, and even death.
- Risk factors for GI tract diseases are often environmental, with the food we eat and our lifestyle choices playing a significant part in how healthy our digestive systems remain.
- Surgery can offer treatments for many diseases of the GI tract, but may come with its own complications such as colostomies or shortened bowels.

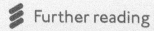

Further reading

Ryan-Harshman, Milly, and Aldoori, Walid 'Diet and colorectal cancer' *Canadian Family Physician* 2007 53(11), pp 1913–1920. https://www.ncbi.nlm.nih.gov/pmc/articles/PMC2231486/

An examination of the scientific evidence regarding foodstuffs and supplements which have been thought to play either a causative or protective role in the development of bowel cancers.

Shreiner, Andrew B, Kao, John Y, and Young, Vincent B 'The gut microbiome in health and disease' *Current Opinion in Gastroenterology* 2015 31(1), pp 69–75. Author manuscript, available in PMC 1 January 2016. https://www.ncbi.nlm.nih.gov/pmc/articles/PMC4290017/

A fascinating, in-depth look at how our gut microbiome functions, and how it may influence diseases of many different organ systems in the body.

Discussion questions

5.1   Think about any themes which run through the different diseases of the GI tract. Are there any risk factors which are more or less universal? How do you think we should manage them, if so? Should the responsibility for risk reduction be placed on the individual, or the state?

5.2   What do patients need to know about any gut operation they are due to have before they can give informed consent?

5.3   Recovery of full gut function after the reversal of a colostomy or ileostomy is often very slow. Reflect on the reasons why this may be so.

6 THE BONES OF THE BODY

You probably didn't think much about how you opened this book but the physiology and biomechanics required to perform this simple action involve a seamless interplay between your nerves, brain, muscles, and skeleton. The brain and nerves may control the body, but it requires the muscles and skeleton for movement to take place.

The musculoskeletal system offers both protection for our organs, and a means of moving to gather resources or escape from danger. The skeleton is a rigid, calcified scaffold made up of separate bones, linked at smooth surfaces called joints. Muscles act as contractile units pulling the joints into new positions to allow movement. The interplay between dozens of muscles controlled by hundreds of thousands of neurones produces the coordinated movement required for survival. But what if these systems are damaged? What if the physiology behind the muscle function goes wrong? What happens when bones break or muscles tear?

Damage to the musculoskeletal system is a common occurrence—a large percentage of emergency admissions to hospitals, and patients in surgery, are due to traumatic injury to these systems. Trauma to the body is common in day-to-day life, but it doesn't usually result in injuries. Any damage caused is a reflection of the forces applied, the area of the body affected and the physiology of the patient. A trip leading to a fall would not be an issue for a toddler, or a healthy twenty-year-old, but the same injury in a frail eighty-year-old could lead to a fracture and ultimately a decline in health leading to death (see Figure 6.1). Similarly, the impact of a cricket ball could cause serious injury if applied to a single finger, but would not be an issue if it hit the thigh or forearm.

In this chapter we will look at the basic physiology of the musculoskeletal system, along with key muscle groups and their joints. We will explore some of the conditions affecting the musculoskeletal system, along with some common injuries. We will also examine the potential of surgical or conservative management, along with some of the potential complications.

Figure 6.1 The body can survive high-impact forces during day-to-day life—and even doing high-risk sports—thanks to the strength of the musculoskeletal system, but as we get older changes in our bones and muscles make injury more common, and surgery more challenging.

Skier: © Ridofranz/iStock. Woman on floor: © KatarzynaBialasiewicz/iStock.

The skeleton

The organs of the body rely on the skeleton and muscles for protection, and to move them around. The ability to mobilize is vital for survival, to escape predators, to hunt, to reproduce and to transport resources. Movement is a complex biochemical feat achieved by the contraction of a muscle or muscles causing changes in the forces applied to a joint where two bones meet. This in turn results in a change in alignment of the bones and ultimately, movement.

What are bones?

When you look at a skeleton, it is either dead bone or made of plastic—and so it is easy to think of bone as nothing more than an inert scaffolding material. In fact, nothing could be further from the truth. Both muscles and bones are complex physiological constructions in their own right. We will start by looking at the formation and structure of bones.

Bones are hard, calcified organs with three well-known functions.

- They support the body within vertebrate animals.
- They protect the internal organs of vertebrate animals.
- They enable movement.

Bones, however, do so much more than this—they have multiple other functions along with their roles in locomotion, support, and protection. Bones are the centre of production of red and white blood cells, they provide a store of calcium and other minerals for the body, and they release hormones

Figure 6.2 Bones can be categorized according to their shape, which also affects their structure, location, and function.

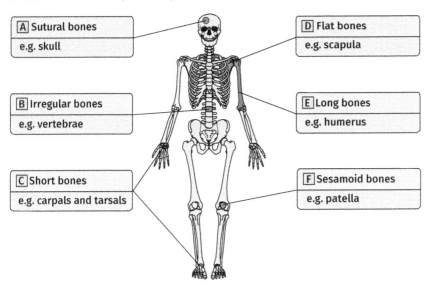

| A Sutural bones |
| e.g. skull |

| D Flat bones |
| e.g. scapula |

| B Irregular bones |
| e.g. vertebrae |

| E Long bones |
| e.g. humerus |

| C Short bones |
| e.g. carpals and tarsals |

| F Sesamoid bones |
| e.g. patella |

that modulate metabolic pathways. A bone is not a homogeneous object but is made of several different types of structures and cells. Bones come in many different shapes and sizes, but are often classified into one of several categories based on their outward appearance (see Figure 6.2).

This wide variety of shapes allows each bone to support or protect specific areas of the body. The bone types have different properties and roles, but all contain both non-living highly calcified connective tissue and specialist **osteocytes** or bone cells. The calcified areas provide the strength and structure of the bone, while the different osteocytes are involved in the maintenance and healing of bones. It is important to remember that bone is not a static material. The bones of your skeleton are constantly remodelled, with material built up or removed as the forces you apply to your skeleton, and the muscles you use in everyday life, change. Add in growth, if you are relatively young, and repair and maintenance throughout life—and you begin to see bone as the dynamic structure that it really is.

Osteoblasts are cells involved in the formation of new bone, either for growth, remodelling or healing. They secrete a protein mixture known as osteoid around themselves. Osteoid is rich in collagen, an insoluble, fibrous protein—in fact, collagen forms about 25 per cent of the protein in your body! The osteoblast deposits calcium phosphate onto the collagen, which is then hardened by the addition of alkaline ions to form a new layer of bone. As the osteoblast surrounds itself with the osteoid, when it is hardened it ends up encased in hard bone—once this happens it is known as an osteocyte.

Osteoblasts are also involved in the regulation of ions such as calcium and phosphate in the body, along with releasing hormones such as prostaglandins.

Osteocytes are effectively inactive osteoblasts, trapped within the bone in spaces known as lacunae. They are the most common type of cell within bones. Many have cellular processes that meet with other osteoblasts or osteocytes for communication. It is thought they have an important role in sensing mechanical stress, and so in coordinating the remodelling of bones during long-term, strenuous exercise.

Osteoclasts are large cells with multiple nuclei found within the bone structure, and they are responsible for reabsorption of bone. Like almost all tissue in the body, bone is being constantly broken down and replaced, which is important for the constant remodelling and restructuring of bones to adapt them to their use. Osteoclasts secrete enzymes and absorb the products of the breakdown process. Osteoblasts then follow to secrete new bone in its place.

Osteoclasts, like osteoblasts, play an important role in the regulation of calcium ions in the body. Calcium ions play a crucial role in muscle contraction—including the contraction of the cardiac muscle which makes up the heart—so maintaining sufficient levels in the blood and tissue fluid is very important. There are three main structures involved in calcium ion regulation in the body. Calcium comes into the blood from the gut, depending on the food eaten. Calcium then travels from the blood into the bones where it is used by the osteoblasts, and it is returned to the blood by the osteoclasts when they break down bone material. The kidney either conserves calcium or excretes it in the urine, depending on the levels of calcium ions in the blood (see Figure 6.3). The bones, controlled by the osteoblasts and osteoclasts, are the main calcium sink and source, especially if the amount of calcium in your diet is limited.

Figure 6.3 The gut, the bones, and the kidneys are all involved in maintaining a dynamic equilibrium of calcium ions in the blood and tissue fluids.

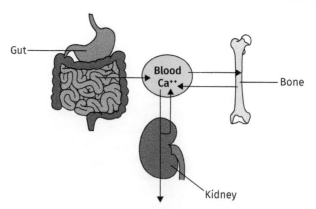

Bones are not homogeneous, solid organs; they possess two distinct types of tissue: **trabecular bone** and **cortical bone**. These have different properties, and both are important for the functioning of the bones.

- **Cortical bone** is dense and very hard. It is found in almost all bones and is largely responsible for the strength of the bone. It forms the exterior layer of the bone and is responsible for the characteristic smooth, white appearance. It is formed of organized microscopic columns of compact bone matrix called **osteons**. Each osteon surrounds a central channel which contains capillaries. These channels are known as **Haversian canals** and they provide a blood supply for the osteocytes within the bone matrix (see Figure 6.4). The columns run in parallel to the bone, with their organized structure improving strength of the bone. The outside of the cortical bone is coated in a highly innervated structure known as the **periosteum**. The interior of the cortical shell is coated in **endosteum**, which separates the two layers of bone.

- **Trabecular bone** is found in the centre of bones and it has a porous, highly vascular interior structure. Trabecular bone isn't always present—it is mainly found in the larger bones such as long bones, as they are big enough to house it. The porous nature of trabecular bone provides a large surface area inside the bone and increases its flexibility, but is less strong than cortical bone. The large surface area is important, because trabecular bone houses bone marrow. Bone marrow is the fatty, gelatinous tissue where red and white blood cells develop. Partially differentiated stem cells called mesenchymal stem cells reside in bone marrow. These stem cells can develop into different types of white blood cells, vital for the immune response, or red blood cells needed to carry oxygen (see Figure 6.4).

Figure 6.4 The organized structure of bone provides it with the strength and flexibility necessary to survive impact forces during everyday activity.

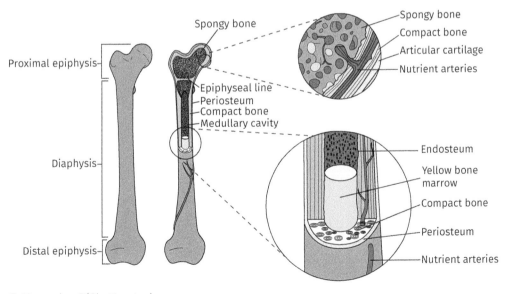

Figure 6.5 The human body undergoes several growth spurts on its way to adulthood, but enlarging a complex organism like a human is not simple.

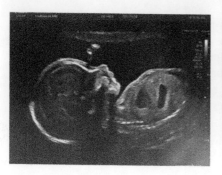

© Ann Fullick.

Skeletal growth

Have you ever looked at pictures of yourself as a baby? It's hard to believe you were once that tiny (see Figure 6.5). All parts of us grow as we develop from infants to adults, and many organs simply increase the number of cells and expand, but how do bones grow?

At the start of our lives, our skeletons are not rigid, hard structures. The early human embryo is just a ball of cells. As the foetus develops the skeleton is formed by two mechanisms. Some bones, such as the flat bones of the face and the collarbones, form directly from **mesenchymal cells**—these are the cells of an undifferentiated connective tissue that develops into much of the muscle and soft tissue of the body. The mesenchymal tissue differentiates into osteoblasts, which in turn secrete an uncalcified version of the bony matrix. This is then hardened over a few days as calcium is absorbed into it. These bones are not fully calcified at birth and continue to grow and develop until adolescence (which is why your face shape can keep changing until you are in your early twenties).

Other bones, such as the long bones of the arm and leg, are laid down in the foetus initially by special cells called **chondrocytes**. These chondrocytes produce tough connective tissue called **hyaline cartilage**, and this acts as a precursor to the bone itself. As the cartilaginous skeletal precursors grow, the very central section starts to become calcified, until eventually the chondrocytes in the centre can't receive enough nutrients from the limited blood supply reaching them. The chondrocytes die, causing the disintegration of the central section of cartilage. The space they leave allows new blood vessel formation, and this delivers cells which differentiate into osteoblasts. This central calcified part of the cartilaginous bone precursor is called the **primary ossification centre**. The osteoblasts within the ossification centre then form new bone which spreads from the centre of the bone towards each end. As we grow into childhood, new vessels form within the distal parts of the bone to form **secondary ossification centres**. These grow to form the articulating processes on joints. This entire process is called 'ossification' (see Figure 6.6).

Figure 6.6 The first skeletal structures in a foetus are made of cartilage—but by the time a child is running around, the bulk of the skeleton is bone.

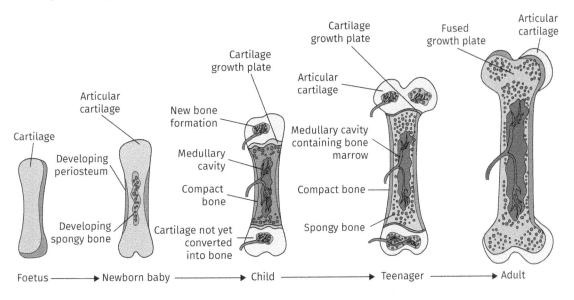

© naulicrea/Shutterstock.

Once the majority of the bones of a child have ossified, that child can still grow. In children and young people until the end of puberty, there are cartilaginous areas at the ends of the long bones between the shaft of the bone and the secondary ossification centres known as the **epiphyseal plates**. Cartilage is laid down and expanded on one side of the plate, before being removed and replaced with bone on the other side. This process is under the control of growth hormone produced by the pituitary gland. During puberty there is an increase in growth hormone, which triggers the adolescent growth spurt. However, another impact of puberty is a big increase in the level of the sex hormones, oestrogen and testosterone. Oestrogen is the dominant hormone in girls and testosterone in boys, but both biological sexes make both hormones—and it is oestrogen which scientists think is particularly linked to the closure of the epiphyseal plate and the end of growth. As the oestrogen concentration in the blood rises, the amount of cartilage in the epiphyseal plate reduces until it is finally replaced with bone to form the epiphyseal line. This change—which takes place at slightly different times at different epiphyseal plates in the body—gives anthropologists, including forensic anthropologists, the information they need to accurately age individuals who die in their teenage years or early adulthood from their skeleton alone. If an individual does not make enough oestrogen, then they will continue to keep growing long into adulthood, which can cause further problems if it results in giantism.

The bigger picture 6.1
Issues with skeletal growth

The growth of the skeleton is closely controlled. It is governed by a combination of genetic factors and the environment in which a child grows. Nutrition is the most important factor affecting bone growth, starting even in the womb. Lack of certain nutrients can cause issues with bone development and growth.

One of the most important nutrients for bone growth is vitamin D, a fat-soluble vitamin which is manufactured by the body from cholesterol. It is responsible for the regulation of calcium in the body, including the absorption of calcium from the gut, the reabsorption of calcium by the kidney, and the resorption of bone via activation of osteoclasts. These mechanisms increase blood levels of calcium and allow the formation of healthy bone. Lack of vitamin D can cause decrease in bone strength through a loss of calcium from the bones.

Vitamin D is synthesized naturally by our bodies in a three-stage process. The initial stage takes place in the skin, and needs UV radiation from sunlight to occur. The sterol 7-dehydrocholesterol (produced in your body) reacts with UVB radiation to form a compound called **cholecalciferol**. This cholecalciferol is then carried in the blood to the liver, where it is metabolized to calcidiol. The calcidiol is then carried in the blood to your kidneys, and here it is converted to the active form of vitamin D, calcitriol (see BP 6.1 Figure A).

BP 6.1 Figure A Natural vitamin D formation in the body.

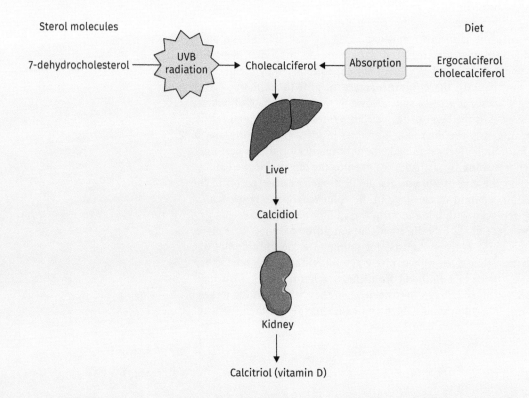

The initial step of production is vital to provide the liver and kidneys with cholecalciferol to convert to active vitamin D. To form enough vitamin D, the body has to be exposed to sunlight directly outdoors. The wavelength of radiation needed to catalyse the breakdown of 7-dehydrocholesterol to cholecalciferol cannot penetrate through clothes, or even glass windows. This can cause problems in some parts of the world. In the UK, for example, the optimal time for exposure to sunlight is between 11am and 3pm, April to September. No wonder it is often very hard to provide our skin with enough exposure to sunlight while also ensuring, particularly if we have pale skin, that we do not get sunburn!

In addition to the logistical factors affecting exposure to the sun, people with more melanin in their skin (such as those of African, African-Caribbean, or South Indian descent) will need longer exposure to sun as the melanin in their skin naturally protects them against UV radiation. With such a brief window of time to manufacture vitamin D, many people are at risk of developing a deficiency and while vitamin D can be absorbed from food, it is not very plentiful in natural sources. Oily fish, red meat, and eggs all contain vitamin D, but in relatively small amounts. Some cereals and other foodstuffs are fortified with vitamin D to compensate for this and help people get the vitamin D they need.

Vitamin D deficiency is a problem because it decreases the amount of calcium in the body and bloodstream. This in turn means that there is less calcium available for osteoblasts to use in the production of bone. Bones without calcium are weaker and more prone to malformations and fractures. In childhood, vitamin D deficiency causes the disease **rickets**, where the developing long bones are soft and bow outwards with the weight of the body (see BP 6.1 Figure B). In adults a lack of vitamin D can cause osteomalacia—a weakening of the bones due to decreased calcium. This can cause bone and joint pain, bone malformation and weaker bones that are more prone to fractures. Vitamin D is one of the few vitamins where taking supplements really can help!

BP 6.1 Figure B Rickets used to be a common condition—yet it is easily avoided.

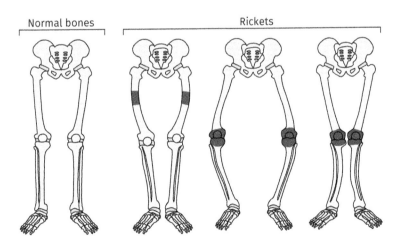

© Double Brain/Shutterstock.

The magic of muscle cells

The ability to move demands a system able to contract or relax to create tension and move joints in a reliable and controllable way. This system has to manage large, high-strength activities such as walking along and fine, delicate movements such as manipulating tools. The importance of both reliability and control are seen all too clearly when watching a small child learn to walk, and then run, or struggle to manipulate a small toy (see Figure 6.7).

There are several different types of muscle cells. Smooth muscle is found throughout internal organs of the body, including the gut, the airways, the bladder, and in the blood vessels. Cardiac muscle makes up the structure of the heart (see Chapter 3). Here we will focus on striated muscle, also known as voluntary muscle, the muscle tissue which moves the skeleton—and so moves us about.

Striated muscle cells are specially adapted for movement. They contain complex molecular mechanisms enabling them to contract. The cells form organized bundles collectively known as muscles. Each muscle consists of millions of muscle cells aligned to provide contractile forces that shorten the muscle when stimulated. This contraction acts to pull on one side of a joint and cause movement (see Figure 6.8). Muscles cannot extend

Figure 6.7 It takes a small child time and practice to gain control of their muscles—and develop the strength they need.

© Anthony Short.

Figure 6.8 Muscles form functional pairs that act on either side of a joint.

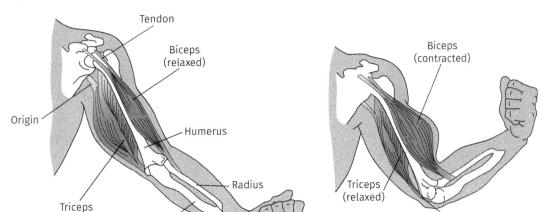

© stihii/Shutterstock.

themselves. Once a muscle has contracted, the cells relax and then have to be 'pulled' back to their original length by the contraction of an opposing muscle. Muscles have evolved to form functional pairs on either side of joints to allow flexion and extension of that joint.

Muscle cells contain many myofibrils lying parallel to each other; each myofibril contains the functional units of a muscle cell called the sarcomeres. A sarcomere is largely made up of the proteins actin and myosin, as you can see in Figure 6.9. The cytoplasm of the myofibrils is called the sarcoplasm. Unsurprisingly, it contains large numbers of mitochondria, needed to supply the ATP needed for muscle contraction. Running through the sarcoplasm we find the sarcoplasmic reticulum, a network of membranes which store and release calcium ions.

As you can see in Figure 6.9, a sarcomere has overlapping regions of actin and myosin. So how does muscle contraction work? Looking at striated muscle under a microscope provides many of the clues. Whatever the state of the muscle—contracted or relaxed, the A band remains the same size. However, the I band and the H band get shorter when a muscle fibre contracts, and return to their original state when the fibre relaxes. This evidence supports the sliding filament theory of muscle contraction—that actin and myosin move over each other. Our current model of the mechanism is as follows.

- Actin is a thin protein with active sites protected by an even thinner strand of protein called tropomyosin. Tropomyosin in turn is bound to another protein, troponin. Troponin has three subunits—one binds to actin, one binds tropomyosin and one binds calcium ions.

- When the muscle cell is activated, calcium channels in the sarcoplasmic reticulum open, causing an inrush of calcium ions.

- These calcium ions bind to the troponin, changing its shape so it pulls on the tropomyosin molecules, exposing the actin binding site.

Figure 6.9 The detailed structure of striated muscle.

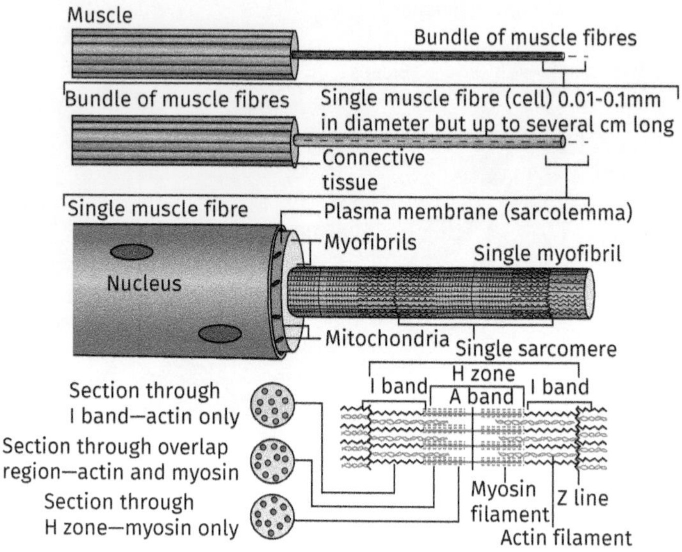

© Ann Fullick, *Edexcel A2 Biology* (Longman, 2009), p 142, fig. 7.2.1.

- The thicker myosin strands have many branching stalks with bulbous heads on the end. Each of these heads binds to the actin, forming an actomyosin bridge.
- Once coupled ADP and Pi are released from the myosin head and the myosin changes shape—the head bends forward and moves along the actin filament, shortening the sarcomere.
- Free ATP in the sarcoplasm then binds to the myosin head, causing another shape change so that it decouples from the actin strand.
- This activates ATPase in the myosin head, in a reaction which also needs calcium ions to work. The energy from the bond breaking in the hydrolysis of the ATP allows the myosin head to return to its original position, with ADP and Pi bound to it—so it is primed and ready to go once more.

If the stimulation continues, calcium ions remain in the sarcoplasm and the cycle is repeated. If not, the calcium ions are pumped back into the sarcoplasmic reticulum in an active process, so troponin and tropomysin return to their original positions on the actin strand, the contraction stops and the muscle fibre relaxes. This is the mechanism by which all voluntary muscles contract.

Soft tissues: tendons and ligaments

Bones on their own would not provide enough support and structure to allow us to move about—they'd fall apart! Just adding muscles wouldn't solve the problem either. A significant amount of the stability and strength in our joints comes from soft tissues such as tendons and ligaments, which hold the joints in place and provide stability. They allow the joints to move, within certain degrees of freedom, without popping out of alignment or damaging themselves.

Rather like skeletal muscle, tendons have a very organized structure—much of their mass is made of non-living collagen fibres supported by specialized cells called tenocytes. Tendons anchor muscles to bone through specialized insertion points and play a key part in the stabilization of joints. The main body of a muscle may be some distance from the point where its tendons are anchored to the bones, and this allows large muscles to control small joints. For example, bending and stretching our fingers (flexion and extension) is not controlled by muscles in the fingers themselves but by muscles in the forearm. The tendons run all the way down our arms and connect to the distal end of our fingers. The fibrous connective tissue of the tendons has different properties depending on where in the body they are found. Some tendons, such as the Achilles tendon at the back of the ankle, provide an elastic recoil rather like a spring—this provides energy to our stride and makes walking and running more efficient. Others, such as the long tendons controlling our fingers, are much more stiff and static. Perhaps counterintuitively, this allows finer movement control. The insertion points of tendons on bones may come under immense stress during vigorous exercise or trauma, and so they are a common site of injury (see Figure 6.10).

Damage to tendons can cause either bony or soft tissue injury. If the injury puts strain on the tendon, the tendon itself may remain undamaged, but the forces transmitted to the insertion site at the bone can cause a

Figure 6.10 The forces developed in sports such as rugby can be huge—no wonder sport is a common cause of tendon and ligament injuries!

© Yu Chun Christopher Wong/Shutterstock.

fragment of bone to be pulled off. This is known as an **avulsion fracture**. If a tendon is stretched beyond its elastic limits it may tear—either partially or totally. Damage to tendons affects muscle function, but as tendons have both a poor blood supply and relatively few nerve endings, such injuries are often not particularly painful. Patients often present following injury with loss of muscle function affecting one joint—but it doesn't really hurt. Repair of a tendon injury depends on the site and extent of the injury. Some smaller injuries to fingers can be treated simply by placing the finger in a splint, which brings the two ends of the tendons together. The tissues slowly heal and, although there may be residual weakness in the tendon, patients often have a good result. If larger tendons such as the quadriceps in the front of the thigh or the Achilles at the back of the ankle are damaged, they may require surgical intervention to suture (stitch) both ends of the tendon together.

Ligaments are formed from fibrous connective tissue. They are mainly collagen and they hold the bones in a joint firmly in place. Their main role is to stabilize joints and limit their movement to ensure that the bones remain aligned correctly and the joints are not damaged when you move. Most ligaments have a small amount of elasticity and return to their resting size when relaxed, but unlike muscles, if they are overstretched, they cannot return to their original state. This means that damage to ligaments is often permanent and can significantly affect the stability of a joint.

If enough force is applied to a joint, the two bones will separate, an injury known as a **dislocation**. Dislocations are usually extremely painful, and they cause significant trauma to ligaments as they stretch them far beyond their normal elasticity. If the joint is not relocated promptly, the ligaments may be permanently damaged, decreasing the stability of the joint and increasing the risk of further dislocations in future. Ligaments are not living tissue but are made up of layers of collagen fibres with a poor blood supply, and so they have very little ability to heal following injury. A torn ligament will weaken a joint, and may make it unstable and prone to dislocation, collapse or further injury later on. The good news is that ligaments can be repaired, either by replacing them with a section of ligament or tendon taken from another area of the body or by using artificial ligaments. The joint remains unstable until the new ligament is fully integrated, so a ligament injury is often followed by a long period of physiotherapy and recuperation. This makes it a particularly difficult injury for those who compete in professional sports—a broken bone, whilst initially more dramatic, often heals much faster.

Joints—and when they go wrong

An entirely solid skeleton would be fine for protection and support—but no use at all for movement. It is the movement between bones that allows us to move about. Where two bones meet a joint is formed, allowing rotation, flexion, or extension between the two bones. As you saw earlier in the chapter, bones come in many different sizes and shapes, which means that joints also come in a variety of forms with different functions, as you can see in Figure 6.11.

Figure 6.11 There are many different types of joints within the skeleton, each with a different range of movement. The ball and socket joint of the hip, for example, offers multiple dimensions of movement, whereas the hinge joint of the knee is rigid and can only flex or extend.

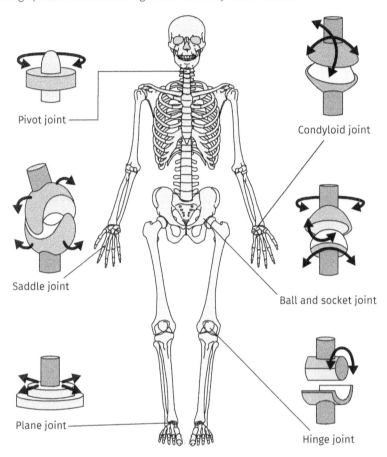

Pivot joint

Condyloid joint

Saddle joint

Ball and socket joint

Plane joint

Hinge joint

© VectorMine/Shutterstock.

There are several classification systems for joints which look in detail at the type of movement, presence of cartilage and structure of the joint. Here we will focus on **synovial joints**, the joints which allow the biggest range of movements, and which are most commonly affected by problems which require the attention of orthopaedic surgeons. Synovial joints are contained within a fibrous joint capsule. The two bone surfaces are coated in smooth cartilage and the capsule is filled with synovial fluid which acts as a lubricant and cushioning factor between the bones. Some joints have additional features such as strengthening ligaments connecting either side of the joint or fat pads within the joint to further protect the cartilage. Joints like the shoulders, hips, and knees (see Figure 6.12) are all synovial joints, an important factor when considering joint replacements. We've already established the importance of joints in movement—so what goes wrong with joints, and what can we do about it?

Figure 6.12 The simplified structure of a synovial joint.

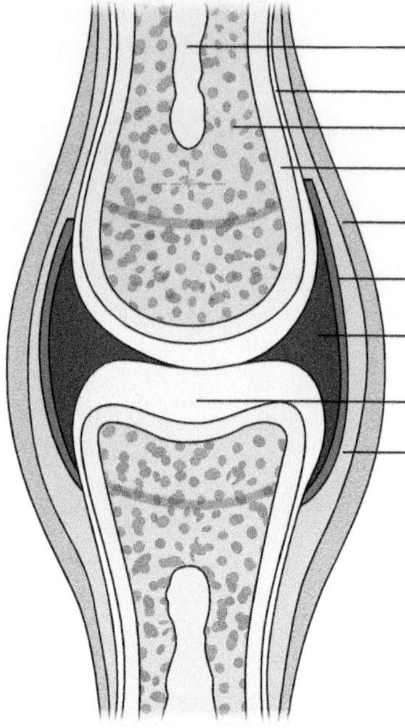

- Yellow bone marrow
- Periosteum
- Spongy bone
- Compact bone
- Ligament
- Synovial membrane
- Joint cavity (contains synovial fluid)
- Articular cartilage
- Joint capsule (reinforced by ligaments)

Wear and tear

The cartilage covering each side of the bones in synovial joints allows easy, pain-free movement between the two articulating surfaces. The type of cartilage coating the joint surface is known as hyaline cartilage, a very specialized subtype of cartilage that is exceptionally smooth with a highly organized structure. It provides a perfect articular surface for joints. Our joints experience thousands of articulations on a day-to-day basis, which over a lifetime contributes towards the breakdown of this specialized surface. Contributing factors to this breakdown include obesity, diabetes, and hypermobile joints. You cannot change the mobility of your joints, or avoid type 1 diabetes. However, by avoiding obesity, and so reducing your risk of developing type 2 diabetes, you can help to protect your joints and minimize the effects of wear and tear.

As the cartilage begins to become less organized and break down, the joint may become stiff or reduce in flexibility. This breakdown of the articulating cartilage is known as **osteoarthritis**. Commonly, as the cartilage is worn further, greater stress is placed on the innervated bone and this causes pain. This pain can be severe enough to limit the mobility—many patients do not move much because it hurts so much. Initial management of the earlier symptoms of osteoarthritis may include weight loss, painkillers, physiotherapy, and walking aids to help alleviate symptoms. Eventually, however, when the pain and lack of mobility is having a significant impact on the patient, surgery is used to replace the joint with an artificial one.

Joint replacements

If a joint is worn down by osteoarthritis, and conservative management has not helped, then the joint can be replaced by a prosthetic version. Only certain joints are amenable to this surgery as it requires finesse and precision to line up the artificial joint with the normal biomechanics of the limb. The shoulders, hips, and knees are the most commonly replaced joints, but there are occasions when fingers or even toes are given artificial joints. The generic name for the procedure replacing a joint is an **arthroplasty**.

There are many factors to consider before carrying out an arthroplasty, focusing on the patient and which approach and type of joint would be most appropriate for them. Some patients are relatively fit and active, and desperately want to return to an active lifestyle. Others are less worried about being very active, but want to be able to live their lives free of pain. Some patients are much older than others, and some are much heavier than others. The surgeon and the team have to take all of these factors into account when considering the make and type of prosthesis inserted. The most common materials used in joint replacements are a metal base or stem (either titanium or a cobalt–chromium alloy) and a ceramic articulating surface (see Figure 6.13). The specific composition of the prosthesis will differ depending on the patient and the joint replaced.

As a joint is made of two bones articulating, replacements either replace one (hemiarthroplasty) or both articulating surfaces of the joint (total arthroplasty). Whether the surgeon uses hemi or total replacements depends on how long they feel the joint needs to last, or how much use it will have. In elderly patients a less long-lasting but less extensive procedure is

Figure 6.13 Different joints require different materials to ensure maximum longevity.

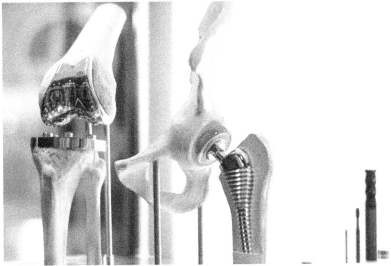

© Monstar Studio/Shutterstock.

warranted, to minimize the risk of the surgery, and so they are often suitable for hemiarthroplasty. A younger patient is much more likely to require, and to be able to withstand, the surgery needed for a total arthroplasty. Like the natural joints they replace, prosthetic joints don't last forever. In fact, they usually have a much shorter lifespan than the natural joint, and some may need to be replaced more than once. In 2019, articles were published in *The Lancet* based on metadata analyses of a number of studies looking at the longevity of replacement joints. They found that for around 85 per cent of patients, a new hip will last around twenty years, and for 58 per cent of patients, the new hip will last twenty-five years. In a similar metadata analysis of replacement knees, the team found that total knee replacements lasted twenty-five years in 82.3 per cent of patients and partial replacements lasted twenty-five years in around 70 per cent of patients. The surgeon has to consider this when thinking about which joint replacement to use.

The replacement of a joint normally requires the removal of a section of bone and replacement with the prosthesis. This needs specialist tools including saws, aligners, and even hammers. Although this sounds a bit like carpentry, the orthopaedic surgeon has to be very skilled to align the prosthesis in the correct way to ensure that the joint functions properly. In modern operating theatres, the accuracy of the surgery is further improved by X-rays or CT scans of the patient, which can be displayed on monitors, allowing the surgeon to review and plan the replacement before even starting the operation.

Case study 6.1
The puzzle of metal-on-metal joints

In the early days of hip replacements, the new joints often did not contain the articulating layer of ceramic or polyethylene which is common today. These bare metal-on-metal arthroplasties were thought to be excellent for younger patients, as they reduced wear on the ceramic plate and could potentially last a lot longer and endure higher levels of activity. They had a resurgence in the 1980s, until a trend began to appear of failure rates in patients with metal-on-metal (MOM) hips. Around 1–2 per cent of patients complained of increased pain, a decreased range of movement, and swelling. Scans of the patients demonstrated inflammation and oedema surrounding the joints. No bacteria grew when aspirating the joints and the patients did not have raised inflammatory markers, so the swelling and other problems weren't due to infection.

Looking at samples from these patients under the microscope, it became clear that there were large inflammatory reactions taking place in the joints, but that they were more characteristic of a hypersensitivity reaction than a response to infection. The mystery remained why MOM hips were causing this, but not metal-on-ceramic, and why only a subset of MOM patients were affected. As prosthetic hips are used, the articular surfaces rub together. This friction causes tiny particles to be shaved off over time. These particles are

CS 6.1 Figure A Metal particles from an MOM hip replacement seen using an electron microscope. In some patients, these particles cause problems and compromise the value of the new hip joint.

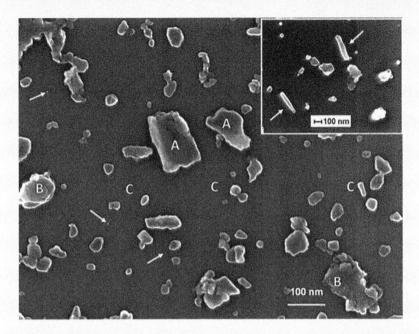

Clinical Orthopaedics and Related Research®.

thought to be why an immune reaction can develop, but MOM hips demonstrated significantly less erosion over time than metal-on-ceramic hips, which potentially means *fewer* irritating particles. Interestingly, although there is smaller volume of wear on MOM hips, they produce particles of smaller size, which may contribute more to an immune response. A study looking at patients who developed this immune reaction suggested that those who had a hypersensitivity to the metal hip were already five times more likely to be hypersensitive to metal than the general population, and so it could be that those who developed symptoms would have been affected because of their genetic predisposition.

The issue is complex and has been discussed at length in journals over the world. It is now common practice for orthopaedic surgeons to consider all factors, including the sensitivity of a patient to metals, before going ahead with MOM arthroplasty.

? Pause for thought

What other factors apart from the potential sensitivity of a patient to metals might influence an orthopaedic surgeon when they make a decision about what kind of joint to use?

Trauma and fractures

Trauma describes the injury of the body due to external forces. This could be from a fall, a penetrating injury, a gunshot, or a car accident. The force applied by these external factors causes damage to the body tissues. If the force is mild this may only be some bruising or damage to the skin, but in the case of high-impact trauma the injury may be enough to kill. These traumatic injuries, which have the potential to have life- or limb-threatening consequences, are known as 'major trauma' in medicine. They represent a small percentage of the cases seen in the emergency department, but have a high likelihood of poor outcomes unless managed well right from the start. In the UK, there are trauma networks of hospitals which help assess and direct trauma cases to the most appropriate location, decreasing transfer times and ensuring that patients get the care they need for their injuries.

In trauma, the nature of an injury is intrinsically linked to the physical forces exerted on the body. An understanding of anatomy, physiology, and physics is important for the physician when considering the trauma sustained. The pressure exerted by the impact is very important. The area that a force acts on determines how much pressure is exerted.

A force exerted over a large area (like a basketball) will cause less trauma than if it was exerted over a small area (like a knifepoint). Crucially, however, the trauma will only occur to that specific area, and so a knife will easily pierce muscle and skin, but only injure the areas it strikes. A large enough force, such as a car, will cause tremendous damage even if it hits the whole side of a person, as it carries a lot of force.

Alongside any immediate and obvious damage, doctors need to consider the site and direction of the injury. Direct forces next to the skin will cause deep transmitted impacts which may precipitate bleeding, whereas twisting injuries to limbs can cause complex fractures and amputation. When considering how an injury occurred, it is important for the doctor to consider what other injuries may have been caused—for example, someone who has fallen from a high building or cliff may have fractures in their legs, but as they land the force will be transmitted to their spine, and they may have spinal injuries as well.

Traumatic injuries to the musculoskeletal system

The musculoskeletal system has a key role in support and protection for the body, and as such it is one of the most commonly injured systems in trauma. This may be damage to the muscles via tearing, lacerations, or bruising, or damage to the skeleton with breaks or fractures. Once again, the site and forces applied will determine the extent and nature of the injury sustained.

The bones are very strong and are able to withstand significant impacts, but if the forces applied are greater than the strength of the bones, they will break. This is known as a fracture. A fracture can occur anywhere along the bone. Fractures are classified according to several different characteristics including the site, fracture pattern, and whether they are displaced or not (see Figure 6.14).

Figure 6.14 Fractures can be classified in several different ways, but each tells healthcare professionals important characteristics of the fracture.

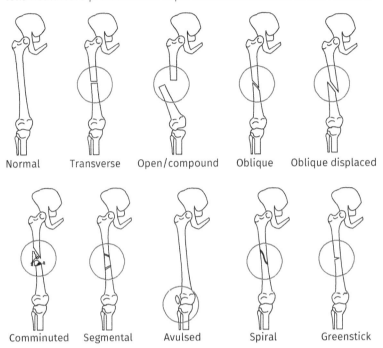

Normal   Transverse   Open/compound   Oblique   Oblique displaced

Comminuted   Segmental   Avulsed   Spiral   Greenstick

© Alexander_P/Shutterstock.

Like many other parts of the body, the bones have the remarkable ability to heal themselves—however, to do this, the broken ends of the bones have to be close enough to allow formation of new bone to bridge the gap. Sometimes, if a fracture is closed and stable, it simply requires stabilization with a hard cast surrounding it. It is important that the broken bone is immobilized (kept still), because it is very painful. The pain comes mainly from the highly innervated periosteum, or connective tissue layer surrounding the bone, rather than from the bone itself. If the fracture is not stable, then the two ends of the bone rub together, causing intense pain from the periosteum. When it is stable, the bone heals easily without causing pain. In modern medicine, the cast needed to immobilize a stable fracture is placed over a layer of gauze or cotton wool to protect the skin, and is made from bandages impregnated with plaster of Paris (a powdered form of the mineral gypsum which hardens after being exposed to water). Many ancient texts document different ways people have tried through history to create similar hardening casts, using resins or starch, but the cheap, rapid drying plaster of Paris has remained popular for over a century.

Sometimes, if the two parts of a fracture are significantly displaced, the bone cannot heal over and the fracture needs to be relocated or 'set'. This involves the surgeon holding on to one side of the break and carefully manoeuvring the fragments together. As discussed above, without anaesthesia this can be very painful! Sometimes a small amount of nitrous oxide or sedation is required, but for larger bones the patient may need to be entirely anaesthetized to give doctors the time they need to relocate the fractured bones successfully.

The fracture may also require an operation to repair it if the bone is shattered and in many pieces, or has broken through the skin. The bone needs to remain stable, and there are several ways this can be achieved. A plate can be inserted on top of the bone and the fragments of bone fixed together using screws, or a pin or rod can be placed inside the bone to hold the fragments together. These plates or pins come in a wide variety of sizes—a finger bone only requires a very small pin, but the femur (thigh bone) requires very large rods or plates if it is broken. If there are multiple fragments then the fracture may require an external fixator, which holds the bone in place using pins that run through the skin to a fixation device surrounding the limb (see Figure 6.15). During these operations it is vital that the theatre is as clean as possible, as introducing foreign material like metal provides a place where bacteria can easily grow. Special positive pressure air flow is used to blow cleaned air down onto the patient, stopping any dust or dirt from entering the operating field. Because of this increased risk of infection, most fixation devices like pins and plates will be removed in a further operation once the fracture has healed.

If the injury includes a joint, then surgeons may need to replace the joint itself. Hip joints in particular have a complex blood supply, meaning that fractures to the hip are more likely to result in poor healing. Many hip fractures therefore result in a hip replacement, like those described above, but carried out as an emergency operation. Hip fractures are common in medicine, accounting for more days in hospital due to trauma than all other fractures combined.

Fractures and the elderly

Fractures of all types are more common in the elderly. It is important for surgeons and anaesthetists to understand the physiology of ageing, to help

Figure 6.15 Fractures can be fixed via external or internal fixation, depending on the site and complexity of the fracture.

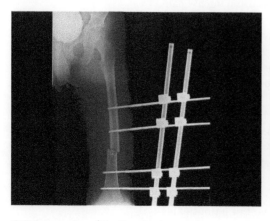 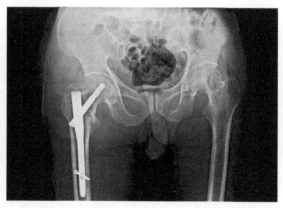

© Yok_onepiece/Shutterstock.

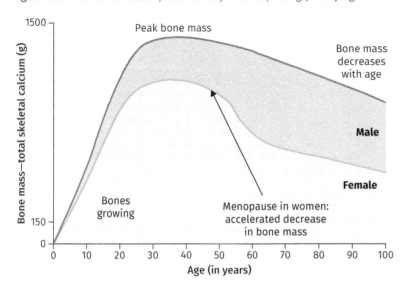

Figure 6.16 Our bones reach peak density at a surprisingly early age.

them ensure that older people make a good recovery from such significant injuries. Among all the physiological changes of ageing, the effect of decreased bone density and age-related muscle loss predisposes this subset of the population to traumatic bone injury.

The density of our bones dictates how strong they are and is a useful tool for estimating our risk of fractures from mild to moderate injury. The human skeleton reaches peak density at around thirty years old (see Figure 6.16) and declines steadily afterwards. This means that as we grow older our bones become more brittle and prone to fractures. Even smaller injuries such as tripping and falling may cause a fracture. This is compounded by age-related loss of fat and muscle, which decreases cushioning and stability respectively. This increased risk of fractures means that the vast majority of trauma patients in the UK are elderly, making surgery more challenging for the surgeon and the anaesthetist (see Chapter 2 on the anaesthetic challenge of the ageing patient).

It is not only physiological factors which affect the rate of fractures in the elderly—sociological factors are important as well. If someone is unable to afford heating, and so wears thick slippers and bulky clothes to keep warm, they are more likely to stumble and fall. Deterioration in eyesight makes tripping over furniture more likely. Forgetting to drink, or being unable to remain hydrated, means that older people are more prone to low blood pressure and fainting. All of these factors play a role in increasing the risk of falling, something that GPs in the community and workers in care homes have to consider every day. In addition to this, those most at risk of fractures are also those who are at most risk from surgical or anaesthetic complications. A thorough review of patients by a specialist orthogeriatrician (a physician in old-age medicine who specializes in caring for those who present with fractures) is required to review their medication, their living conditions, and other major aspects of their medical and social history.

One of the key conditions increasing the risk of fractures in the elderly is **osteoporosis**, where bone resorption exceeds bone formation. This can occur naturally, as part of the ageing process, or as a result of a lack of calcium or vitamin D in the diet. It may also be the result of certain medications, such as long-term steroid use, which are known to have side effects including a reduction in bone mass. The excessive resorption of bone leads to weaker bone structure and therefore increased risk of fractures. Patients at risk may have a bone density scan known as a DEXA scan (Dual-Energy X-ray Absorption scan). This uses two beams of different energy X-rays to measure the density of key bones such as the hips. This data can then guide therapy to improve the density and strength of the patient's bones, reducing the risk of fractures and all the associated problems.

Chapter summary

- The musculoskeletal system is key to protecting our other organ systems and allowing locomotion. It relies on organized muscles acting as antagonistic pairs to pull joints into position.
- Joints come in many shapes and sizes, depending on their location and role within the body. They represent weak points that can be vulnerable to damage via age-related changes or injury.
- Injury to the musculoskeletal system is common through traumatic mechanisms. A good understanding of physics is important to gauge the severity and likely injuries sustained following trauma. Current medical terminology recognizes major trauma as a life- or limb-threatening emergency.
- Joints or bones that are damaged through trauma or age-related changes can often be replaced or repaired. The options available are varied and are guided by the mechanism and type of injury sustained.
- As humans age, there are various changes to the musculoskeletal system which expose it to greater risk of damage. This is mirrored with the increased risk of surgery and anaesthesia, meaning careful consideration of all available options is required between the surgeon, anaesthetist, and patient.

Further reading

National Health Service 'Trauma and orthopaedic surgery' n.d. https://www.healthcareers.nhs.uk/explore-roles/doctors/roles-doctors/surgery/trauma-and-orthopaedic-surgery
Basic but comprehensive overview of the career and lifestyle of an orthopaedic surgeon. It includes a nice section on the common procedures and interventions that orthopaedic surgeons perform.

Subramanian, P, Kantharuban, S, Subramanian, V, Willis-Owen, S A, and Willis-Owen, C A 'Orthopaedic surgeons: As strong as an ox and almost twice as clever? Multicentre prospective comparative study' *British Medical Journal* 2011 (15 December) 343. https://doi.org/10.1136/bmj.d7506

There is a stereotype in the field of medicine that orthopaedic surgeons are intellectually less gifted than other specialities, relying on brute strength during their operations by wrangling with tough structures and metal implants using electric tools and mallets. This endearing paper published in the Christmas edition of the *British Medical Journal* in 2011 aims to argue against this, comparing anaesthetists (a common source of the light-hearted mockery) with orthopaedic surgeons. The study suggests that orthopaedic surgeons possess both superior grip strength and higher overall intelligence scores! This article brought a lot of amusement within operating theatres and remains often-quoted repartee to this day.

Uppal, Sulaiman 'Pursuing a career in trauma and orthopaedics: using behavioural science as a skeleton' British Orthopaedic Association, 2021. https://www.boa.ac.uk/resources/pursuing-a-career-in-trauma-and-orthopaedics-using-behavioural-science-as-a-skeleton.html

An award-winning short essay by a fifth-year medical student on the challenges facing the pursuit and selection of orthopaedic surgeons. It raises some very important points about gender disparity in the field and the risks of overconfidence in one's abilities.

 ## Discussion questions

6.1   What aspects do you think surgeons and anaesthetists have to consider when a very frail patient requires an operation for a fracture?

6.2   Many surgical procedures on the skeletal system are done to correct the effects of 'wear and tear' and ageing. Suggest arguments for and against having this surgery earlier rather than later in life.

6.3   In the UK, the National Health Service (NHS) advises the public to take vitamin D supplements during autumn and winter. What scientific evidence would have been needed to reach the conclusion that vitamin D supplements do indeed help prevent bone problems?

7 THE SEAT OF SELF AND NEUROSURGERY

We have seen how modern advances have enabled us to replace or repair almost any part of the human body. If organ systems such as the heart or kidneys fail due to damage or disease, there are machines to optimize or even replace their function. But the brain, the organ so vital for life, is one of the rare examples where it is currently beyond the realm of science to replace damage or dysfunction with machinery (see Figure 7.1).

We saw in Chapter 1 that evidence of rudimentry 'brain surgery' in the form of trephining has been found in remains dating back thousands of years. We have come a long way since then—but not perhaps as far as we might have hoped. In this chapter we will explore the workings of our nervous system and some of the ways we can—and cannot—repair any damage.

Figure 7.1 The human brain is a complex and still largely mysterious organ—we know less about the workings of the brain than any other system in the body.

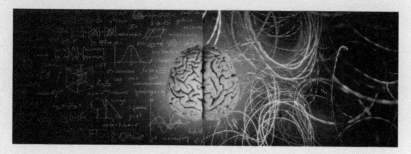

© Triff/Shutterstock.

The brain and nervous system

We saw in Chapter 2 that the nervous system is basically organized into two parts, the central and the peripheral nervous system—but what makes up these parts? Common to all of the nervous system is the nerve cell or neurone. This is a specialized cell with long processes called dendrites or axons that allow it to reach out to other neurones or cells and form synapses with them. The cell body is the hub of the cell containing the nucleus, and it is responsible for creating most of the proteins vital for the cell to function. Many of the proteins created will be neurotransmitters or cellular channels which allow the maintenance, creation or transmission of electrochemical signals down the neurone. Dendrites carry these signals towards the cell body and axons carry signals away from the cell body (see Figure 7.2). A collection of neurones is called a nerve; a nerve may contain only motor neurones or sensory neurones but is more often a mixture of both. Nerves carry information to and from all over the body, often connecting to the same or closely related organs, skin, or muscles.

The brain and spinal cord are made of very similar cells to those that make up the peripheral nervous system, but neurones in the CNS often have far more communications between each cell; a single neurone in the brain may connect to dozens or even hundreds of different neurones! The separation of the central and peripheral nervous system becomes important in disease, as damage to a single peripheral nerve will only disrupt a small amount of sensory or motor information, but damage to the central nervous system can have life-threatening consequences.

Figure 7.2 There are several different types of neurones which carry different types of signals within the central and peripheral nervous system.

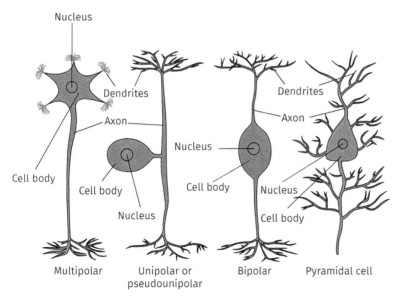

Figure 7.3 A sea anemone and an insect both have simple nerve systems which allow coordinated, and in some cases very complex, behaviour.

© Anthony Short.

Structure and function of the central nervous system

What *is* a brain?

The brain is the only known object in the universe to have named itself. Once animals get to a certain size, almost all of them demonstrate a collection of specialized neurones which form a nervous system. In animals such as a sea anemone (see Figure 7.3) this nervous system is a simple network which enables the body to act as a coordinated whole. In insects, neurones are found clumped together in ganglia of from 100,000 to 1 million cells which act as a coordinating centre of simple brain. This might sound like a lot of neurones—but a human brain contains around 86 billion (86,000,000,000) neurones!

In a human brain, the neurones process inputs from the rest of the body and formulate the outputs and actions which maintain normal physiology or aim to improve survival. While modern science has mapped connections and anatomical features extensively within the human brain, we are decades from decoding exactly how it creates the complex idea of consciousness. Much of the research carried out today focuses on very precise areas of the brain, and involves advanced techniques such as radioactively labelling neurotransmitters in animals to expose the connections of just a handful of neurones. Previously in history, mapping of the functions of the brain required observing what happened when bits of it were damaged—either by trauma or on purpose. Even now, when people suffer brain damage through accidents or disease, we sometimes gain new insights into the working of the brain.

Anatomically the brain is split into three sections: the **cerebrum**, the **cerebellum**, and the **brainstem** (see Figure 7.4). Compared to other animals, humans possess a very large and highly developed cerebrum, split into two hemispheres, the right and the left. Each side controls the opposite side of the body, for most functions. Sometimes people talk about 'left-brained' and 'right-brained' people, to describe someone who is particularly logical or artistic. In truth there is no evidence at all that dominance of either

Scientific approach 7.1
Discovering how the brain works

Much of the human brain is still a mystery, not least because it is widely regarded as unethical to experiment on human brains when they are still inside living people. Although we discover the common features of the mammalian brain from work on other mammals, the human brain, with its ability for self-awareness, is something different. Here we consider two of our major sources of information: injury and disease.

External brain injuries

The classic example of how brain injuries enhance our knowledge and understanding of the brain is the story of Phineas Gage. Gage was an American railway foreman in the nineteenth century, horrifically injured when a large iron tamping rod passed through his skull and brain as the result of an explosives accident. The rod destroyed much of his left frontal lobe, but amazingly he survived and continued normal life for many years afterwards. From contemporary reports, it appears that the brain injury initially had a clear impact on his behaviour and personality, but that his recovery continued for years. After Gage died in 1860, doctors and scientists examined his skull and tried to build a picture of the normal role of the parts of the brain destroyed in the accident (see SA 7.1 Figure A).

Internal brain injuries and disease

In a stroke, an area of the brain is damaged either by a bleed or a blood clot that prevents oxygenated blood reaching the tissue. Tumours may damage or destroy areas of brain tissue, and diseases affect the levels and types of neurotransmitters, in turn impacting behaviour. Here are three examples of how internal brain problems have improved knowledge and understanding.

- Mrs S suffered a massive stroke affecting the deep, rear portions of her right cerebral hemisphere. Her intelligence, humour, and speech were unimpaired but she lost all perception of the left side of her body. She would only make up the right side of her face and only ate the food on the right side of her plate. She showed no awareness at all that the left existed. This loss of perception of one entire side of the body gives scientists insights into the division of the labour in the brain, and how the right side of the brain processes information from the left side of the body, and vice versa.

- Mr J presented with right-sided arm and leg weakness. His family reported that he was speaking 'utter nonsense' but he appeared calm and collected with the ambulance crew. When asked how he arrived at the hospital he replied, 'We stayed with the water over here at the

SA 7.1 Figure A The skull of Phineas Gage is still giving doctors unexpected insights into the working of the brain, using images of the injury built up from the original remains using modern scanning and computer technologies.

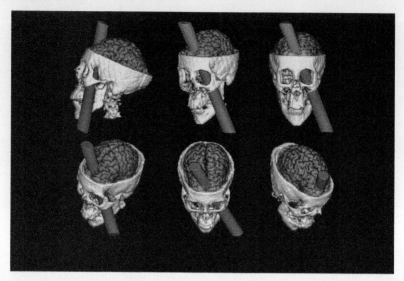

© Patrick Landmann/Science Photo Library.

moment and talk with the people for them over there. They're diving for them at the moment, but they'll save in the moment held water very soon, for him, with luck, for him'. He didn't seem to understand questions or that he was not speaking clearly. He had a stroke affecting Wernicke's area on the left side of his brain. Damage to this area causes an inability to comprehend speech, so Mr J couldn't understand what was said to him or what he was saying. Patients with damage to this area get Wernicke's aphasia—they speak fluently but it is nonsense!

- Mr H had a long history of alcohol abuse and told a story to a paramedic of falling over a hedge. In hospital he told the doctor he was exploring Africa and got hit by a landmine. He continued to tell random and bizarre stories to different medical staff, and was eventually diagnosed with Wernicke–Korsakoff syndrome, caused by a lack of thiamine (vitamin B1). Thiamine is a vital cofactor in several enzyme pathways and is only available from a varied diet. Alcoholics often lack thiamine as a result of poor nutrition, but it also presents in other diseases. The characteristic symptom is **confabulation**—falsification of memory with amnesia. Patients answer questions promptly with 100 per cent conviction, but the stories they provide are inaccurate and often bizarre. They 'make up' a new past every time they are asked, but are unaware of this—to them it is true. Sadly, this level of damage is not reversible.

These are examples of how some situations, disastrous for the individuals concerned, give doctors and scientists insights into the human brain which are of benefit to many.

Figure 7.4 The human brain has a very large cerebrum compared to other animals, but the cerebellum and brainstem also have vital roles in normal movement and homeostasis.

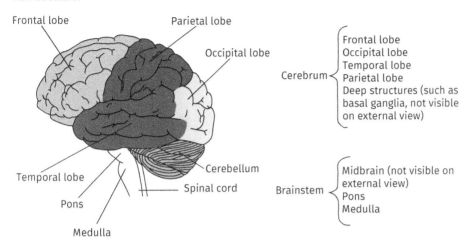

side of the brain can dictate personality traits. The idea probably originated from the knowledge that the left brain controls the dextrous right hand and contains language centres, while the right brain contains centres used to control spatial awareness; however, both sides have cross connections and complex interactions that make such compartmentalizing far too simplistic.

The cerebellum means 'little brain' and sits underneath the cerebrum. This specialized area of the brain is mainly involved in coordination and the organization of tone and movement of muscles. Muscle movement is initiated in the **motor cortex** in the cerebrum. The cerebellum 'fine tunes' these movements, using the feedback it gets from other sensory centres. Almost all vertebrates have a cerebellum so we know its evolutionary origin was very early in the vertebrate lineage.

The brainstem, however, is the oldest part of the organized brain and it is the first section to develop from the spinal cord. The brainstem is split into the pons and medulla, both with vital roles in unconscious bodily processes such as breathing and heart rate. Damage to the brainstem disrupts these functions and is almost inevitably fatal.

Protecting the brain

The brain is a vital and irreplaceable organ, and needs to be protected. It sits within the skull, covered by thick bone, wrapped in three layers of membranes that cover the brain and the spinal cord (the meninges), and suspended in cerebrospinal fluid, or CSF.

The CSF is continually produced by the brain and is vital for its normal function. It provides a chemically stable environment for the brain, with highly controlled levels of salts such as potassium, chloride, and sodium present. It also reduces the effective weight of the brain by suspending it in fluid, reducing the weight from around 1,500 grams to around 50 grams. This in turn reduces the pressure the brain would otherwise feel from the

Figure 7.5 The brain is well protected, floating in the cerebrospinal fluid within the meninges and the skull.

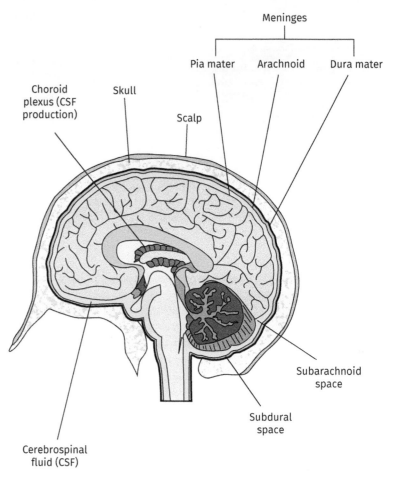

force of gravity as it rests against the floor of the skull. CSF also acts as a cushion or shock absorber, significantly reducing transmission of external forces on the skull to the brain suspended in the fluid (see Figure 7.5).

The brain is supplied with a lot of blood—around 50cm³ per 100 grams of brain tissue per minute, which is around 15 per cent of the heart's output! This is because the brain requires a constant supply of oxygen and glucose to function. The blood supply to the brain comes from the carotid arteries, on either side of the neck. Once in the skull, they form a complex 'loop' of blood vessels at the base of the brain, which then snake upwards to supply the left and right hemispheres, the cerebellum and brainstem. This circulatory loop attempts to counteract the effect of any blockages in some of the blood vessels, by ensuring that some blood can still get through. The downside of this complex blood supply is that it creates lots of potential weaknesses in the vessel walls. The blood is delivered to the brain via capillaries, and then runs into large 'sinuses' located around the outside of the brain.

These run into the large jugular veins, again on either side of the neck, then into the superior vena cava and into the heart.

The meninges

Surrounding the brain is a specialized layer of protective membranes called the meninges. There are three layers.

- The **dura mater** is a thick, fibrous membrane that sits right at the outside, sticking to the bone of the skull and helping contain the brain.
- The **arachnoid mater** is named after its spider-web-like appearance. It sits between the dura and pia mater, acting as a cushioning system to absorb external forces. It is crossed by cerebral veins—this is where CSF is reabsorbed.
- The **pia mater** is a very delicate membrane that sticks to the surface of the brain.

The spinal cord

Outside of the skull, the central nervous system is referred to as the spinal cord, a complex highway of neurones travelling to and from the peripheries. It sits protected within the spinal canal of the vertebrae making up the spine. The spinal cord has different input and output neurones clustered together into specific pathways called 'tracts'. These tracts are sensory or motor and have connections to cell bodies that lie within the deeper part of the spinal cord. This allows reflex arcs, and modulation of signals before they even reach the brain. Sensory information is received via the back or 'posterior' aspect of the spinal cord, whereas motor information leaves via the front or 'anterior' aspect of the spinal cord. These two nerve roots then merge to form one spinal nerve (Figure 7.6).

Figure 7.6 The vertebrae protect the spinal cord, which is a very organized structure processing large numbers of signals on a second-by-second basis.

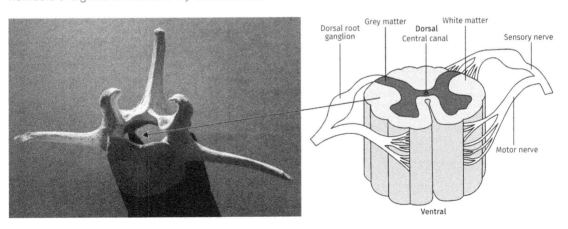

Photograph: © Anthony Short. Diagram: © Emre Terim/Shutterstock.

The peripheral nervous system

The spine is made of separate vertebrae allowing it to bend and move. The spinal cord sits within the spinal canal in the vertebrae which protects its delicate structure. To communicate with the rest of the body, the neurones within the spinal cord exit the spine at each joint through a hole called the **vertebral foramen**. Once they exit the foramen, each root is known as a spinal nerve. These nerves carry various different types of neurones which combine into different specific nerves, classified in several different ways—for example, motor nerves and sensory nerves, or the **autonomic nervous system**; the **sympathetic nerves** and **parasympathetic nerves**.

Motor nerves connect the central nervous system to the muscles, allowing us to move and manipulate the world around us. The nerves contain large, myelinated neurones, which allow signals to travel through them at up to 120 metres per second. This ensures that accurate and timely information is sent to muscles, allowing us to make tiny adjustments to our bodies—in evolutionary terms, this was especially important when millisecond judgements could mean a successful kill or avoiding a predator. Today, it enables us to react when driving vehicles at speeds far greater than any human could run!

Sensory nerves are slightly smaller than motor neurones, and transmit sensation from the body back to the brain. Some neurones innervate the skin, while others carry sensory information from the joints or internal organs. This is important as they convey different types of information depending on where the neurones end and what sensory receptor they terminate with. Neurones within the tendons and ligaments surrounding a joint convey information about the position of that joint to the brain, a sense called proprioception that allows our brain to know what position our limbs are in, even if we cannot see them. Sensory nerves to the skin supply sensations such as pressure, fine touch, or vibration. We have sensory receptors which respond to changes in temperature, to pressure, to carbon dioxide concentration, and even to pain. This allows us to form a detailed picture of what internal and external stimuli are affecting our body.

The autonomic nervous system is active without our conscious control. It is responsible for controlling organ systems related to vital functions and survival. It is split into two different systems, the sympathetic and parasympathetic (see Figure 7.7). The sympathetic nervous system can be thought of as the 'fight-or-flight' system. It increases heart rate, constricts blood vessels, and makes our body ready for movement and action. In contrast, the parasympathetic nervous system can be thought of as the 'rest-and-digest' system. It is responsible for increasing gastric secretions, activating the muscles in the gut, and relaxing other organs when energy-saving mechanisms are important. These systems work in harmony to control all our organs without us ever thinking about it. Life would be very different if we had to control the actions of our heart, lungs, gut, and blood vessels consciously.

The nervous system is very complex. It is devastating when it becomes damaged or injured. How can modern surgery help?

Figure 7.7 The sympathetic and parasympathetic nervous systems innervate the same organs but have very different functions.

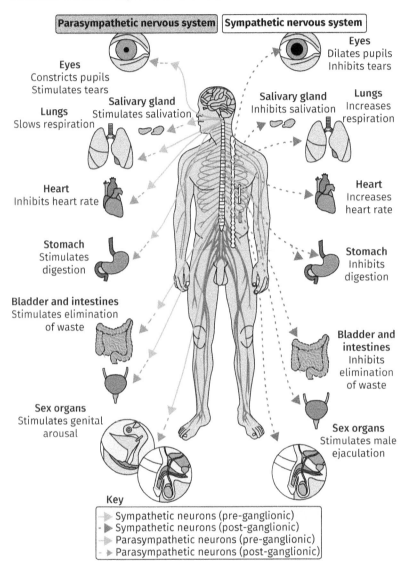

© M Jarvis and P Okami, *Principles of Psychology* (Oxford University Press, 2019), p 97, fig. 4.11.

The brain, trauma, and emergency operations

Your brain controls pretty much everything about you—and damage to your brain may have catastrophic effects (see Scientific approach 7.1). In terms of eventual outcomes for an individual, traumatic injuries to the brain are time-dependent. If there is damage to the brain, it can easily become worse over hours, decreasing the chances of survival and increasing risks of permanent damage to the patient. Brain damage is very challenging to reverse, as neurones are one of the few cell types that have virtually no ability to regenerate themselves; once they're gone, they're gone! As with many types of surgery, our understanding and management of brain injuries has been influenced greatly by the management of battlefield injuries. Here we will examine the two stages of traumatic brain injuries, how we try to preserve brain tissue and limit damage, and the surgical management options.

Primary brain injury

The protective bony case of the skull is not impenetrable, so the brain is not invulnerable. Trauma occurs by high-velocity projectiles piercing or breaking through the skull and physically damaging brain tissue, or by high-impact forces causing transmitted trauma through the skull itself. Sometimes the initial injury comes from an arterial aneurysm in the brain itself which spontaneously ruptures and causes bleeding (see Chapter 3). These external or internal events cause a **primary brain injury**. This describes the cells destroyed or damaged by the initial traumatic event, which cannot be altered by medical intervention. The only way to prevent primary injury is by prevention; this is the reason for many health and safety considerations for those working in high-risk scenarios—and even those of us doing everyday things like riding a bike or driving a car.

Secondary brain injury

The skull is a fixed space, strong and protective—but the volume is fixed. The skull vault is made up of about 80 per cent brain tissue, 10 per cent CSF and 10 per cent blood by volume. If any of these increases in volume, either the other volumes have to decrease or the pressure within the skull increases. This is known as the **Monro–Kellie doctrine**. In practical terms, if there is bleeding within the skull due to trauma, the intracranial pressure (pressure within the skull) will increase, squeezing the brain and causing further damage.

The **secondary brain injury** describes the damage that occurs to areas surrounding the primary injury due to processes including oedema (swelling), hypoxia (lack of oxygen), and **free radical** damage (when highly reactive compounds react with fatty acids and proteins within cell structures). This type of damage normally occurs more slowly than the primary brain injury, often over hours. It can be mitigated or limited by careful management of the patient and, if appropriate, by early surgery.

Initial management and the anaesthetic team

After a traumatic brain injury, the normal processes and functions of the brain are disrupted. The symptoms depend on which part of the brain has been damaged. In moderate injuries a patient might suffer a transient loss of consciousness, but in severe injuries they could be deeply unconscious for a long time, placing them at severe risk of a worsening of the injury via secondary processes.

The bigger picture 7.1
Bleeds, bruising, and bone

After a head injury, the vast majority of intracranial events involve bleeding or oedema. The anatomical location and origin of these bleeds or injuries gives important information for their treatment and prognosis.

- **Subarachnoid bleeds** begin underneath the arachnoid layer and are most commonly caused by spontaneous rupture of aneurysms. The blood spreads under and around the brain on both sides under high pressure from the arteries.

- **Subdural bleeds** are caused by a break in the delicate veins crossing the arachnoid space to get outside the dura mater. They are most common in the elderly, as the brain shrinks with age-related loss of neurones, pulling the veins taut and making them more liable to break. Even minor head injuries in the elderly can have serious consequences. As the veins carry blood at relatively low pressure, the blood pools around one side of the brain in a crescent appearance.

- **Extradural bleeds** originate from the carotid circulation: some of the arteries run outside the dura mater and they may be damaged by skull fractures which lacerate the tough arterial walls. The high-pressure arterial blood 'peels' the tough dura away from the skull in a lens pattern. This type of injury requires a very high impact, and is commonly seen in people who injure themselves in extreme sports.

- **Intracerebral haemorrhage** are relatively rare bleeds that occur deep within the brain tissue or spaces within the brain called **ventricles**. It is often caused by critically high blood pressure, malformations in blood vessels and cocaine use.

- **Contrecoup/concussion** occurs when the brain tissue itself is bruised and damaged by impact. Because the brain is floating in CSF, it is sometimes smashed against one side of the skull by an initial impact and then collides with the opposite side as well, by the momentum from the impact. This dual impact is called a 'contrecoup' injury and is often identified by oedema on both sides of the brain.

- **Penetrating injuries** are another type of pathology that can cause damage to the brain besides blunt trauma. Shrapnel, edged weapons, and bullets can easily penetrate the skull and cause devastating injuries to the soft tissues underneath.

Now you have learned about some of the injuries that can happen in brain trauma, take a look at the CT scan in BP 7.1 Figure A. Which pathology does the scan show: a penetrating injury, a subdural bleed, or an extradural bleed?

Hint: In CT scans bone is shown as bright white, blood shows up as dull white or pink, while brain is grey or black.

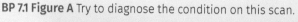

BP 7.1 Figure A Try to diagnose the condition on this scan.

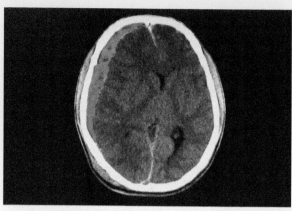

As our consciousness level drops as the result of an injury, our muscles and motor processes also become less coordinated. This includes the muscles which hold our airways open. When these relax, they produce a snoring-type sound, indicating that the patient is about to lose their airway and thus their ability to breathe. Anaesthetists often initially deal with head injuries, because airway support with an endotracheal tube—a procedure requiring the patient to be anaesthetized and paralysed to tolerate it—is part of their everyday work (see Chapter 2).

Once the patient is **intubated**, they require ventilation to keep them breathing, but this raises further issues and risks for the patient's brain. In order to minimize secondary brain injury, there are four main areas to consider: the pressure within the skull, the blood flow to the brain, and the oxygen and carbon dioxide levels in the blood.

Intracranial pressure

The Monro–Kellie doctrine tells us that increased blood and swelling within the skull after an injury causes an increase in pressure. This causes further damage and therefore further swelling, setting up a vicious cycle which continues until there is no more space for the brain. At this point, the brain begins to squeeze out of the base of the skull, compressing the brainstem and killing the patient.

There is little that we can do to lower the intracranial pressure without surgery. Often the patient is elevated to a head-up angle of 30 degrees to improve the rate of the blood returning in the veins and so decrease pressure. The endotracheal tube is stuck with tape to minimize any compression of the veins in the patient's neck. Sometimes a drug called Mannitol is given, moving fluid from tissues including the brain by osmosis for excretion by the kidneys. This reduces swelling in the brain, but is not hugely effective in the management of acute head injury.

Cerebral blood flow

Disruption to the blood supply to the brain results in anaerobic respiration in the cells, increasing lactic acid production, the release of free radicals and swelling leading to secondary brain injury. As pressure rises inside the skull, the blood must be delivered at higher pressure to adequately supply and perfuse the brain, or the likelihood and severity of secondary brain injury increases. Sometimes we use drugs to increase the blood pressure and get enough blood to the brain.

Oxygen within the blood

The amount of oxygen in the blood is sensed by blood vessels within the brain. If oxygen levels drop, these vessels dilate to increase cerebral blood flow, delivering more oxygen to the brain. This preserves cell function but the increasing blood volume has the side effect of increasing intracranial pressure (Monro–Kellie again). This is one reason why patients are intubated—to allow doctors to monitor and control the oxygen delivered to the body. Often an arterial blood sample is analysed to check oxygen or carbon dioxide levels in the blood.

Carbon dioxide in the blood

Carbon dioxide is the waste product of metabolism and a rise in carbon dioxide levels in the blood is the main normal stimulus to breathing. If the CO_2 levels get too high, the blood vessels in the brain relax and blood flow increases to remove carbon dioxide from the cells. If CO_2 levels are too low, the blood vessels contract and blood flow reduces. Either situation may cause problems. Controlling the patient's breathing by intubating and ventilating them helps reduce secondary brain injury.

Emergency neurosurgery

Once a patient has been stabilized, they will often need to be transferred to a hospital or surgical theatre with neurosurgical capabilities. The only thing that will definitively stop the swelling of the brain is to expand the fixed cavity it sits in and/or remove the pooling blood within the skull. The management of traumatic bleeding within the skull is most commonly done through either a burr hole (see Chapter 1) or a **craniotomy**.

Burr hole surgery—modern day trephining

Burr hole surgery is a generic procedure that allows access to the skull through which a variety of procedures can be done (see Figure 7.8). It is the nearest we come in modern times to the trephining tried over thousands of years ago—and it is so very different! The patient has a scan on their brain allowing the surgeons to locate and plan the operation. Often neurosurgery theatres have large interactive screens allowing the scan to be displayed for reference during the surgery—some even have additional

Figure 7.8 Burr hole surgery is used to save lives after brain injuries of many types.

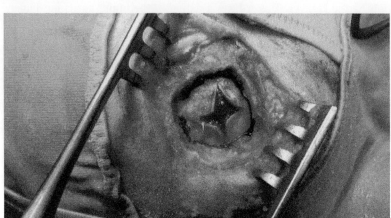

Massimo Lama/Alamy Stock Photo.

software indicating in real time exactly where the surgeon is in the brain. Any movement of the patient can have disastrous consequences, and so their head is often fixed in position by metal screws attached to a scaffold to ensure no movement during the procedure. Preparing the head for surgery involves shaving and sterilizing the area, before the surgeon carefully dissects through the skin down to the skull. The burr hole itself is made using a specially designed drill—once activated, the surgeon advances it through the skull to form a small hole about 14mm across. The drills stop as soon as a loss of resistance is detected, so they don't damage the delicate brain. Once the hole is made the surgery begins. Depending on where the blood is, the surgeon may have to carefully suction it out or dissect further into the brain, to evacuate the blood and relieve the pressure. Operating through such a tiny hole is not easy—so surgeons are aided by microscopes, cameras, and magnifiers giving them better views while they operate.

Craniotomy

Craniotomy is used in operations where a larger hole is required, because of the size or the location of the bleed. It involves removing an entire section of the skull. Although there are many similarities with burr hole surgery, these operations are often significantly longer and more complex. One big advantage of a craniotomy is that the larger field of view makes it easier for the surgeons to get inside the skull, so they can remove clotted blood or damaged tissue if needed.

Neurosurgery and neuroanaesthesia

The emergency operations described above are needed immediately when the brain is threatened. Fortunately, there are also times when operations are needed in a less acute setting. Cancers and tumours within the brain tend to be slow-growing, offering time for detailed planning and preparation for the surgery. This is important as neurosurgery is not without risks—removing or disrupting areas in the brain can cause bleeding, infection, or damage to surrounding structures with potentially devastating results. Neurosurgical procedures can be used to improve a variety of the pathologies within the brain, including the following.

- **Brain lesions:** The position of masses or lesions in the brain affects the symptoms, so a thorough history and a multitude of scans and tests are often required to help diagnose exactly where the surgeon needs to operate.

- **Pituitary tumours:** The pituitary is a tiny pea-sized gland that sits right at the base of the brain, suspended by a tiny stalk. It is made of both neuronal and glandular tissue, and it is responsible for a number of important hormones and hormone-stimulating and -releasing factors which impact on other endocrine glands around the body, such as the ovaries and testes. These hormones include those that regulate the kidneys, the adrenal glands and the production of growth hormone. When cells within the pituitary gland grow out of control, any of the hormones can also be over-produced.

- **Meningiomas and gliomas:** When cells grow out of control but retain good differentiation, they are often called benign tumours because they don't generally spread or invade other tissues. Unfortunately, in the brain even benign tumours can cause significant symptoms, because of the increase in pressure they create within the skull. These tumours form almost anywhere within the brain, and often spread throughout the tissue, making extracting them very challenging.

- **Aneurysms:** As you saw in Chapter 3, most aneurysms are asymptomatic, but if they are found by chance, they often need to be treated. If an aneurysm bursts in the brain, surgeons have very little time to repair it before the patient suffers irreparable brain damage.

- **Hydrocephalus:** The CSF circulates both around the brain and also within it, in the series of spaces called ventricles. If there is a blockage in one of these ventricles or an overproduction of CSF, then the brain can be put under higher pressure. This is called **hydrocephalus**. Sometimes anatomical variations before birth can cause hydrocephalus, but it can also be caused by infection or bleeding within the brain.

Types of operations

We have already covered burr holes and craniotomies, used to gain access to superficial areas of the brain and meninges. When surgeons need to reach deeper brain structures, these techniques are inappropriate, as a large amount of healthy brain would need to be destroyed to get to the problem. Other procedures are required which allow closer access and minimal trauma to healthy brain tissue.

Trans-sphenoidal surgery

The sphenoid bone sits behind the nose and forms the front part of the base of the skull. It communicates with the nasal cavity through the sphenoid sinus, a hollow formation in the centre of the face. The sphenoid bone contains a small hollow called the **sella turcica** (which translates to 'Turkish saddle'). Within the sella turcica sits the pituitary gland. Pituitary tumours are often operated on through the nose via the sphenoid sinus (see Figure 7.9), a technique known as the trans-sphenoidal approach. The pituitary gland weighs only 0.5g, so the operation requires tiny precise movements of a camera and equipment, threaded through the nose, but even so it often is a relatively short procedure lasting around two hours.

Posterior fossa surgery

So far we have only considered operations on the cerebrum, but the cerebellum and brainstem (see Figure 7.4) can also become injured or damaged. The cerebellum and brainstem are housed in the posterior fossa, an area

Figure 7.9 The pituitary gland may initially seem impossible to reach, as it is buried deep in the brain, but operating via the sphenoid sinus makes it far easier to gain access and remove tumours.

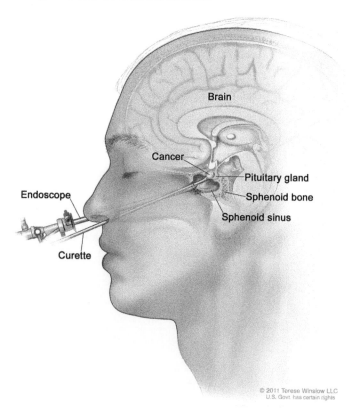

© 2011 Terese Winslow LLC
U.S. Govt. has certain rights

at the back and base of the skull which is not easy to access surgically. Unfortunately the presence of tumours, or vascular or anatomical malformations of the cerebellum can cause symptoms which only surgery can resolve. For example, in Chiari malformations the cerebellum is malformed and protrudes down through the exit of the skull. Amazingly, many people have no symptoms, but some have a range of problems including dizziness, headaches, numbness and tingling in the arms and legs, and issues with vision, swallowing, and hearing. Surgery in this area carries many risks, as it takes place near the brainstem which houses vital control centres for breathing and the cardiovascular system. It also poses challenges to the surgical and anaesthetic team, as for surgeons to reach a Chiari malformation the patients must be positioned sitting upright (although this is rare), on their front in the 'prone' position, or lying on their side *after* being anaesthetized lying on their back. This makes the possibility of injury or pressure damage more likely.

Aneurysm clipping and coiling

Aneurysms in the brain usually only pose risk of rupture once they are larger than 5mm, but some may require fixing as a preventative measure. They can be clipped, using a surgical approach, or 'coiled'. Clipping of aneurysms requires a craniotomy with cameras threaded deep under the brain to the blood vessels before spring clips are deployed around the aneurysm. Coiling is a newer technique which involves threading a microcatheter up through the patient's femoral artery into the brain under radiological guidance. Once the aneurysm is reached, tiny platinum coils are passed through the tube into the aneurysm, blocking the blood flow and stopping the risk of rupture. These procedures are considered high-risk, as there is always a chance of these aneurysms rupturing during the operation.

Surgery without anaesthesia—the awake craniotomy

Modern science is a long way from understanding how our brains create our emotions and experiences. This raises issues during neurosurgery, where the difference between tumour and vital parts of the brain may be only millimetres apart. In certain types of surgery, the brain needs to be 'mapped out' during the operation to accurately identify certain regions to avoid damaging them. We sometimes use awake surgery when removing tumours, to reduce the danger of removing important brain tissue, while other procedures such as deep electrode placement also use awake surgery to see the effect of the electrode before fixing it in place.

Anaesthetic challenges

These operations are possible because the brain has no neurones capable of sensing pain, and so can be operated on without anaesthesia. If someone pokes the surface of your brain, you can't feel it! However, the initial stages of a brain operation, such as fixing the head in place and opening the skull, are understandably incredibly painful. The patient needs to be anaesthetized for these first stages, with anaesthetic drugs that work quickly and then wear off, so the patient is relaxed and calm but awake. Anaesthetists now often use the asleep–awake–asleep technique. The patient is fully

Figure 7.10 A patient plays her violin during the removal of a brain tumour.

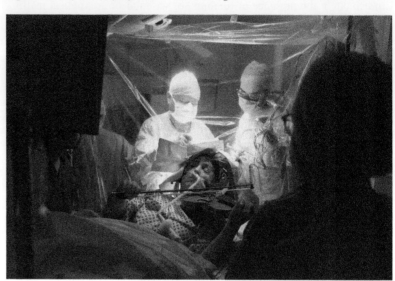

© King's College Hospital NHS.

anaesthetized and a supraglottic airway is inserted (that doesn't require muscle relaxation). The patient is then positioned and fixed before the skull is opened. Once the surgeons have located the tumour, the patient is woken up and the airway removed. During the procedure the anaesthetist may sedate the patient mildly to ensure they remain calm, but this isn't always necessary. At the end of the operation the patient is anaesthetized again while the skull is replaced and the skin sutured. These transitions are relatively dangerous, but provide incredibly useful information to surgeons and give good outcomes for patients.

Surgical benefits

An awake patient can communicate with the surgical team during the procedure, helping them differentiate between tumour and functional brain tissue. This is particularly important if the patient requires specific motor control for their career, such as playing an instrument. In some cases, patients have brought their instruments into theatre to play while the surgeon is operating (see Figure 7.10). The surgeon tests the area of brain with a stimulating electrode. If vital neurones are present, the patient will display symptoms of damage to that area, such as muscle weakness or speech dysfunction. The surgeon can then attempt to excise around these vital centres.

Looking to the future: the regeneration of neurones

Neurones are remarkable cells capable of transmitting impulses at hundreds of metres a second, and creating the unparalleled complexity of the brain. However, for all of their incredible abilities, neurones have one significant weakness—once they are damaged or injured, they cannot heal or regenerate. There are no stem cells in the brain/nervous tissue, so injuries to the brain, spinal cord, or peripheral nerves are permanent. As signals cannot pass through the damaged neurones, any of the functions they perform are affected, including supplying motor function to muscles or sensory information from the skin. If the peripheral nerves are damaged, then only a small aspect of limb function may be affected, whereas damage to the brain or spinal cord can cause permanent loss of function of entire limbs.

Modern medicine is still working towards being able to heal nerve cells, but because the nerves do not normally heal themselves, this is a big ask! Scientists are investigating entirely new processes of cell healing to reconnect the neurones. Here are some of the most promising ways that neurosurgery can offer treatment to those with nerve damage.

Neuronal cell transplant

The inability of neurones to heal after injury is a major limiting step in encouraging regeneration of function after brain, spinal cord, or nerve injury. There is, however, one group of neurones that *do* regenerate. The olfactory nerve is responsible for our sense of smell. It is found in the skull running from the medulla to just above the nasal cavity (see Figure 7.11) where it forms a swelling called the olfactory bulb. At the olfactory bulb, connections are made to a special type of nerve cell called the olfactory receptor neurone (ORN). These neurones project into the nasal cavity and possess unique receptors. When we smell something, molecules in the air we breathe activate these receptors, depolarizing the ORN and activating

Figure 7.11 The olfactory nerve ends in the olfactory bulb at the top of the nasal cavity. Olfactory receptor neurones run into the nasal cavity and allow us to smell.

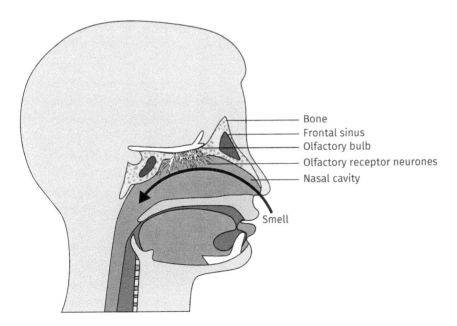

Case study 7.1
Repairing the irreparable

Darek Fidyka was a Polish volunteer firefighter. In 2010 he was attacked with a knife and stabbed eighteen times, leaving him paralysed from the waist down—the knife cut almost completely through his spinal cord. This form of spinal cord injury is very uncommon—most injuries involve a crushing or compressive force instead of a sharp transection. After two years of intense physiotherapy, the paralysis of Darek's lower limbs was unchanged. He volunteered for experimental surgery to help reconnect the distal section of his spinal cord using his own olfactory ensheathing cells.

The research was largely led by an English professor of neuroscience named Geoffrey Raisman, who had a prolific amount of published research on the nervous system and the potential to reconnect injuries using OECs—but no one had tried using a human subject before. He and the Polish lead neurosurgeon Pawel Tabakow proposed a way to potentially reconnect the spinal cord and offer Darek some movement or sensation of his legs (see CS 7.1 Figure A).

The project started in 2012.

- Darek was assessed to document his muscle strength, nerve conduction and to plan for the surgeries ahead.
- Surgery 1: remove the left olfactory bulb, and culture it to produce a collection of Darek's OECs.
- Surgery 2: open up Darek's spine and carefully remove scar tissue surrounding the spinal cord. Place several lengths of nerves across the damaged cord to provide a 'scaffold' for the OECs to grow into. Place over 100 micro-injections of OEC collections around and into the severed spinal cord.

CS 7.1 Figure A Professor Geoffrey Raisman and Dr Pawel Tabakow—pioneers of neurosurgery to repair a severed spine.

PA Images/Alamy Stock Photo.

CS 7.1 Figure B Darek Fidyka used a stationary bicycle to gain strength and eventually cycled outside along forest rides. He remains the only person to benefit from this pioneering surgery—but who knows where it will lead in the future?

© Maciej Kulczynski/EPA/Shutterstock.

After recovering from the surgery Darek began an intense physiotherapy course with regular assessment of his muscle strength, sensation, and nerve function. After six months he regained some feeling in his lower limbs, and after a year he began to move his legs. In 2014, two years after the operation, he could walk with the aid of a frame. In 2016 he had recovered sufficient muscle mass to ride a tricycle. Darek remains the only person in the world to have this form of pioneering surgery performed (see CS 7.1 Figure B).

The research team are keen to find others with this form of severed spinal cord. If the technique is conclusively proved to work for these rare injuries, it may also prove beneficial for the more common compressive spinal cord injuries. Darek's recovery is ongoing but he remains undeniable proof that these injuries have the potential to be treated—truly the stuff of science fiction!

neurones in the olfactory bulb. A unique property of these ORNs is that they only have a lifespan of six to eight weeks before new neurones are grown to replace them. The ORNs cannot do this alone—special supportive cells called olfactory ensheathing cells (OECs) facilitate this process. These two specialized cells have been explored since the mid-1990s for their potential to regenerate neurones and therefore heal damage to the nervous system.

In animal studies, ORNs and OECs have provided some ability to regenerate neuronal connections between injured sections of the nervous system, both in the CNS and peripherally. There is still a long way to go before we can reliably restore significant function via this technique, but it remains a hot topic of research and a promising avenue for healing nerve injuries.

Integrated prosthetic technology: rebuilding the body

Every time you move your brain is sending signals to the muscles in your body, but what happens if the body itself is damaged or missing? During high-impact trauma limbs may be severed or damaged beyond repair. In amputated limbs the nerves still run in their previous configuration, often up to the site of amputation, but they have no muscles to innervate. The concept of melding man and machine, to create artificial limbs which respond to our nervous system, has long been possible only in the realm of science fiction—but it is increasingly becoming a reality.

Myoelectric signals

As nerves synapse onto muscles, they form a connection known as the neuromuscular junction. It is here that neurotransmitters are released onto the muscle to cause it to depolarize and contract. As these depolarizations also use electrochemical signals they can be sensed by electrodes on the outside of the skin and translated into stimuli for mechanical limbs.

This sounds exciting and feasible—but there are limiting factors; the myoelectric signals are crude and weak, so often only two electrodes can be used—one on each side of a limb (such as the front and back of the forearm). This allows opposing actions such as opening and closing of the hand but not detailed manoeuvres such as opening different fingers. This hurdle is being overcome by programming different settings to perform different movements, for example, if the patient wants to select a pointed finger, they think of opening and closing their hand two or three times to select 'pointed finger' mode on the limb. These limbs are life-changing for the patients who receive them (see Figure 7.12) but they cost tens of thousands of pounds, so they are not yet available to most people who need them.

Targeted muscle reinnervation

Myoelectric limbs receive signals from the depolarization of the muscles of the patient, not from the nerves themselves. This means that they can only be used for a single joint function (such as opening and closing the hand).

Figure 7.12 This amazing bionic hand is available for people who have amputations from the forearm down.

Otto Bock Healthcare Products GmbH.

If amputation occurs higher up the limb, for example, just below the shoulder, then a more complex solution is required.

Multiple nerves supply the arm (or the leg), but they all come from a single collection of nerves called a plexus. For the arm this is the brachial plexus, and for the leg, the lumbar and sacral plexuses. In these plexuses, a wide variety of spinal nerves come together to form a much smaller number of nerves that enter or leave the limb and supply all motor and sensory function. In high-limb amputations, near the shoulder or the hip, these are severed at the level of the amputation. It is possible to relocate the ends of these nerves to separated muscle groups in the shoulder or hip. These nerves supply designated muscle movement and so when separated and 'plugged in' to muscles they can stimulate myoelectric sensors. This allows control over several joints using only myoelectric sensors. This technology is very new, requires a complex neurosurgical procedure and is currently only available in research trials—but it has very promising results!

The future of bionics

Bionics is the application of biological systems to engineering systems and computer technology, and the hope is that one day bionics will enable us to develop truly integrated replacements for lost body parts. The implementation of true, integrated bionics is, however, still a long way away. Nerves carry far too much information to be sensed and interpreted reliably through the skin. But there are other ways to monitor nerve impulses—either by sensing peripherally from the nerves themselves, or centrally from the motor cortex of the brain. The signals in the motor nerves can be sensed by placing electrodes within or around the nerves. This data is more reliable and specific than information from the skin, and can offer much more fine control of robotic limbs. The electrodes we use are still very crude compared to the natural function of the nervous system, but the research is encouraging. Nevertheless, it is still very experimental and a long way from providing long-term prosthetics. In patients who have experienced damage to the brain or spinal cord rather than the limbs, the alternative can be placing electrodes within the motor cortex that then allows them to control robotic limbs which are not attached to their body. This can mean that someone paralysed from the neck down can still control a robot to feed or offer drink to themselves. This technology is very much in its infancy, and it requires a complex and invasive neurosurgical procedure to place the electrodes, but if it becomes more successful in the future it may allow people to control robotic limbs or even an exoskeleton or mobility aid to allow them to move and care for themselves again. The fact we are even considering these possibilities is hugely exciting and has the potential to offer incredible benefits for hundreds of thousands of people—but true bionics remains currently the realm of science fiction.

Chapter summary

- The nervous system is composed of two distinct anatomical components—the central and the peripheral system. They provide control and communication to the body.
- The brain possesses many secrets we have yet to unlock, but slowly research is exposing more and more information that we can use to help heal and improve outcomes for people with brain damage, disease, or injury.
- The nervous system is as susceptible as any other organ to damage through trauma. The danger is increased due to the inability of the nervous system to repair damaged neurones. This makes emergency management of traumatic damage vital to improve survival.
- Neurosurgery offers ways to manage both acute and subacute damage to the brain and spinal cord, but remains a high-risk procedure.
- There is a wealth of new research into the brain and the field of reconstructive neurology and bionics to improve outcomes after brain or nerve damage.

Further reading

Herr, Hugh 'The new bionics that let us run, climb and dance'. TED, 2014. https://www.ted.com/talks/hugh_herr_the_new_bionics_that_let_us_run_climb_and_dance
A fascinating talk by Professor Hugh Herr, a biomechanical engineer who lost his legs in a climbing accident and now works at the leading edge of prosthetic research at MIT.

Sacks, Oliver *The Man Who Mistook His Wife for a Hat*. Picador Classic, 2015. (Originally published 1985.)

A very readable exploration of the mysteries of the human mind, and how scientists and doctors can use evidence from brain injuries and diseases to learn more about the way the brain works.

Werner, C and Engelhard, K 'Pathophysiology of traumatic brain injury' *BJA: British Journal of Anaesthesia* 2007 99(1), pp 4–9. https://doi.org/10.1093/bja/aem131

A review of the mechanisms causing traumatic brain injury. A complex article but with an interesting look at the history of the physiology and studies from which current guidelines have been developed.

Wilson, M et al. 'Emergency burr holes: "How to do it"' *Scandinavian Journal of Trauma, Resuscitation and Emergency Medicine* 2012 20, article 24. https://doi.org/10.1186/1757-7241-20-24

A guide for clinicians on how to perform emergency burr holes in critical scenarios where neurosurgery may be too far away to be feasible to transfer the patient. A very interesting article which outlines the anatomy and technique for burr holes outside of the operating theatre.

 ## Discussion questions

7.1   When are traumatic brain injuries most likely to occur? What challenges may this present in the pre-hospital setting?

7.2   Consider the awake craniotomy from a surgical, anaesthetic and patient perspective. What questions would you have as a patient, and how would you prepare a patient for the operation if you were an anaesthetist or neurosurgeon?

7.3   Consider the possible future implications for bionic limbs. Discuss the ethical implications of bionic limbs or exoskeletons, both now and in the future.

GLOSSARY

Accessory muscles muscles in the thorax and abdomen which work to increase and decrease the thoracic volume during active breathing

Adjuvant used to improve the effectiveness of a treatment. Adjuvants may be added to a vaccine, for example, to improve its effectiveness. Adjuvant chemotherapy or radiotherapy is given at the same time as other treatments, to improve the likelihood of remission

Allogeneic a transplant using cells or tissue from a donor

Anaesthesia a state of temporary, controlled loss of sensation or awareness which is induced for medical purposes

Analgesia reduction in sensation of noxious or painful stimuli

Analgesic a drug or substance designed to relieve pain

Anastamosis a connecting point in a tubular structure such as the lungs or bowels. Anastamoses may be naturally occurring, or they may be created by surgery or disease

Angina temporary chest pain—often exertional—experienced by individuals with narrowing of the coronary arteries

Anosmia loss of sense of smell

Arachnoid mater a delicate layer of connective tissue between the dura and pia mater around the brain, named after its filamentous, spider-web-like appearance

Areflexia inability of the body to produce movement, including reflex movements

Arteries muscular-walled blood vessels which transport blood away from the heart

Arthroplasty generic name for surgery replacing a joint

Aseptic entirely free from contamination by potentially harmful microbes

Aspiration pneumonia an infection in the lungs caused by accidentally inhaling food, saliva, or vomit into the airways

Atheromatous plaques deposits of fatty materials in the wall and lumen of a blood vessel

Autologous a transplant using cells or tissue from the patient's own body

Autonomic nervous system division of the peripheral nervous system that supplies organs and glands. It enables the body to function efficiently without conscious thought and controls the resting state along with the fight-or-flight mechanisms

Autopsy the examination of a dead body by dissection, often performed to examine the possible cause of death

Avulsion fracture fracture where a small section of bone is pulled off as a result of strain applied to a tendon

Awake surgery brain surgery carried out while a patient is awake, usually performed after a period of anaesthesia to prepare and open the skull

Biopsy a small sample of tissue taken from the body to be examined under the microscope for signs of disease

Blood–brain barrier highly selective barrier made up of specialized endothelial cells surrounding the blood supply to the brain. It helps protect the brain from toxins, bacteria, and other harmful chemicals while selectively allowing transport of glucose and other important molecules

Bolus a ball-like mixture of food and saliva

Botulinum toxin a neurotoxic protein, produced by the bacterium *Clostridium botulinum*. It prevents the release of neurotransmitters from the nerves to the muscles, and results in a flaccid (floppy) paralysis of affected muscles

Brainstem the area of the brain at the top of the spinal cord. Consisting of the pons, the midbrain, and medulla oblongata, the brainstem controls many of the automated functions of the body, such as breathing, swallowing, heart rate, and blood pressure

Bronchiectasis the airways to the lungs become permanently widened, leading to a build-up of mucus and increasing the vulnerability of the lungs to infections

Bronchoscopy passing a fibreoptic camera (a bronchoscope) into the lungs for visual inspection

Buffer a compound/solution that resists pH changes

Bullae blisters, or blister-like structures within the body. Singular: bulla

Bullectomy surgery to remove large bullae from the lungs in COPD sufferers

Burr hole a small hole allowing access to the brain produced surgically enabling surgeons to reduce pressure, remove blood etc.

Cadavers dead bodies used for the study of anatomy, physiology, and pathophysiology

Capillaries tiny, thin-walled blood vessels which connect the arterial and venous system together

Cardiac cycle the cycle of contraction and relaxation of the atria and ventricles of the heart which pumps blood to the lungs and to the body in a coordinated way

Cardiomyocytes cardiac muscle cells—one of the three types of myocytes (muscle cells) in the human body

Cataract a cloudiness of the lens in the eye, reducing vision

Catheter a hollow tube which is inserted into the body

Cerebellum this vital structure sits below the cerebrum—the name is Latin for 'little brain'. It is vital for motor and sensory processing, and maintaining balance and stability

Cerebral oedema swelling of the brain tissue, often caused by a traumatic injury or a stroke

Cerebrovascular event (CVE) damage to an area of the brain caused either by ischaemia or by haemorrhage

Cerebrum the largest and most highly evolved part of the brain containing the cerebral cortex, hippocampus, and basal ganglia

Cholecalciferol a compound formed in the body when the sterol 7-dehydrocholesterol reacts with UBV radiation

Cholecystectomy removal of the gallbladder, from the Latin 'cholecystis' meaning gallbladder, and the suffix '-ectomy' meaning surgical removal of

Chondrocytes specialist cells that reside within cartilage and are responsible for producing and maintaining the cartilaginous matrix. Within the foetus they lay down the long bones in the form of hyaline cartilage

Chyme a mixture of food and digestive juices in the stomach or small intestine

Claudication exercise-induced discomfort in the legs or buttocks, caused by chronic narrowing of the blood vessels to the lower limbs. Discomfort eases at rest

Colonoscopy endoscopy where the tube is inserted into the gut through the anus to examine the lower end of the digestive system

Colostomies procedures which involve bringing one end of the large intestine out of the abdominal wall to form a stoma

Commensal micro-organisms on or in our bodies which are beneficial to us

Comorbidities health problems which exist alongside the primary problem being discussed

Computed tomography an imaging technique which uses computers to blend together many different X-ray images taken at different angles to produce cross-sectional images of part of the body

Conducting zone the airways from the oropharynx down to the level of the bronchioles—the part of the respiratory tract primarily concerned with the movement of air rather than gas transfer

Confabulation a clinical sign of Wernicke-Korsakoff syndrome characterized by falsification of memory with amnesia. A patient will give random and varying accounts of events but be unaware that they are fabricating these memories

Congenital present from birth

Cortical bone dense, hard bone largely responsible for the strength of the bone structure

Craniotomy the removal of an entire section of the skull to allow more access to the brain for surgeons, e.g. to remove clotted blood or damaged tissue

Crohn's disease inflammatory condition found in any area of the gut, affecting the whole intestinal wall, and often starting and ending very abruptly. In severe cases it causes ulceration of the affected tissues. It may affect tissues outside the GI tract

Culture medium a medium, usually solid or liquid and often containing specific nutrients, used to grow microorganisms in the laboratory

Cystic fibrosis an inherited condition where thick sticky mucus builds up in the lungs, the digestive system, and the reproductive system affecting the functions of each

Cytotoxic damaging to cells. Chemotherapy is often cytotoxic

Diastole the period of the cardiac cycle characterized by relaxation of the chambers of the heart

Dislocation an injury where sufficient force is applied to a joint to separate the two bones, putting great strain on the ligament capsule that normally holds the bones together

Dissection the dismembering of a body in order to learn more about its anatomy and features

Dura mater outermost and strongest layer of meninges covering the brain and spinal cord. It is made of relatively tough, interlaced fibrous connective tissue

Echocardiogram ultrasound examination of the heart—used to assess valvular disease and heart function

Endogenous ligand a specific substance formed in the body that forms a complex with a receptor or enzyme to exert its effect

Endoscopy technique for seeing inside the digestive system involving a long thin tube with a light and a camera at one end. It may also involve instruments for the removal of tissue samples (biopsies)

Endosteum layer separating the cortical and trabecular bone

Enflurane/isoflurane halogenated ethers that are structural isomers of each other. They are used to produce general anaesthesia via inhalation of their vapour

Epiglottis flexible piece of cartilage which obscures the opening to the trachea during swallowing to prevent food or fluid going down the airways to the lungs

Epiphyseal plates cartilaginous areas in the long bones that enable growth to continue until they become ossified after puberty

Erectile dysfunction when a man cannot achieve or maintain an erection

Erythrocytes red blood cells responsible for the transport of oxygen throughout the bloodstream

Ethoxyethane/ether $(C_2H_5)_2O$ a colourless and highly volatile liquid at room temperature, the vapour is sweet-smelling and produces anaesthesia in high doses

Exhalation the process of breathing out

Exocrine pancreas the parts of the pancreas which secrete digestive enzymes, along with water and sodium hydrogen carbonate

Exudate a collection of cells and fluid, which often occurs as a result of infection

Fibrillate to quiver due to uncoordinated contraction of muscle cells

Fistula an abnormal connection or track which forms between two body parts

Free radicals highly reactive and unstable molecules produced during metabolism, which have the capacity to damage cells

Fundus the most superior aspect of the stomach

Gastroscopy endoscopy where the tube is inserted into the gut through the mouth to examine the upper end of the digestive system

G-protein-coupled receptors (GPCRs) serpentine (snake-like) proteins that span the cell membrane and contain two key elements: an extracellular receptor site (where ligands bind); and an intracellular binding site which has specialized 'G proteins' attached. When a ligand binds to the receptor site a conformational change alters the G proteins and exerts an intracellular effect

Greater omentum large, apron-like structure that lies in front of the abdominal organs and is the site of fat deposition when people eat more than they need

Haematemesis vomiting blood

Haemoptysis coughing up blood

Haemorrhage loss of blood from a ruptured blood vessel

Halothane alkyl halide which was inhaled to produce general anaesthesia—old-fashioned and rarely used in modern anaesthesia

Haversian canal the central, capillary-containing canal within osteons

Heartburn an uncomfortable burning sensation in the centre of the chest, usually caused by gastric juices or food in the oesophagus

Hyaline cartilage a specialized subtype of cartilage that is exceptionally smooth with a highly organized structure

Hydrocephalus abnormal buildup of cerebrospinal fluid within the ventricles of the brain, usually caused by either a blockage or overproduction of cerebrospinal fluid

Hyoid bone a U-shaped bone in the anterior neck. Muscles attached to the hyoid bone aid in tongue movement and swallowing

Hypnosis the loss of awareness and memory formation which characterizes general anaesthesia or deep sedation

Hypopharynx the part of the upper respiratory tract below the pharynx. Usually extends down to the level of the larynx

Iatrogenic caused by medical intervention—often used to refer to unwanted consequences of medical treatment

Idiopathic a disease with an unknown cause is said to be idiopathic in nature

Ileostomies procedures which involve bringing one end of the small intestine out of the abdominal wall to form a stoma

Inhalation the process of breathing in

Intubated the process of inserting an endotracheal tube into a patient's trachea to support the airway

Ischaemic stroke loss of blood supply to an area of the brain, causing permanent damage to brain tissue. Usually caused by plaque rupture or thrombus formation

Isoflurane/enflurane halogenated ethers that are structural isomers of each other. They are used to produce general anaesthesia via inhalation of their vapour

Keyhole surgery see laparoscopic surgery

Laparoscopic surgery a surgical discipline utilizing small incisions and cameras to view the internal organs of the body and, if necessary, to operate on them. Also known as keyhole surgery

Laparoscopy technique using a laparoscope – very similar to an endoscope – which is inserted through a small incision in the body wall to examine various internal organs

Laryngectomy surgical removal of the larynx

Larynx the voicebox, a cartilage structure containing the vocal cords which make sounds as air passes over them

Leaflets the separate sections which together form a complete heart valve

Ligand-gated ion channels cell membrane spanning pores that contain an extracellular binding site. When a ligand binds to this site the pore opens or closes, allowing ions such as sodium or calcium to be let in to or move out of the cell

Lingual lipase lipid-digesting enzyme secreted by the tongue

Lumen the space in the centre of a blood vessel

Macrophages a specialized type of white blood cell

Magnetic resonance imaging (MRI) see NMR

Mediastinum the membranous partition between the lungs in the chest cavity containing the heart, oesophagus, thymus gland, and other structures

Melaena stool containing blood from the upper digestive tract (stomach and small intestine). Partially digested blood turns the stool black and tarry

Meninges three layers of protective tissue surrounding the brain

Mesenchymal cells cells of an undifferentiated connective tissue that develops into much of the muscle and soft tissue of the body in the embryo

Metaplasia a change in the cells of a particular type of tissue. May be cancerous (neoplastic) or precancerous (dysplastic)

Metastasis the spread of cancerous cells—either locally within a region of the body, or throughout the entire body

Monro–Kellie doctrine a theory describing the volume/pressure relationships within the skull

Motor cortex a strip of outer cerebrum which is dedicated to the initiation of motor control. It has a highly organized structure with very little variance from person to person. The motor cortex on the left side of the body controls the right side and vice versa

Motor end plate the specialized area of a muscle cell which responds to the neurotransmitters released from the presynaptic membrane of a motor neurone, causing contraction

Mucolytics medications used to reduce the viscosity of sticky sputum

Myelinated neurones myelin is a fatty substance held in specialized cells called Schwann cells which surround certain types of neurones in a band called a sheath. The presence of a myelin sheath increases the speed of conduction in a neurone

Myocardial infarction damage to the heart muscle caused by reduced blood flow through one or more coronary arteries

Necrosis death of an area of tissue, caused by a source external to that tissue—such as trauma, or reduction in blood supply

Neoplasia the uncontrolled growth of cells which are not under the usual cellular control mechanisms. A cancerous process

Neurotransmitters chemicals released at the axon of a nerve terminal that cause either excitatory or inhibitory effects at the post-synaptic membrane

Nitrous oxide N$_2$O a colourless, pleasant-smelling gas used for its analgesic and dissociative effects in short procedures and during childbirth

Nuclear magnetic resonance (NMR) an imaging technique which uses powerful magnets to affect the rotation of atoms within the body. Radio waves are used to detect these rotations, and sophisticated computers process the data into detailed images of the soft tissues of the body in a cross-sectional fashion. Also known as magnetic resonance imaging (MRI)

Oedema an abnormal accumulation of fluid within body tissues, causing swelling

Open-heart surgery operations which require the patient's chest cavity to be opened, exposing the heart

Opioids a class of drugs which mimic the action of opium. These may be illegal street drugs, such as heroin, or legal painkilling medications such as codeine, tramadol, or morphine

Osteoarthritis joint condition characterized by the breakdown of the articulating cartilage for example as a result of ageing, wear and tear, diabetes, hypermobility, and obesity

Osteoblasts cells involved in the formation of new bone, regulation of mineral ions including calcium and releasing prostaglandins

Osteocytes cells formed from an osteoblast nestled within mature bone in specially formed spaces known as lacunae

Osteoclasts large cells with multiple nuclei responsible for the reabsorption of bone

Osteons the organized columns of compact bone matrix

Osteoporosis condition where bone resorption exceeds bone formation and the bone density is reduced, increasing the risk of fractures

Otitis externa an inflammation or infection of the external auditory canal

Otitis media an inflammation or infection of the middle ear, behind the tympanic membrane

Otolaryngologists surgeons who specialize in diseases of the ears, nose, and throat

Parasympathetic nerves a division of the autonomic nervous system that increases absorption of food and synthesis of glycogen. It is often known as the 'rest and digest' division, but it affects a multiple of other organs too

Parenchyma the elastic connective tissue of the lung

Partial pressure the pressure a single gas within a mixture of gases would exert if it were the only gas occupying the same volume as the mixture

Pathogenic something which causes a disease or disease process

Peristaltic progressive wave-like movements of muscles (mainly in the oesophagus, stomach, and intestines)

Periosteum highly innervated structure covering the outside of the cortical bone

Peritonitis infection or inflammation of the peritoneum

Phagocytosed engulfed and broken down by phagocytes, specialized white blood cells of the immune system

Physiology the normal functioning processes of the body

Pia mater a very thin and delicate layer of connective tissue that adheres very tightly to the brain and spinal cord

Pleurodesis therapeutic process putting mildly irritant compounds into the space between the pleural membranes, causing inflammation and adhesion so the membranes stick together, preventing the build-up of fluid in the pleural space

Pneumothorax condition when air gets into the pleural cavity through an injury to the lungs or the chest wall

Post-mortem examination of the body after death, with a view to determining a cause for the death

Prehabilitation pre-emptively getting patients into the best possible condition for surgery using physiotherapy, exercise, psychological and nutritional support to maximize their physiological reserve and minimize post-operative complications

Primary brain injury the immediate and irreversible injury to the brain as a result of direct injury or bleeding

Primary ossification centre the first central part of the foetal skeletal system to become bone

Prolapse the displacement of a body part from its normal position – in the case of prolapsed heart valves, they are too soft and floppy and fold the wrong way, allowing backflow of blood in the heart

Prostatectomy removal of the prostate gland

Pulmonary excretion the removal of waste products via the lungs

Pulmonary hypertension high blood pressure in the pulmonary arteries, the blood vessels that supply the lungs

Pulmonary surfactant a substance secreted by type 2 alveolar cells that reduces the surface tension at the air/liquid interface in the alveoli, preventing alveolar collapse

Pus a thick white or green material sometimes seen around wounds, consisting of dead white blood cells, dead bacteria, and tissue debris

Radiofrequency ablation the targeted destruction of tissue using heat

Radio-opaque something which does not permit the passage of radiation. In medical terms, this usually refers to a substance, dye, or material which does not allow the passage of X-rays, and which therefore shows up as a solid opaque mass on X-ray, CT, and fluoroscopy

Recurrence something occurring again. Often used in the context of malignancy to refer to the reappearance of a cancer some time later

Resection the cutting out or removal of a localized area

Respiratory zone the part of the lungs directly involved in gas transfer—between the terminal bronchi and the alveoli

Rickets common name of a bone disease resulting from lack of vitamin D or calcium in the diet or lack of sunlight on the skin

Rigors shivering episodes associated with high fevers

Sarcoidosis a relatively rare condition where areas of swollen tissue which do not function normally occur in body organs, including the lungs and lymph nodes

Secondary brain injury the damage to the brain which results from the after-effects of a primary event which may be reduced or mitigated by appropriate medical or surgical interventions

Secondary ossification centres distal centres of bony growth that develop during childhood and adolescence

Sedation a state of calmness or drowsiness. When used as a medical term, usually implies the use of medication to induce this state in order to perform a medical or surgical procedure

Sella turcica small hollow in the sphenoid bone where the pituitary gland sits

Sepsis a condition caused by overwhelming infection of the body, rapidly leading to death if untreated

Serous fluid a body fluid similar in composition to serum in the blood. Pale, straw-coloured, and transparent, it often fills spaces within body cavities, such as the pericardium

Skin graft transferring skin from a healthy area of the body to a damaged area

Soft palate the soft tissue which makes up the posterior part of the roof of the mouth

Sphincter a muscular ring which maintains the closure of a bodily orifice, relaxing to allow the orifice to open

Sputum mucous secretions from the lungs

Squamous cell carcinoma a malignant growth originating from squamous cells. It may occur anywhere in the body where squamous cells are found, from the skin to the lining of the respiratory tract

Stenosis thickening or stiffening of the valves of the heart so they do not open fully

Stoma an opening in the skin, which is formed to allow the connection of a colostomy or ileostomy. This allows the passage of faeces into a bag attached to the stoma

Stridor a harsh sound heard on inspiration if there is a blockage or partial blockage in the upper respiratory tract

Suture a medical stitch, used to hold the edges of a wound together

Sympathetic nerves a division of the autonomic nervous system that readies the body for activity by redirecting blood supplies to muscles, increasing respiratory and heart rate and various other effects. It is often known as the 'fight-or-flight' division

Synapse the communicating junction between one neurone and another, or between a neurone and a muscle or gland

Synergistic producing a combined effect greater than the sum of each individual effect

Synovial joints specialized joint which allows large movements and contains lubricating synovial fluid

Systole the period of the cardiac cycle characterized by contraction of the chambers of the heart

Telepresence the use of technology to make a person feel as if they are present, or to exert an effect, from a place other than their actual location

Thorax the cavity within the human body enclosed by the ribs, breastbone, and vertebra; also known as the chest cavity

Thrombus a clot which forms within a blood vessel

Tinnitus a ringing, buzzing, or humming noise heard within the ear

Trabecular bone porous, highly vascular bone found in the centre of the bone structure, providing it with lightness and flexibility

Tracheostomy a tube reaching from the trachea (below the level of the larynx) through the skin on the front of the neck, allowing a patient with an airway occlusion to breathe

Transient ischaemic attack (TIA) temporary disruption of the blood supply to an area of the brain, causing symptoms similar to a stroke, but which last for a few minutes to a few hours, and have completely resolved after twenty-four hours

Trephining an ancient surgical technique, involving cutting a small round hole in the skull

Trichloromethane/chloroform CHCl$_3$ a colourless and pungent liquid that was previously used for anaesthetic and analgesic purposes

Tyrosine kinase receptors cell membrane-spanning protein complexes with extracellular receptor sites. When a ligand binds to the receptor sites, the intracellular portion transfers a high-energy phosphate group to various proteins (depending on the subclass of receptor), which alters intracellular activity

Ulcerative colitis (UC) inflammatory condition found mainly in the colon, which can also affect tissues outside the GI tract. The inflammation only affects the mucosa of the intestine and affects large regions of the bowel wall

Unmyelinated neurones neurones which are not surrounded by Schwann cells and so do not possess a myelin sheath. This means the speed of conduction of their impulses is slower than in myelinated neurones

Vascular dementia memory loss caused by many small ischaemic changes in the brain over time

Veins thin-walled blood vessels which transport blood back to the heart

Ventricles hollow spaces deep within the brain that contain cerebrospinal fluid

Vertebral foramen an opening or space between two vertebra that allows spinal nerves from the spinal cord to exit

Video fluoroscopy a moving X-ray, taken when an individual is swallowing, to assess the swallowing process

Vivisection the dissection of living animals for scientific or experimental purposes

INDEX